The Wars in VIETNAM

1954–1980

C H I N A

Red River

Dien Bien
Phu

Hanoi   Haiphong

Gulf of Tonkin

L A O S

Luang Prabang

N.
VIETNAM

HAINAN I.

Vientaine

Udon   Nakhon Phanome

DMZ

T H A I L A N D

Danang

MEKONG RIVER

Ubon

Korat

Bangkok

Anghor Wat

Ton le Sap Lake & River

C A M B O D I A   S.   VIETNAM

Phnom Penh

Sihanoukville

Saigon

South
China Sea

Scale 0   50   100 150
                    Miles

MAP. I

Edgar O'Ballance

The Wars in VIETNAM
1954—1980

New Enlarged Edition

HIPPOCRENE
BOOKS, INC.

NEW YORK, N.Y.

Contents

Maps

Acknowledgements

This account of the War in Vietnam is primarily compiled from information I have gained during my visits to Vietnam, official briefings, interviews, tours, discussions and notes made in my practical researching, but I would like to record that I have read with interest, profit and pleasure the following works, and I would like to make grateful acknowledgement to the authors, compilers and editors of them:

Burchett, Wilfred G., *Vietnam: Inside Story of the Guerrilla War*, International Publishers, New York (1965).

Cooper, Chester L., *The Lost Crusade*, MacGibbon and Kee (1971).

Dawson, Alan, *Fifty-five Days: The Fall of South Vietnam*, Prentice-Hall, Inc., Englewood Cliffs, 1978.

Halberstam, David, *The Best and the Brightest*, Random House, New York (1972), Barrie and Jenkins, London (1972).

Lacouture, Jean, *Ho Chi Minh*, Penguin Press (1968).

Pike, Douglas, *Viet Cong*, The M.I.T. Press, Massachusetts (1966).

Sihanouk, Norodom and Burchett, Wilfred G., *My War with the CIA*, The Penguin Press (1973).

US State Department, *Aggression from the North*, White Paper issued in 1965.

US Defense Department, *History of US Decision-making Process on Vietnam Policy*, (The Pentagon Papers – a summary published in the New York Times, from June 13th–18th and July 1st–5th, 1971).

Vo, Nguyen Giap, *People's War, People's Army*, Foreign Languages Publishing House, Hanoi (1961).

Vo, Nguyen Giap, *Big Victory, Great Task*, Pall Mall Press (1968).

Preface

This is a brief account of the course of the war that took place in Vietnam between 1954 and 1973, and which could be aptly subtitled the Second Vietnam War. The first was the Indo-China War,* which lasted from 1945 until 1954, being fought by the Viet Minh against the French Colonial Power immediately after World War II. Unfortunately the Third Vietnam War is now in progress. Many books and articles have been written about the Vietnam War, but most seem to deal with a particular aspect, or subject, or show a strong bias, and as there does not at the time of writing seem to be a concise account of the conflict, this book may fulfil a background need as a handy reference work.

The War in Vietnam was the type of struggle which has become familiar in the 20th Century, and is usually loosely referred to as guerrilla warfare. It is a dedicated form which involves fanatical and complete political involvement waged by Communist forces intent on forcing their political beliefs and domination on a country. Although the methods used by Communist revolutionary guerrillas have become familiar, and the pattern seems to be predictable, Western nations do not yet seem to have discovered a universally successful and simple counter. Perhaps further study will enable one to be developed, and this book may be of some assistance.

This war was an example of how conventional forces can be sucked into the guerrilla morass. America, anxious to stem the tide of Communism which it believed was flooding eastwards, gave military and economic aid that continually had to be increased, in the mistaken theory that just a little more military help would tilt the scales decisively against the Viet Cong. It never did and as always more aid was needed – and given. It was a crusading era, and the Americans were unable to understand why they could not successfully fight 'half a war'. American involvement in Vietnam coincided with the era of the Whizz Kids; blinded and bemused by their own brilliance, understanding only

* *The Indo-China War 1945–54:* A study in Guerrilla Warfare by Edgar O'Ballance (Faber and Faber, 1964).

technical data and statistics, they did not comprehend the human element and were unable to compute the factors of morale, political indoctrination and stamina accurately. The 'think tanks' miscalculated Communist resolve and Viet Cong staying power and toughness.

When considering American lack of success, it should be remembered that the war was not completely controlled by the US; it was only "assisting the Government of SVN", which was technically in charge of military operations. American Advisers were in SVN in plenty, but at times their advice was not sought, at others if asked for it was ignored, while when proferred it was often refused; also there were wide differences in view between the SVN and the American generals.

I have endeavoured to narrate the main events in a chronological sequence, which at times has meant flitting from subject to subject and from battle-field to battle-field before the fight was over, but this has been done in the attempt to produce a clear logical account that is readily understood by the general reader. It was a war of countless small battles, skirmishes, patrol actions, ambushes, assassinations and terrorism, which were continually in progress throughout the length and breadth of SVN. Clearly, all cannot be mentioned individually, and a detailed catalogue of all incidents, large and small, would weary and bore. Those mentioned are either the main events or examples to show the general trend of the fighting and the course of the war.

This was a war that aroused conflicting emotions, and propaganda played a large part on both sides. Practically everyone has strong views on some aspect of the fighting in Vietnam, and illogical as it may seem, for example, there was always a ready cry of horror at the mention of the use of war gases – no matter how non-lethal – and methods of defoliation, but hardly a gasp was raised over the use of flame-throwers by the Viet Cong or their ruthless terrorist activities. I have tried to divorce myself from emotion and to tell the story as it really happened, which may not be quite as many would have liked it to be told.

There is continuing dispute over casualty figures, both generally and for individual engagements, and those quoted, unless otherwise stated, are those issued either by the US Defense Department or by the MACV in Saigon. Sometimes there are even differences as to the exact dates on which battles were fought. The usually accepted Westernised spelling of names, places and people has been used. Some provinces were renamed in 1956 by President Diem; for example, Thu Dau Mot became Binh Duong, and Xuan Loc became Long Khanh. Confusion still lingers over some of them as neither the NLF nor the GDRV would recognise the changes, and continued to refer to provinces and places by their former names.

Edgar O'Ballance

Preface to the 1981 Edition

Two up-dating chapters have been added for the new American edition to include events up to January 1981, since the first edition of this book, printed early in 1975, brought the account only up to January 1973. The first of these covers the "Third Vietnam War", when the "North" fought against the "South" after American forces had withdrawn, a struggle that ended in a Communist victory and the re-unification of the two parts of Vietnam under Hanoi rule. The final chapter describes subsequent events in neighboring Laos and Cambodia, Soviet and Chinese involvement, and the Sino-Vietnamese War of February-March 1979.

E. O'B.

Two Vietnams   1

"Political activities [were] more important than military activities, and fighting less important than propaganda" Vo Nguyen Giap *People's War: People's Army*.

The brilliant victory of General Vo Nguyen Giap at the Battle of Dien Bien Phu, which ended on May 8th, 1954, finally brought home to the Colonial Power that it could no longer continue the struggle to retain its former position of authority in Indo-China. This shock defeat sapped the French will to win the unpopular and much misunderstood war being fought so far from Paris in South-East Asia which had been dragging on since 1946. French Indo-China had been occupied by the Japanese during World War II, but when that war ceased the French fully expected to return, to resume their former overlordship where they had left off. But they were forestalled and thwarted by Ho Chi Minh, the veteran Asian Communist leader, who on September 2nd, 1945, entered Hanoi in triumph to proclaim the existence of the Democratic Republic of Vietnam (the DRV).

Struggling by force of arms to re-assert their presence, the French had initial successes; Ho Chi Minh had to flee to the mountains of northern Tongking, while his small group of Viet Minh* fighters under Giap had to leave the cities and towns and take to the mountains and jungles to preserve themselves. The Viet Minh expanded and became adept at guerrilla warfare as enunciated by Mao Tse-tung. After a period of protracted warfare, in which the French Expeditionary Force suffered successive reverses, Viet Minh formations surrounded and defeated a large entrenched French force at the far-inland village of Dien Bien Phu in a conventional siege-type battle.

* From Viet Nam Doc Lap Dong Minh Hoi, meaning the League for the Independence of Vietnam.

International talks in progress at Geneva eventually produced the Geneva Agreements of 1954: the former French Indo-Chinese territory was to be divided up; Cambodia and Laos were each to become independent states; Annam (including the province of Tongking) and Cochin China, reverting to their original name of Vietnam, were to be provisionally and arbitrarily split into two parts, divided at the 17th Parallel, across the narrow waist. This artificial partition was only intended to be for an interim period, to allow the turmoil and emotions that had been aroused to subside sufficiently for elections to be held on both sides of the Parallel to elect a regime that would unite and govern both parts of the country. It was prescribed that these re-unification elections should be held by 1956. Neither America nor South Vietnam signed the Geneva Agreements, but North Vietnam did. Armistice agreements between the French and the Viet Minh came into effect on July 21st, 1954, and a timetable for the withdrawal of French troops was produced, the last leaving in March 1956. An International Control Commission, the ICC, of representatives from India, Poland and Canada, was established to supervise the military evacuation and population exchanges. The French seemed to lose heart and interest immediately.

The line of the 17th Parallel became a Demilitarised Zone (DMZ), which extended to three miles on either side of the eastward-flowing Ben Hai River. When the time limit for free movement was up it was firmly shut, thus creating two Vietnams – North Vietnam (NVN)* and South Vietnam (SVN)* – which in turn created both political and economic problems that caused them to draw apart. The main political problem was that the Communists, under Ho Chi Minh, had gained power to the north of the Parallel, while to the south of it, the so-far French-supported regime of Bao Dai was strongly anti-Communist. The economic problems were that the South, especially the Mekong Delta, had traditionally supplied rice and food for the North, but possessed hardly any minerals or industrialisation, while the North, which had deposits of coal and iron and ample hydro-electric potential, was short of food; formerly the two had economically complemented each other.

Two major population exchanges occurred. Christian missionaries had been busy in Indo-China for many years, and about 85 per cent of the 900,000 Catholics in the North, fearing to live under a Communist regime, after having helped and been in sympathy with the French, moved as refugees into SVN. The other population move, although of smaller proportion, was from South to North, of about 90,000 Viet Minh and Communist personnel, who had been fighting or hiding in the mountains,

* These abbreviations will also be used to denote North Vietnamese and South Vietnamese.

jungle and population centres until the cease-fire, and who were ordered to move northwards. A period of 300 days was allowed for this 'free movement'. Many others, at least 5,000 Viet Minh, referred to as the "stay behind cadres"*, were instructed to remain in the South and continue open political activity in the villages. So too were the thousands of regional and village militia members, who were told to hide their arms in secret caches and become ordinary peasants, but to be alert for any signal to arouse them into insurgent activity again, should that become necessary.

When these moves had been completed, NVN was left with an area of about 63,000 square miles and a population of about 18 million, of whom the majority were Buddhists, but there were also groupings of Catholics and hill tribesmen. Most of the people were huddled into the Red River Delta region, the most fertile part of the country, the remainder of the territory being far less hospitable. SVN was left with an area of about 66,200 square miles and about 17 million people, again the majority of them being Buddhist, but also many were Catholics, Chinese and hill tribesmen. The two tottering 'half-countries', hostile to each other, unsure of themselves or each other, both gave urgent priority to mending their fences and putting their own houses in order.

Ho Chi Minh, who was President of NVN and also Premier, was for the moment less interested in SVN than he was in consolidating a firm Communist country under his control, and he looked almost complacently southwards at the chaos left by the departing French. Believing there would be re-unification elections within the prescribed time, he anticipated that SVN would fall to him easily through the ballot box. However, he did appreciate the possibility of American military participation on the Korean pattern, so he gave priority to regularising, strengthening and modernising his armed forces, but he made only slow progress.

Ho Chi Minh had a ready-made, battle-tested army of about 325,000 well-trained and disciplined regular troops, formed into six divisions and a number of independent regiments and units. It was an infantry army, strong in manpower, but weak in guns and transport; in victory its morale was extremely high. When the French evacuated Hanoi on October 5th, 1954, the 308th Viet Minh Division, in recognition of its conduct at Dien Bien Phu, moved in on their heels, triumphantly marching through the city displaying its war trophies. The name of the Viet Minh army was changed to that of the Vietnamese People's Army (VPA) and as befitted the now open character of the Government, General Giap, who had been mainly instrumental in raising, training

* The term 'cadre' is the usual translation of the Chinese 'Can Pu', which means junior leader, and is usually applied in a political context.

and directing it, became the Defence Minister. Three divisions were immediately moved towards the DMZ in a blocking position while the remainder were scattered about the country. Small amounts of military equipment, mainly trucks, were received from China during the next two or three years, until the VPA possessed about 100 armoured fighting vehicles and about 500 field guns.

The supporting, part-time militia, which became a home-defence force, available for emergencies and to back up the regular element, was lightly armed and territorially based, eventually settling down about the 200,000 mark. The armed border and security police numbered about 40,000, and a system of conscription, selectively applied, ensured that a sufficient intake of youthful manpower was brought in to the armed forces to maintain these numbers. The nucleus of a small navy and air force was established.

The command system was the Communist type of authority shared by the military commander and a political commissar, the latter having the power of veto. This inevitably caused some friction and although it was always played down, occasional glimpses showed through. The military were regarded as the elite of the nation, favoured as regards rations, clothing and housing. Ho Chi Minh saw the VPA as a counter to the power of the Lao Dong Party,* or Worker's Party of Vietnam, the only permitted one, which was, of course, Communist.

An 11-man Politburo, or Cabinet, was formed from the Central Committee of the Lao Dong Party in 1945, its membership being unchanged, and a 366-seat National Assembly was Communistically elected. Pham Van Dong, a veteran Communist, trained at Chiang Kai-shek's Whampoa Military Academy in 1925, who was an able organiser and administrator and had worked with Ho Chi Minh in China in World War II, became Premier in 1955. Truong Chinh was made Secretary-General of the Lao Dong Party, thus becoming the second most powerful person in the hierarchy to Ho Chi Minh. Throughout their struggle with the French, the Communists, under Ho Chi Minh, had a strong, united leadership, but following the cease-fire and the inevitable relaxation of certain stresses, differences of opinions became apparent. Certainly all members of the Government were united when it came to the principle of communising their country, but divergent views arose on how much aid and influence should be accepted from China and the Soviet Union. There arose a pro-Chinese and a pro-Soviet group within the Politburo which Ho Chi Minh skilfully played off one against the other, as traditional nationalistic prejudices clashed with ideology.

Pham Van Dong and Giap represented the pro-Soviet faction, and Truong Chinh the pro-Chinese one. Partly because of Truong Chinh's

* Dang Lao Dong Viet Nam.

14

influence and partly because the military leadership – dazzled by Mao Tse-tung's victory on the Chinese mainland – looked to China for military inspiration and help, the years from 1954–1956 can be regarded as the pro-Chinese period in NVN. A small Chinese military advisory group was sent to the VPA, but its scope was extremely limited, and late in 1956, following the Chinese example (itself copied from the Russians) VPA officers blossomed out in gaudy uniforms, colourful epaulettes, glittering badges of rank and shining medals. This atmosphere did not last and tended to give way to a pro-Soviet period, mainly because the Vietnamese were inherently fearful and suspicious of the Chinese, who for centuries had conquered, occupied or dominated them. The fact that Annam in Chinese means 'pacified south', may give some clue to this complex.

General Giap, who had acquired a high military reputation for his conduct of the war against the French, tended to be abrasive, and so was at loggerheads with some of his Politburo colleagues, especially the powerful Truong Chinh. Giap, who had visited the Soviet Union on several occasions, tended to be anti-Chinese and an admirer of Soviet military technology, and he always put NVN interests before those of Communism. His authoritarian manner did not help him in his relations with his colleagues, and he was progressively down-graded in the hierarchy, until he was only sixth or seventh in order of importance, although throughout he retained the Defence portfolio.

Like other Communist leaders, Ho Chi Minh ran into difficulties in forcing his ideology on his people. About two-thirds of the peasants in NVN owned the plots they worked, the remainder of the land being owned by landlords, and as a first step, a three-year land reform programme was put into operation by Truong Chinh, the Secretary-General of the Lao Dong Party. Both landlords and peasants with any sizeable holdings were ruthlessly dispossessed as dedicated reformers marched in to strip them of their possessions, the expropriated land being redistributed on lease by the Government to landless peasants. Truong Chinh, the son of a mandarin, who was reported to have let his parents be executed rather than do anything to save them (saying the People's Court which condemned them was correct), soon found that people with an acre of land were hard to find, so he coined the expression 'landlord mentality' to dispossess those whose ancestors had been landlords or had owned land or livestock. Radio Hanoi later reported that 325,000 families had each been given about one-fifth of an acre.

The peasants were surly and unco-operative, but those who resisted or objected, were dealt with harshly. All produce had to be sold to the Government at low prices, which led the peasants to conceal part of their crops, thus creating a Black Market. Food shortages caused ration cards to be issued, but there were large-scale evasions of the regulations, while mismanagement and chaos at the rice distribution centres meant that workers sometimes had to spend several days there each month waiting to receive their rations – a vicious circle that simply resulted in more lost production. In 1957, there were armed risings and demonstrations, particularly in Catholic areas, in the provinces of Vinh, Phat Diem and Than Hoa, and also near Hanoi, when the VPA had to be brought in to suppress them. Refugees who escaped by boat down the coast to Tourene* (later to be renamed Danang) told harrowing stories.

Anxiously, Ho Chi Minh stepped in to prevent a national insurrection, and in November 1956, he dismissed Truong Chinh from his post as Secretary-General of the Lao Dong Party, who in true Communist fashion after being formally denounced by Giap for having "resorted to terror and having executed too many people", took the blame and confessed his failure to implement the land reform programme. This triggered off the only real crisis within the NVN leadership in the early years, but it was successfully handled by Ho Chi Minh, who read out an apologetic letter over Radio Hanoi to the people, released some 12,000 peasants who had been detained, and the 50,000 who had been killed resisting land reforms, many of whom it was suspected were first tortured or had died unpleasant deaths, were declared to have been "executed by mistake" and proclaimed "national heroes". Dispossessed landlords and peasants were promised their land back and compensation, but this was easier decreed than implemented, as those to whom it had been Communistically given, were reluctant to quit, and in their resentment killed livestock, destroyed irrigation systems, burned barns, smashed tools and cut down trees. Such a wave of bitterness and recrimination followed, that in June 1957, President Ho Chi Minh again spoke on Radio Hanoi, urging the peasants to "forgive and forget" and to "abrogate their moment of revenge". He then toured dissident areas to persuade them to rebuild the dikes before the monsoon rains began.

Le Duan, the senior Viet Minh commander in SVN during the struggle against the French, who had also attended the Whampoa Military Academy in 1925, was appointed acting Secretary-General of the Lao Dong Party, a post in which he was formally confirmed in 1960 when the title was changed to First Secretary. Truong Chinh, who retained his seat on the Politburo, was not in disgrace for long, and in 1958 he was appointed a Chairman of the National Assembly, which gave him precedence over the Premier, and he was reinstated politically. During 1957 Ho Chi Minh re-organised the Lao Dong Party.

* On October 22nd, 1956 a SVN Presidential decree changed the names of certain provinces, but the NLF and the GDRV would not recognise them, which tended to add confusion to communiques.

Many peasants had been reluctantly pushed out from the Red River Delta into the hinterland to cultivate marginal plots, and the resultant discontentment and rioting in 1957 were such that the VPA had again to be brought into action. Owing to rigid censorship little was known in the outside world of the depths of Ho Chi Minh's difficulties with his people and his programmes, which were considerable. In a rare flash of candour, Radio Hanoi reported on November 26th, that there had been riots in the Nghe An province, where "gangs of reactionaries taking advantage of the mistakes committed during the implementation of land reform, molested soldiers and cadres, seized quantities of arms and blocked traffic. Some local units also joined in and General Hoang Sam's 304th Division had to be called in, which drove the insurgents into the hills where they set up a guerrilla resistance". Nghe An province was the birthplace of Ho Chi Minh,* but it had a large Catholic population.

As if he did not have enough on his hands with mis-managed land reforms, Ho Chi Minh also had to weather a financial crisis, as the rate of the 'dong' sank so low that even Communist countries refused to accept it, and all international trade had to be conducted by barter. Domestically, paper money was worthless, so taxes had to be levied in sacks of rice, and wages also calculated in that commodity. Huge quantities of rice were confiscated to pay wages, and the paper dongs given in exchange could not be redeemed, which caused serious discontent. Although forbidden by law, swarms of beggars haunted the streets of Hanoi and Haiphong.

Chinese influence was being overshadowed by that of the Soviet Union, but it was still strong, and despite protests by members of his Politburo, Ho Chi Minh allowed a NVN version of the Chinese Hundred Flowers Campaign† to be adopted. Like the Chinese original, it rapidly got out of hand, becoming known as the Revolt of the Intellectuals, and was harshly put down. By this time the pro-Soviet Ministers, such as the Premier and his following, were in the ascendant. NVN was entering fully into its pro-Soviet period and it seemed that Hanoi was more in step with Moscow than with Peking. Ho Chi Minh was a realist and a nationalist, who did not relish his country becoming a satellite of China, and he limited military aid from that country drastically, as he feared that if he accepted too much it would virtually mean Chinese military occupation. All in all, Ho Chi Minh was more than fully engrossed in both domestic and foreign problems during the first five or six years after the

* The town of Kim Lien.
† In full it was "Let a Hundred Flowers blossom, and a Hundred Schools of Thought contend", and was intended originally to allow a mild criticism by intellectuals as a safety valve.

Geneva Agreements, and had little time to spare to look southwards to SVN, which in turn was also having severe difficulties, but on the face of things seemed to be solving them better than he was able to.

To the south, in 1954, great chaos and confusion existed in SVN, where the writ of the Government barely extended beyond the environs of Saigon and other major cities. Most of the countryside, and indeed many of the provincial capitals, were in the hands of the Viet Minh fighters, private armies and bandits. In addition, nearly one million refugees had to be absorbed. The new state of SVN lacked any sense of unity, being an uneasy, disparate conglomerate of cities, towns, regions, religions and tribes, all subjected in various ways to the pressures of 15 years of war.

In the absence of any more compliant candidate, the French had attempted to govern through Bao Dai, who at the best was their reluctant ally, suspected and distrusted by his own people was well as the French, but they could find no one else of sufficient stature to work for them. The former Emperor of Annam, Bao Dai was persuaded to return from exile in 1949, had dropped his royal title and assumed that of Head of State. Bao Dai was in France in 1954, when the Geneva Agreements were finalised, and he refused to return to a divided country or to share power with Ho Chi Minh.

Meanwhile, on June 16th, 1954 Ngo Dinh Diem, a Catholic politician from a mandarin family, returned from voluntary exile to become Premier in Saigon. Diem had been Minister of the Interior in Bao Dai's Government in 1933, but had resigned because his proposals for reform were not accepted, after which he stayed out of politics for some years, before going into exile in 1949. Few reckoned his chances of survival, let alone success, to be very high, and most predicted his downfall within weeks with increased chaos resulting.

The Vietnamese National Army, raised by the French, defeated and demoralised, had sunk to a strength of about 100,000. Conscription had been decreed in 1953, but there were large scale evasions and deferments, and it badly needed re-organising, re-arming and re-training before it could be regarded as effective. Although external defence was a high priority, Premier Diem was determined to extend his authority over his country, so first of all he turned to deal with the three private armies which the French had allowed to be maintained on the pretext that they were defending certain areas for them against the Viet Minh. The French, who were desperately short of troops in Indo-China, had armed and paid the soldiers in these private armies, over which they had little real control. Early in 1955, the French stopped paying the subsidies, and Diem saw his chance to step in and draw their teeth.

The first of these private armies, numbering about 5,000 men, belonged

N

PROVINCIAL BOUNDARIES --------

L A O S

DMZ
Bo Ho Su
QUANG
TRI
Quang Tri
Dong Ha

Hue
THUA
THIEN
MUI DA NANG
Da Nang
QUANG
NAM
Hoi An
Tam Ky
QUANG TIN
Quang Ngai
QUANG
NGAI
Mo Duc

T H A I L A N D

KONTUM
Hoai
Nhon
Kontum
BINH
DINH
Pleiku
PLEIKU
An Tuc
Qui Nhon
Song
Cau
PHU
Hau Bon
Song Ba
BON
PHU
YEN
Tuy Hoa

DARLAC
Ban Me
Thuot
KHANH
HOA

C A M B O D I A

QUANG
DUC
Gia Nghia
Bo Duc
Phuoc
TUYEN
DUC
Da Lat
Nha Trang
CAM RAN
NINH
THUAN
Loc
Ninh
An
Loc
PHUOC
LONG
LAM DONG
Bao Loc
Phan Rang
TAY
NINH
Tay
Ninh
BINH
LONG
Phuoc Vinh
BINH
DUONG
LONG
KHANH
BINH
THUAN
Song
Phu Cuong
BIEN
Bien
Hoa
BINH
TUY
HAU
NGHIA
Gia Dinh
SAIGON
Xuan
Loc
Mo
Hoa
Phu
Chau
KIEN
PHONG
KIEN
TUONG
Cho Lon
HOA
Phan Thiet
MUI KE GA
CHAU
DOC
Cao Lanh
DINH
GIA
Phuoc Le
PHUOC
TUY
Ham
Tan
Ha Tien
Long
Xuyen
AN
My Tho
DINH
TUONG
Tan
An
Vung Tau
KIEN
GIANG
Sa Dec
Go Cong
GO
CONG
Duong
Dong
DAO
PHU QUOC
(Vietnam)
Can
Tho
Vinh
Long
KIEN HOA
PHONG
DINH
Truc Giang
Rach Gia
Vi Thanh
Phu Vinh
VINH
BINH
CHUONG
THIEN
BA
XUYEN
Khanh
Hung
Quen
Long
BAC
LIEU
Vinh
Loi

AN
XUYEN

MAP 2

to the Binh Xuyen, a gangster-like organisation that for years had preyed on river traffic coming into Saigon, and its twin city, Cholon. Unable to police these two cities properly, in 1953, with French acquiescence, Bao Dai had 'sold' this 'army' the right to do the job for him, with the inevitable result the Binh Xuyen ran a gigantic protection racket and had a stranglehold on the capital. The second private army numbered about 15,000, and belonged to the Coa Dai Sect, which was a confused mixture of several religions and had a reputed following of over 300,000. The other also numbered about 15,000, and belonged to the religious Hoa Hao Sect loosely modelled on Buddhism. Both these Sects operated freely in certain areas in SVN, and that of the Cao Dai was particularly strong in the provinces surrounding Saigon.

Armed clashes between elements of the SVN National Army in April 1955 in Saigon, culminated in a successful counter-attack on the 28th, which drove the Binh Xuyen from the city, after which Diem formed a new police force to look after the capital. Next, National troops moved against the Hoa Hao Sect in the provinces which was brought to heel by June. This was followed by action against the Cao Dai Sect, in which, after some skirmishing, its military leadership was won over by subterfuge. Although these private armies still retained their arms, their military power had been shattered, but nevertheless they remained politically powerful, controlling large sectors of territory. These sharp military actions chastened potential rivals for power, strengthened Diem's hand, and allowed his army to look northwards towards the DMZ. He made little or no attempt to penetrate the countryside to eliminate the Viet Minh, bandits and other armed groups known to be there, probably anticipating they could be dealt with individually in due course.

The American Administration had been cool and suspicious to Premier Diem at first, but his victory over the gangster-like Binh Xuyen, swung it over to his side: it looked as though someone in SVN was at last achieving something, and so the Eisenhower Administration promised economic and financial support. To understand this American decision, and the fears and hopes of those days, it should be mentioned that only six years previously the Communists had seized China, barely two years had passed since the Korean War had drawn to a wary, suspicious close, and in Europe the Cold War was at its height. The American Government eyed with foreboding what it saw as the flood-tide of Communism sweeping westwards across Asia, and to try and stem this surge it had, in September 1954, concluded the South East Asia Treaty Organisation (SEATO).*

* Signed by America, Australia Britain, New Zealand, Pakistan and the Philippines.

20

According to the Geneva Agreements, the USA was allowed to keep 342 military personnel in SVN – the number that happened to be there on the cease-fire. After sending a letter to Premier Diem, in which President Eisenhower said he would in future send US aid direct to him, and not channel it through the French authorities, the Americans announced on May 10th, 1955, that they had been asked to train and re-arm the National Army, a statement that merely removed French obstruction. An additional 350 US military personnel were sent to SVN in May 1956, nominally to help the Diem Government to recover military material abandoned by the French, and when this task was completed they stayed on, becoming part of the newly formed US Military Advisory and Assistance Group, MAAG. Clouded by their Korean experience, the American military appreciation was that the larger and much more efficient VPA might try to cross the DMZ in strength and move southwards, so Diem was persuaded to send some of his formations northwards to be in a blocking position just south of it.

On June 6th, 1954, there had been NVN demands for talks to arrange the re-unification elections, but on the 18th (only two days after his appointment as Premier) Diem had said he refused to take any action in this respect unless there were 'free' elections in NVN. A year later, on July 16th, with American support, Diem cancelled the re-unification elections called for by the Geneva Agreements, which he refused to acknowledge on the grounds that SVN had not signed them. He realised that if the elections were held, the Communists, as the only politically well organised body in SVN, would be able to dominate and manipulate the ballot box, and so take over the country. Later, President Eisenhower was reported to have said the Communists would have won the re-unification elections anyway.

In the summer of 1955, Diem launched a "Denunciation Campaign" in which between 60,000 and 80,000 people were detained, mainly his political opponents. He also returned land that had been distributed out by the Viet Minh to the original landlords. Diem realised that his country needed a period of firm rule to unify it and put it on its feet, but Bao Dai in Paris disagreed with his policies, and intrigued to have him removed from the Premiership. Instead, tables were turned and after further consolidating power into his own hands, Diem held a referendum in which he was elected President. A Republic of Viet Nam (RVN) was declared, and the absentee Head of State, Bao Dai, was pushed from the scene.

President Diem next turned to Cholon, the twin city of Saigon, in which lived over half a million Chinese, who tended to be self-contained and aloof. Cholon means Big Market in Chinese. Most of the one million Chinese in SVN, who controlled two-thirds of the economy of the country, and who invariably retained their Chinese citizenship, and regarded China as 'home', even though many had never been there, gave their loyalty to the Chiang Kai-shek Government. Diem was obviously anxious in case they be persuaded to change loyalties and accept Mao Tse-tung as their leader, as the Chinese community in Cambodia had done, when they would be in a position to strangle his economy. President Diem demanded that the resident Chinese become 'Vietnamised', and with some difficulty got his way, insisting they become RVN citizens, and prohibiting 'foreigners' from engaging in many trades, some of which, such as rice-milling, had almost become a Chinese monopoly.

In May 1957, when President Diem visited President Eisenhower in America, he had an impressive balance sheet to show. In almost three years he had seemingly worked wonders: not only had he survived, but had brought order and stability out of chaos, brought the private armies to heel, quietened the Chinese in Cholon, settled at least half a million refugees from the north, and with US aid had commenced a number of projects, that included irrigation schemes, road construction and land reform. SVN seemed to be progressing so much better than its northern rival in all respects. The Eisenhower Administration and America smiled on Diem, the Catholic anti-Communist who seemed to be halting the surge of Communism in South East Asia. Diem pledged himself to fight Communism, and Eisenhower pledged to continue to give him aid.

In September 1959, in a general election (in which Communists were debarred from voting) President Diem, leading his National Revolutionary Movement, won 78 out of the 123 seats in the National Assembly, the reminder going to rigl t-wing independents, one of whom was Madame Ngo Dinh Nhu, his formidable publicity-seeking sister-in-law, who acted as the President's Lady on official occasions, Diem being a bachelor. A determined lady of forceful character, Mme Nhu worked to gain women's enfranchisement, to uplift their status and generally to win more rights for them. Feeling far more secure in power, President Diem tended to become dictatorial and aloof in manner.

Attention was paid to improving the armed forces, now known as the Army of the Republic of Vietnam (ARVN)* and its strength slowly rose to the 150,000 mark, conscription having been regularised in 1957 to be for 12 months at the age of 20. But there were still many evasions, and a fairly high proportion of the draftees were found to be unfit for military service. Initially a few political officers were assigned to units with poor morale, who later became known as Psychological Warfare

* The abbreviation ARVN will be used at times to embrace all SVN armed services including Regional and Popular Forces, the Air Force and the Navy.

Officers, who gave lectures and made a feeble pretence of helping the peasants. Morale varied considerably from unit to unit, and the American advisers attached to the ARVN had a hard task.

The ARVN officer cadre was a serious problem. Most senior officers had achieved their commissions and promotion through the patronage of Bao Dai, and gradually Diem removed most of them, replacing them with his own nominees, allowing him to counter-balance the rival factions within the ARVN, which remained a hotbed of patronage. In theory, conscripts with sufficient educational qualifications were eligible for officer-training, but in practice, family and other influences were needed to obtain entry to the National Military Academy at Dalat. The ARVN was under-officered because so many were required to assist the civil administration which was struggling into being.

In his drive to unite his country and solidify his authority, Diem tended to gloss over one vital aspect, that of the pockets of Communist guerrillas remaining in the mountains, swamps and jungles, some of which had not been under any form of central governmental control for many years. This may have been understandable during his first two or three years when he was so preoccupied with other matters, and perhaps also because his American advisers were training his army to be a conventional one, designed to block a land invasion from the north at the DMZ. The ARVN seldom ventured off the main roads into the countryside proper, and studiously avoided areas where Communists were known to be well established, such as the U Minh Forest in the Camu Peninsula. the Plain of Reeds in the Delta, the Ho Bo Wood, some 30 miles north of Saigon, and several other remote strongholds that were difficult to reach or to penetrate easily because of swamp or dense jungle.

Vietnam was a country of villages, into which the people had been first organised by the conquering Chinese in 200 BC, each almost autonomous, with its chief-cum-priest in charge, supported by an elected village council. This system had endured, and the French had never succeeded in undermining it, in their efforts to form larger administrative units. The villager was tied to his village, and many lived throughout their harsh lives without ever travelling more than a score of miles from it. This pattern bred traditional hostility between city and village dwellers, a heritage that still exists, and colours many of the current prejudices. Diem tried to eliminate village autonomy altogether by placing officials appointed in Saigon as village headmen when vacancies occurred, having power over the locally elected councils. Village autonomy worked to the advantage of the Communist guerrillas, as villages were traditionally independent of, and suspicious of, each other, and so reluctant to go to each other's assistance when attacked or in trouble.

From 1954 until 1960, the Communist guerrillas in SVN, who came to be known as Viet Cong (Vietnamese Communists, the VC*) struggled on alone, without outside aid, guidance, or encouragement, Ho Chi Minh, as we have seen, having more urgent problems to deal with. The writ of the Government of the RVN, the GRVN, barely touched a majority of villages, and in manv of them the Communist cadres who had been left behind in 1954, depending upon their individual drive, quality and luck, asserted a degree of influence and control. So, apart from the firm VC strongholds, there arose a disjointed patch-work pattern of Communist dominated areas and villages in the countryside, away from the main routes, within which the VC were able to terrorise the inhabitants safe from legal retribution. This was their period of survival in which they practised the first Communist principle of war. They must have felt lonely and neglected and there were many defections, for the Diem Government generally took harsh measures against Communists whenever it could. Strategic, political and tactical direction was absent, communication with NVN was non-existent, the DMZ was firmly blocked by Diem's troops, the coastline was patrolled by his ships, and to the west lay the unfriendly countries of Laos and Cambodia. Had President Diem recognised that the main Communist subversive threat was in the countryside and not in the population centres, this would have been the most opportune time, when it was at its weakest, to root it out – but he did not and so missed a great opportunity of smothering it before it developed into civil war.

The cancelled re-unification elections in SVN caused the VC cadres to stir uneasily, and from 1957 numbers of former Viet Minh, who had been ordered to the north in 1954, began to trickle southwards, infusing fresh blood and enthusiasm. These 'returnees' were all Southerners, who had spent the intervening three years at guerrilla and political training centres in NVN, and who had been given permission to return to their home villages again. The motivation seems to have been simply that of home-sickness, rather than deliberate direction, as they were so disorganised. Their return journey was made either by sea, creeping along the coast in small craft, down the Mekong River, by tedious jungle trails through Laos, or from the port of Sihanoukville, along jungle trails through Cambodia, methods and routes that were both dangerous and slow. Not all by any means completed the journey, which could take several months, successfully. Back in their home villages their welcome was dubious, as they posed as 'Patriotic Liberators', attempting to rouse the peasants to form themselves into anti-Government 'Patriotic Self-Defence Forces'. Apart from the hard-core Communist areas,

* At times the abbreviation VC will include VPA and any other Communist troops, cadres or workers in SVN.

24

generally Communist morale was low in the remainder of the country-side, and the VC unpopular with the people, who simply wanted to be left alone, but they added fuel to what were the early stirrings of a spontaneous revolt against the Diem regime, by his political opponents, dispossessed peasants, ejected village councils and others who felt themselves badly treated and who seemed to have no redress.

During 1958, there was more positive activity amongst the VC in SVN, and as they were joined by others from the North, some signs of organisation became apparent: liaison between VC groups was improved, as were communications, while the beginnings of an intelligence network was set up. The VC were still left entirely to their own resources, and for instance, had to forage for their own food. The only arms they had were those cached away in 1954, but using them they made a few attacks on small police posts and government offices in remote villages. A terrorist campaign developed, which concentrated upon eliminating the Government appointed officials in the country-side and villages. There had been many murders by the VC already, but most of them could be put down to settling old scores or plain banditry. Killings now became selective, the objects being to demon-strate VC power to the peasants, to win back their former prestige, and to embarrass the Diem Government by demonstrating that it could not protect its own officials. This selective assassination campaign caused a creeping paralysis of fear to settle on villages in certain areas, and an increasing number came under VC control as soon as darkness fell, the ARVN and the police seldom venturing out at night.

More selective killings occurred during the following year, 1959, the ensuing terror furthering the radius of influence of the VC. Attacks on small police posts and isolated paramilitary positions became more daring, until on July 8th, the VC made their first attack on an ARVN outpost, near the airfield at Bien Hoa, about 20 miles north of Saigon, which had US Military Advisers attached to it. In this assault, two Americans were killed, the first US dead of this war, and one was wounded, as well as two ARVN soldiers killed, while an attacking VC blew himself up with a grenade by accident. Incidents became more serious and numerous as the year proceeded. Across the oceans, to the watching American Administration President Diem seemed to be the perfect success story, but unseen, lurking underneath this false picture, the germs of Communist insurrection were breeding fast.

The Ho Chi Minh Trail 2

"Every Communist must grasp the truth 'Political power grows out of the barrel of a gun' " Mao Tse-tung *The Little Red Book*.

The next three events of major importance were the eventual declaration of the neutrality of Laos, the gradual development of what became known as the Ho Chi Minh Trail* – a clandestine mountain and jungle route through the eastern parts of Laos – and the assumption by the GDRV of the direction of the VC activities in SVN. A VC supply route also developed from the Cambodian port of Sihanoukville so it is necessary to look briefly at Laos and Cambodia, as well as SVN, and to appreciate that the precise borders of these three countries have always been in dispute, and the countries themselves traditionally antagonistic towards each other.

Until the arrival in 1893 of the colonising French, who made the present day Laos into a Protectorate, that country had only been united for a short period of history in the 14th century, when it was known as the Land of the Million Elephants and the White Parasol, after which it shattered into a number of principalities and independent tribes. On their return after World War II, the French granted Laos autonomy, merging the Kingdom of Luang Prabang with the two Laotian-speaking provinces of Champassak and Vientiane. Having an area of about 91,400 square miles, the terrain of land-locked Laos was mainly mountainous, with thickly forested valleys and swampy areas near the 1,200 mile length of the Mekong River which flowed through the country. The population was probably about two million – no one knew exactly as there had never been a census, and at least half were primitive hill tribesmen, the Meo, Kha, Lu and over 40 other tribes, that included the Black, Red and White Thais, so-called because of the colouring of their dress, who barely knew they were Laotians.

* So called by journalists – a name that stuck.

26

The majority of the people were able to exist in primitive comfort, without too much hard work, on agriculture or fishing, the only real cash crop being opium. Under the French, Laos had been a comparatively peaceful backwater, existing without railways, newspapers or telephonic communication with the outside world, and managing with less than 500 miles of all-weather roads. There were two capitals, the Royal one at Luang Prabang and the Administrative one at Vientiane, which had been the French government centre.

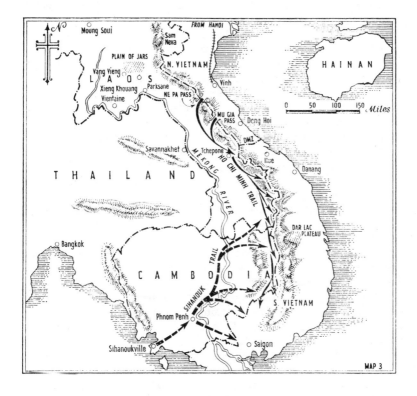

MAP 3

The independence of Laos, formalised by the Geneva Agreements of 1954, allowed the French to retain a garrison of 5,000 troops, and a military mission to train the 25,000-strong Royal Laotian Army. French troops soon withdrew and their military mission was stultified by lack of money as French financial aid to Laos ceased, but the Americans stepped in, providing money and a small advisory mission, that soon consisted of about 70 members, while about another 100 American military advisers joined the French Military Mission to help it train the Royal Laotian Army, only the French then having the legal right to do this.

A Communist-inspired insurrection had been rumbling in the northern part of Laos since before 1953, and the two northern provinces of Phongsaly (which adjoined both China and NVN) and Sam Neua (which adjoined NVN) were occupied by the Communist Pathet Lao troops, under Prince Souphanou Vong. Formed in 1950, and sponsored by the Viet Minh, the Pathet Lao force was about 6,000 strong and roamed sectors of Laos in small groups, trying to impose its creed and influence on the villagers. It was opposed, not only by the Royal Laotian Army, but also by many hill tribes, especially the Meo. The political organisation controlling the Pathet Lao, also led by Prince Vong, was the Neo Lao Haksat (Patriotic Front).

In 1956, Prince Souvanna Phouma became Premier and because of his policies became branded as a 'neutralist'. He negotiated with Prince Vong, his half-brother, and eventually in return for giving him, together with another Communist, seats in the Cabinet, brought the two northern provinces under nominal control of his Government. The issue of integrating the Pathet Lao troops into the Royal Laotian Army was never resolved. In elections held in May 1958, the Communists won 21 seats out of 59 in the National Assembly.

Becoming deeply involved in next-door SVN, the Americans did not like the look of this Communist success, and by withholding financial aid managed to bring down the Government of 'neutralist' Prince Phouma. The USA had been pouring money into Laos for some time in an effort to help it stabilise its government and resist Communism, far more than the simple economy could absorb, which resulted in mismanagement and corruption, hardly any of the money reaching the peasants or those whom it was intended to benefit.

The American Central Intelligence Agency (CIA) found a right-wing anti-Communist, General Phoumi Nosavan, who was pushed into power as Defence Minister, and in August 1958 a Laotian Government was formed without Communists. America sent more military and civilian instructors and advisers, and a Military Assistance and Advisory Group, MAAG, was formed to train the Royal Laotian Army so it would be able to defeat the Communists on the field of battle. American arms and equipment began to arrive in Laos, but the American Government was reluctant to put ground troops into the trackless Laotian expanses. Members of the ICC, supervising the implementation of the Geneva Agreements had been asked to leave Laos, which they had done.

In November 1958, the NVN Government accused Laos of border

violations. This was followed up in July 1959, when a small force of VPA troops, including political cadres, although there were greatly exaggerated reports of its strength, entered Laos, linked up with the Pathet Lao, and supported by groups of Black Thais, in a successful two-month monsoon campaign, re-occupied the provinces of Phongsaly and Sam Neua. In May the following year, the Royal Government demanded that two Pathet Lao units hand in their arms. One, near Luang Prabang, was surrounded and surrendered, but the other, near Xieng Khouang, moved northwards to join the main body. General Nosavan rounded up and imprisoned many Communists, including Prince Vong, the Pathet Lao leader, but later, in April 1960, Vong walked out of prison, taking the prison guards with him.

Suddenly, on the night of August 8th/9th, 1960, an obscure paratroop captain, Kong Le, seized control of Vientiane, when all the members of the Government were away at Luang Prabang, attending the last rites of King Sisavang Vong, who had died the previous November. Kong Le's soldiers had not been paid for months. Professing a neutralist policy, Kong Le established a Revolutionary Committee to negotiate. The Pathet Lao declared its support, enabling him on the 16th, to bring back neutralist Prince Phouma as Premier. On September 22nd, Kong Le captured Paksane from General Nosavan's Royal Laotian Army units, forcing the General to retreat southwards to Savannakhet, but his hopes that Thailand would intervene to help him were not realised. In the north, the Pathet Lao took the town of Sam Neua on September 28th, and on the 27th of the following month, Prince Phouma declared he was accepting Soviet aid, which immediately caused the Americans to cut off theirs. There were now three groups struggling for power in tiny Laos, the Royal Laotian Government, the Pathet Lao and the Neutralists, each having armed forces at their disposal.

In December 1960, with US encouragement, General Nosavan began a drive northwards which succeeded in forcing Kong Le out of Vientiane. Kong Le withdrew to the strategic Plain of Jars, an 800 square mile plateau in north-central Laos (so-called because it was littered with huge granite burial jars, in which human ashes were deposited in ancient times, some weighing up to 100 tons) where he made contact with the Pathet Lao, while the neutralist Premier, Prince Phouma fled into Cambodia.

A military stalemate now set in between the three conflicting armies. The Americans supported the Royal Laotian Army, the Soviet Union sent supplies by aircraft from Hanoi to Kong Le, while the NVN Government sent VPA troops and supplies to bolster up the Pathet Lao. The stalemate was briefly broken during March and April 1961, when General Nosavan moved out to tackle Kong Le and the Pathet Lao, without success. On the contrary, the Royal Laotian Army units were completely driven from the road between Luang Prabang and Vientiane by Kong Le's men, while farther south the Pathet Lao raided towns and villages. This left Kong Le and the Pathet Lao in strong positions on the Plain of Jars.

The British and Soviet Foreign Ministers, as Joint Chairmen of the Geneva Conference, appealed for a cease-fire in Laos, and on May 3rd, 1961, without any special effort being made, the fighting just stopped. America saw that it was backing the wrong horse in General Nosavan, and that he was not the man to fight and defeat the Communists in Laos, so they changed to a different tack – that of making Laos into a neutral buffer state. On May 16th, an international conference was opened at Geneva and on the 22nd of the following month there was agreement to work to form an all-party Government in Laos. But there were delays in putting it into operation and it was not until January 19th, 1962 that one was formed and even then there were differences and squabbles over portfolios.

In April 1962 fighting again broke out in northern Laos, which resulted in more Pathet Lao successes and ended with the flight of the right-wing Government into Thailand. During this period there was international tension, and certain SEATO forces were dispatched to Thailand in case that country was drawn into the anti-Communist struggle. The USA was now officially backing the neutralist Prince Phouma, but there were rumours and suspicions that the CIA still deliberately encouraged General Nosavan and his right-wing faction.

On June 12th, 1962, the various groups in Laos agreed to form a National Union Government, under Prince Phouma, and on July 18th representatives of 14 nations, including America and the Soviet Union, signed the Accord, establishing the neutrality of Laos. The ICC was to supervise the withdrawal of all foreign forces, and America agreed not to station any troops in the country. The armed forces in Laos consisted of the Royal Laotian Army, which had been increased to about 60,000 men, the Pathet Lao, with about 15,000 men, its numbers having been swelled by former Viet Minh personnel, and Kong Le's force of about 5,000 soldiers. The foreign forces in Laos were considered to be the 750-strong US MAAG, a few Soviet pilots and up to 10,000 VPA troops. The Soviet pilots were quickly withdrawn and most of the American personnel were evacuated by October, but there was little sign of any diminution of the VPA forces, which not only remained, but probably increased in number during the ensuing months. By this time the Communists controlled well over half Laos, the eastern half, and the rest of the country seethed uneasily under the Government led by Prince Phouma.

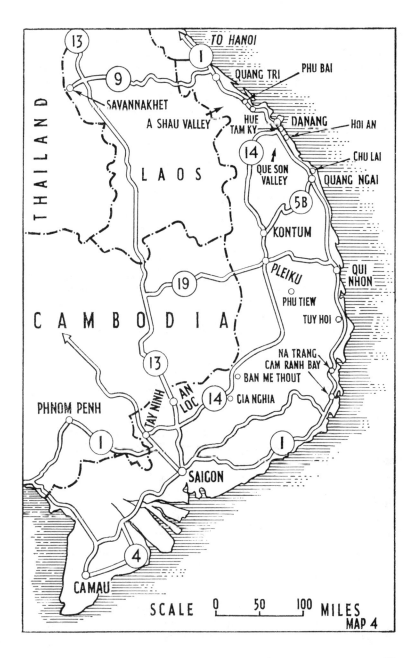

SCALE 0   50   100 MILES

MAP 4

31

To the south of Laos, wedged between SVN and Thailand, lay Cambodia, ruled by Head of State Norodom Sihanouk, and mainly remembered in the West because it contained the remains of a lost civilisation at Angkor Wat. Sihanouk had become King in April 1941 by a complicated process of Royal selection, on the death of his grandfather, but in 1955 he abdicated in favour of his own father. On his father's death in 1960, Sihanouk became Head of State, prior to which he had several times been Premier and Foreign Minister. Even when holding no formal office he had always been a power in the land.

Like Laos, Cambodia, which had become a French Protectorate in 1863, had achieved its real independence by the Geneva Agreements which rid the country of the French and ostensibly of the Viet Minh, who had spilled over into it. Having an area of about 70,000 square miles and a population of only 8·5 million, it was both under-populated and under-developed, its economy being based on agriculture, fishing and forestry products. The majority of the people clustered in the Mekong and Ton Le Sap river valleys, where the main occupation was rice growing – rubber and rice being the main exports. The capital, Phnom Penh, was a river port, and most of the movement was by waterway, there being few good all-weather roads. A short stretch of railway ran from Phnom Penh westwards to the Thailand border, and another south-west to Sihanoukville (Kampong Son) on the Gulf of Siam.

Sihanouk became an adept Neutral, maintaining contacts with both West and East, and taking what aid, without obligations, he could obtain from both. America was early and generous with cash, providing over $120 million in the first three years of independence, and supplying pay and equipment for the 28,000-strong army. But as in Laos, this large amount of money led to corruption. Communist countries weighed in with economic projects, such as factories. Although rejecting Chinese offers of military aid, Sihanouk was on friendly terms with that country, officially recognising it in July 1958, thus upsetting SVN, which incidentally territorially claimed a few Cambodian islands. Sihanouk had to visit President Diem in Saigon the following month to sooth his ruffled feelings, before flying off to Peking. In November, Chou En-lai, the Chinese Premier, visited Cambodia, and while there, he was able to convert the loyalties of the some 300,000 resident Chinese from Chiang Kai-shek to Mao Tse-tung. This alarmed neighbouring Thailand, a traditional enemy, in case the now Communist Chinese in Cambodia should make guerrilla raids across the border. Thailand certainly gave refuge to enemies of Sihanouk and a state of emergency was declared by the Thai Government in the border regions.

There were also about half a million Vietnamese in Cambodia, mainly in the eastern provinces, over which Sihanouk had at the best but sketchy control, and who had direct ties and sympathy with either NVN or SVN. President Diem constantly claimed that Cambodia gave help and refuge to the VC, and that the VC made raids into SVN from Cambodian territory, while Sihanouk counter-claimed there were many violations of Cambodian air space by both SVN and Thailand. Indeed, Sihanouk's hold over vast sections of his country was also nominal, and several dissident groups existed, some with armed forces at their disposal. The main two were the Khmer Rouges, Cambodian Reds, a loose description of Communists and leftists, who were in opposition to the Government, or had been at some time or other, and the Khmer Serai, Free Cambodians, who had associated with and been trained by the Viet Minh.

Sihanouk's studied neutrality did not please the USA, which wanted him to veer towards the West, and on his part Sihanouk was not always pleased with the USA, blaming the CIA for two attempted military coups against him in January and February 1959. Also, in 1960, when he urged that both Cambodia and Laos be recognised as neutral buffer states by both East and West, he blamed America for the failure of this plan. In June that year, disappointed at the slow rate of modernisation of his army by the USA, Sihanouk said he would ask the Chinese for military aid. However, he did not do so, preferring the ever-ready American money which kept his economy healthy, to dubious Chinese support and obligations.

In Vietnam the DMZ remained closed, a barrier between North and South, and so as conditions in both Laos and Cambodia gradually made it possible, especially in Laos when large sections of territory came under Communist control, a route was developed that bypassed it, which became known as the Ho Chi Minh Trail. The Ho Chi Minh Trail was not a single roadway or track, but was a network of jungle and mountain tracks that ran roughly parallel to, and not far from, the western border of SVN, and its length eventually reached to between 600 and 800 miles, depending upon where one thought it started and ended – the edges were blurred.

Once the Pathet Lao gained control of certain sectors of terrain, commencing in 1959, the Ho Chi Minh Trail became the regular route to the south, it being estimated that some 1,800 VC used it that year, and about 2,000 in 1960, a volume of traffic that was not fully realised at the time by either the Governments of SVN or America. Heavily forested terrain made camouflage easy and detection by air reconnaissance difficult. At first small groups of VC made their way along it southwards as best they could, striking eastwards into SVN when they thought they were opposite the area they wanted to reach, but it soon became better organised.

33

The Government of NVN was still largely unconcerned with events in SVN, and for instance, when Le Duan, as early as 1955, urged that the NVN Politburo should abandon the idea of the 'political struggle' for the VC in SVN, for a military one he was voted down. But by 1959, having put his house in order to some extent after his initial difficulties, Ho Chi Minh was able to turn his eyes southwards and think about the re-unification of Vietnam under his leadership. The NVN Politburo was in a pro-Soviet mood, and in August 1959, Ho Chi Minh visited Moscow to attend a conference of Communist Parties, and was promised aid, which surpassed any which the Chinese could give. He was accordingly able to start his first Five Year Plan in 1961, which included over 40 industrial projects. There were many Russians in Hanoi and Soviet influence was growing, but Ho Chi Minh was in the happy position of being able to play off the two Communist giants against each other, especially after 1960, when relations between them began to deteriorate. It was now obvious to Ho Chi Minh that there would be no large scale land assault from South Vietnam across the DMZ, as the ARVN was clearly not capable of mounting such an operation against the VPA, and he did not think America, after its Korean experience, would send an expeditionary force for that purpose, which might embroil them in open conflict with China. Therefore his thoughts turned again to guerrilla warfare. He realised that the static ARVN formations were so positioned near the DMZ, in and around Saigon and protecting other cities, that the countryside was left virtually unprotected against the VC, who, he saw, were not having any great degree of success.

At the Central Committee meeting of the Lao Dong Party on May 14th, 1959, it was decided to take a more direct interest in the war in SVN, and as a political cover a SVN Branch of the Lao Dong Party was formed. The following year, at the Third National Congress of the Lao Dong Party, held in September at Hanoi, Ho Chi Minh stated that "The North is becoming more consolidated and transformed into a firm base for the struggle for national re-unification" and he went on to say "the Party has the new task to liberate the South". Concerned at the seeming stability of the Diem regime and the apparent ineffectiveness of the VC efforts in SVN, the Politburo decided on December 20th, 1960, to assume direction of the war in the South, and for this purpose the National Liberation Front (the NLF) was formed and made to appear to be a coalition of several parties and interests anxious to topple President Diem.

The NLF was a typical Communist front organisation, consisting of about 60 leaders and personalities from many diverse groups and it included representatives of the Catholics, Buddhists, the Cao Dai, the Hoa Hao, the hill tribes, professional and businessmen, teachers and students, and soon had about 300,000 members. It became a coalition of the SVN Branch of the Lao Dong Party, and six major groups (the Farmers, Workers, Women, Youth, Students, Cultural and Liberation Associations) and a number of much smaller ones. A Central Committee of 34 members was formed, which produced a 15-man Politburo and a six-man Secretariat. During the years 1960 to 1965 the Central Committee convened periodically, but the real work was done by the Politburo and the Secretariat. The Chairman was Nguyen Huu Tho, a lawyer who had been imprisoned by both the French and the Diem Government for subversive activities, who was formally elected President at a Congress held somewhere in the "liberated territories" in February 1962; he was not a Communist. There were a succession of three Secretary-Generals, before Huynh Tan Phat who came to be generally regarded as the strategist of the NLF, was appointed to that post in 1964. However, the real power to pull the strings lay with a small group, probably of four people, of the Lao Dong Party Politburo in Hanoi, led by Le Duan, known as the Committee for Supervising the South, who worked through the SVN Branch of the Lao Dong Party, which dominated and directed the coalition.

On January 1st, 1962, the SVN Branch of the Lao Dong Party was transformed overnight into the People's Revolutionary Party (the PRP) with declared Marxist ideas, and membership of over 25,000, which formally took its place in the NLF coalition. With their beaver-like dedicated persistence, the Communists seized and kept the key positions within the NLF.

The fighting elements of the Viet Cong became known as the National Liberation Army, the NLA (Quan Doi Giai Phong). Within the NLF, the PRP and the NLA were closely intertwined, and their high-level directorate became known as the Central Office for South Vietnam, COSVN. This was a physical location of the political and military HQ, which was stationed first of all in Zone D* around Long Khanh, in the Binh Duong province, about 40 miles north of Saigon, but it was mobile and moved several times. All senior members were not necessarily at the COSV at the same time, as many were constantly on the move, partly for security reasons and partly attending conferences and making visits.

The NLF took great pains to keep details of its military leadership secret, but it was most probably a four-man committee, from within the Politburo. Some names quoted as being senior commanders in the NLA were thought to have been aliases or deliberately false to mislead. In mid-1965, for example, a woman, Mme Nguyen Thi Dinh, was widely reported to be the Deputy Commander of the NLA, but nothing was

* So designated on old French military maps.

35

known about her. There is more evidence to support reports that the top NLA military commander from 1964 onwards was Tran Nam Trung, who had been a senior officer in the VPA and who became the Secretary-General of the PRP, the membership of which neared 100,000. Generally military leadership at all levels was deliberately blurred. It was said that in 1962, because the NLA was not doing so well in the field, that General Giap himself took direct control of the war in SVN, but there is little to confirm that he made any special efforts. In any case the overall strategy was dictated by Ho Chi Minh, Le Duan and Giap.

The NLA, which had the usual Communist dual, political and military, command at all levels, ever fearing the rise of a Red Napoleon, consisted of the Main Force, the Regional and the Village Militias. The Main Force, which was about 10,000 strong, was the regular one, with full-time, paid, disciplined and well trained soldiers, who were given the best arms available. The Regional Militia was a part-time body, less well armed and trained, available for operations of limited duration and distance from home, while Village Militia was little more than a pool of labour, but it provided reinforcements for the other two elements when required.

At first the COSVN used the existing six Military Regions inherited from the Viet Minh, but it soon re-divided SVN into three Inter-Zones (groups of provinces), which were the Coastal Plain, the Central Highlands and the former Cochin-China, with Saigon-Cholon-Gia Dinh province, which consisted of some 200 square miles containing two million people, as a Special Area. The chain of command then went down through provincial central committees, district central committees, village committees, hamlet committees, while right at the bottom, forming the solid base were three-man cells. In the population centres the VC command structure went from city central committees, suburban committees to street committees, down to groups of houses, with the three-man cell at the base. Boundaries were deliberately non-concurrent with those of the SVN Government, so that weak junctions could be strongly covered.

The Regional Militia was also based on three-man cells, two of which formed half a squad, and four a full squad of which it was planned there should be at least one in each hamlet, while at village level there were to be platoons, of either three or four squads, up to 48 men. This was the desirable blue-print, which developed in patchwork form as some areas progressed more quickly than others. In places the VC hardly became organised politically, let alone militarily.

The personnel of the NLA at this early stage consisted almost entirely of SVN, but as the cadre structure suffered considerable casualties in late 1962 and early 1963 (the cadres being the dedicated, hard working examples at low levels who always on principle led the way in battle), the Committee for Supervising the South had to send many NVN trained cadres to SVN to make up the shortage, until by 1965, half the estimated cadre strength, of about 25,000, in SVN were Northerners.*

Once the decision to assume responsibility for the war had been taken by the GDRV, the movement southwards along the Ho Chi Minh Trail of men and supplies increased. The route was developed and the traffic controlled and organised. Soon a special transport element of the VPA, which eventually numbered several thousands, directed from Hanoi, was employed to look after the Trail. A large training camp was established at Xuan Mai, near Hanoi, to train and condition the VC who were to be sent southwards. From Xuan Mai personnel were sent to a camp near Vinh for further training, from where they were sent to a staging camp near Dong Hoi, where more training was undertaken if there was time. After a few days rest, the VC were taken by truck across the waist of Vietnam to assembly areas near either the Mu' Gia Pass or the Ne Pa Pass, the usual entry points from NVN on to the Trail.

All this direction and support from NVN was clandestine, as the GDRV did not want to appear to be openly helping the VC, and at the final assembly points the men had to change into 'black pyjamas', the standard VC uniform at this period, and indeed the standard dress of the majority of the peasants too, and had their personal belongings, papers and all means of identifications taken from them. At times, depending upon the military situation in Laos, they were also given a khaki uniform to change into while travelling in Laos.

As the situation in Laos deteriorated, the GDRV became bolder and VPA troops were positioned at intervals along the Ho Chi Minh Trail to deal with fractious hill tribes, such as the Meo. Staging posts were established along the Trail, each one a day's march from the other, a guide taking small groups of usually up to 50 men. Half way to the next staging post, he would be met by the guide from that post to whom he would hand over his charges: the first guide then returned to his own post. In this way there was maximum security, as each guide knew only his own tiny fraction of the route. Tracks were broadened and as most were through densely forested terrain concealment remained simple, and transit camps and supply dumps were established. As many of the travelling VC caught malaria and other tropical diseases, so field hospitals were added to the organisation, where VC could be looked after until they recovered.

The horde of VC plodded doggedly southwards, and included small

* Douglas Pike

37

units ready to be drafted into existing VC units, individual reinforcements, specialists, such as signallers, gunners, medical and logistic personnel, and also political cadres whose tasks might be to settle on districts for propaganda purposes, as well as military ones, sent to form new VC units, regular or part-time. Despite these improvements, it still took at least six weeks for the VC to travel from NVN along the Ho Chi Minh Trail into the northern parts of SVN, and correspondingly longer to points further south, although on longer journeys the use of river transport by night along the Mekong River tended to shorten travelling time.

During 1961, some 3,700 VC reinforcements moved southwards along the Trail, and the number was increased to 5,800 the following year. In this period practically all were Southerners, except for the trained cadres mentioned already, and it is recorded that only one native of NVN was captured in SVN. As the volume of traffic was regularised, it became two-way, with young recruits and cadres going northwards for instruction or training. So developed the famous Ho Chi Minh Trail, which remained a vital factor throughout the conflict.

The Day of Diem 3

"The red scarf quickly became an NLF symbol" Douglas Pike *Viet Cong*.

Just as the year of 1959 had been one of depression for the VC, so 1960 could be said to be one of revival and re-kindled enthusiasm and activity, as they capitalised on peasant discontent. The campaign of terrorism continued with the assassination of village headmen and government officials, sometimes as many as 300 a month, causing many from the smaller villages to move into larger ones at night to sleep. Thus freedom of movement across the countryside during the hours of darkness was increasingly given over to the VC, who took full advantage of it, groups of up to 50 entering villages to kill, kidnap, and seize food and stores. There was a particular flurry of activity between June and October, when the VC presence and influence were strengthened in the Mekong Delta, where about 55 per cent of the population lived and where about 75 per cent of all the rice in SVN was grown. Ambushes at night further deterred the ARVN from operating after darkness fell and troops became defensive-minded.

On October 26th, 1960, President Eisenhower congratulated President Diem on the fifth anniversary of the Republic, assuring him of continued American support, but the issue of Vietnam played only the tiniest of parts in the US Presidential elections. The American Administration fully appreciated the strategic importance of Vietnam in the struggle against World Communism, but was somewhat misled on the progress and extent of the fighting, assuming that with a little extra help, Diem could contain and defeat the VC. Diem wanted the Americans to believe this and deliberately suppressed adverse reports, so in effect this became Diem's Secret War, fought silently in the swamps of the Mekong Delta and the Central Highlands, with only carefully vetted news filtering through.

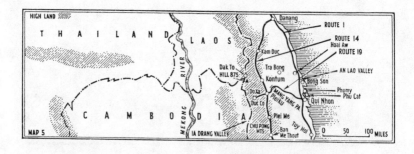

It was not until November 10th, 1960, that for the first time, the GRVN openly charged NVN with direct aggression through Laos. In May 1961, Vice President Johnson paid a fact-finding visit to SVN, and on his return recommended increased military aid, which began to arrive in mid-1961: Diem had said he did not want US combat troops. The main provisions were that the USA would equip and pay for an extra 30,000 soldiers, to bring the ARVN strength up to 170,000; increase the strength of the MAAG; assign more US specialists to train ARVN troops; send US Observers into the field with them and also supply arms for a projected 60,000-strong Civil Guard, to be raised for village protection. Obviously the new Kennedy Administration held a view on the Vietnam problem very similar to that of its predecessor. The question of sending US combat troops was certainly well considered, and on October 11th, the US Joint Chiefs of Staff estimated that "40,000 US troops would be needed to clean out the VC threat, and that a further 128,000 could cope with the possibility of a Chinese or NVN threat".* On November 8th, Defence Secretary McNamara said that any US forces need not exceed "six divisions, or about 205,000 men." On December 14th, it was announced that the build up of US personnel had begun and that already two helicopter companies had reached SVN.

About four-fifths of the ARVN was immobilised blocking the DMZ, garrisoning Saigon, provincial capitals and vulnerable points, leaving only a small number of units available for operations. In May 1961, the five Military Regions were organised into three 'tactical areas', the Northern, Central and Southern, which eventually became Corps Areas as the ARVN expanded. In August the length of military service was increased by six months to two years, to cope with expansion, but there remained many loopholes for the unwilling. The defensive-

* The Pentagon Papers.

40

minded attitude was dictated from the top and enforced by rigid central control, as no major move or attack of battalion-size or over could be made without Diem's personal permission. Casualties were politically bad for him, but nevertheless those of the Government forces of all types amounted to some 500 a month, which indicated there were many small scale clashes between the ARVN and the VC. This attitude stifled the initiative of middle-grade officers and played into the hands of the expanding VC. Despite these drawbacks, during 1961 the ARVN seemed to improve slightly, but was hampered by the slow distribution of US arms and equipment which were so badly needed by units in the field.

During the spring and summer of 1961, the VC strengthened their hold on the Mekong Delta area by terrorist methods and widespread small attacks. It was estimated, for example, that in the two years, 1960 and 1961, they killed nearly 3,000 headmen and officials and kidnapped another 2,500. By mid-summer the VC had complete control of about a quarter of the villages in the Delta area and dominated many more by night. Particularly singled out as targets were buses, motor vehicles, the three-wheeled motor scooters and peasants travelling on foot, the object being to stop all free movement along the roads.

As the VC became able to muster small battalion-sized units for operations they became bolder, especially in the Plain of Reeds, a huge expanse of swamp, waterways and rice fields in the Delta to the south of Saigon. A two-day battle began on July 16th, when two NLA battalions were engaged by ARVN units, which lost 10 killed and 57 wounded, while the VC left 167 dead behind them on the field. Casualty figures for August were 320 VC killed and 357 captured, with 73 ARVN troops killed, 191 wounded and 50 missing, and these figures were typical and indicative of the toll of the 'Secret War'. Another two-day battle began on September 1st, when the NLA captured two small ARVN posts in the Northern Tactical Area, near the Laotian border. The VC were driven out again, but the cost was over 100 ARVN casualties. Farther south, on the 5th, a 500-strong NLA unit clashed with the Cambodian army near the SVN frontier and there was a short battle, after which both sides withdrew. On the 17th, the VC attacked and captured the town of Phuoc Vinh, about 55 miles north of Saigon, killing several government officials and releasing prisoners. ARVN troops were rushed to the area, and the VC were ejected the following day, but the cost was 75 soldiers and civilians killed, but over 100 PLA dead were counted. On October 1st, the VC kidnapped a SVN Liaison Officer, serving with the ICC, when driving about 20 miles north of Saigon and his tortured body was recovered on the 18th.

The intensity of the fighting died down in October 1961, although the constant pin-pricking continued, because the NLA was re-organising and preparing to change strategy. Government successes, VC casualties and shortage of arms, were contributing reasons. Instead of widespread isolated attacks, the new strategy was to concentrate effort upon systematically taking over villages province by province, especially those adjacent to their base areas. The strength of the Main Force had risen to over 12,000, more reinforcements were expected along the Ho Chi Minh Trail and ample volunteers were still available in SVN: the day of VC ruthless conscription had yet to come. At least 27 Main Force battalions had been formed, and were kept in the dozen or so VC base areas, where ARVN troops seldom attempted to venture.

The part-time Regional Militia, available for limited operations, but with limited mobility, had risen to a strength of about 8,000 and had been organised into 43 regional companies, the bulk being in the Delta Area, but they were very poorly armed, while the Village Militia, whose numbers could hardly be guessed at were not armed at all. The NLA had in addition, 21 regular Specialist Units, which carried out such tasks as tax-collecting, propaganda and administration. With the new NLA strategy came the decision to give the peasants more 'carrot' and less 'stick', slackening the terrorism and increasing persuasion, telling the villagers the VC were resistance fighters, and that the Americans were taking the place of the French.

By this time President Diem could no longer gloss over the immensity of the war as he had tried to do for so long, and in any case US Observers were now with ARVN units in the field seeing for themselves at first hand. In a speech to the National Assembly on October 2nd, Diem admitted that SVN was faced "no longer with guerrilla war, but a real war waged by an enemy seeking a strategic decision in South East Asia". His 'Secret War' was at last exposed, and on the 19th, he proclaimed a State of Emergency, and was granted powers to rule by decree.

On that day, General Maxwell Taylor, Special Military Adviser to President Kennedy, arrived in Saigon to assess what further aid was necessary, and on the 26th President Kennedy renewed the pledge to help SVN resist the Communists. In October 1961 there was a major national disaster, when about 25,000 square miles of the Mekong Delta were flooded, the rice crop destroyed and half a million people made homeless. International relief and aid were sent, but this hampered the campaign against the VC, though conversely it also severely retarded that of the NLA. On the recommendation of General Taylor, on November 16th, President Kennedy decided to send more aid to SVN, and by the end of 1961 the first US fighter-bombers and more helicopters had arrived.

The years 1962 and 1963, were ones of increasing American involvement* and while there had only been 948 US military personnel in SVN at the end of 1961, by October 1963 the number had risen to 16,732. On February 8th, 1962, the MAAG organisation was expanded into the US Military Advisory Command in Vietnam (MACV) headed by General Paul Donal Harkins, whose eventual assessment was that it would take five years to defeat the VC. It was decided to provide American arms for a 68,000-strong Regional Force, or Civil Guards, and a 50,000-strong Popular Force, or village militia. US personnel, still in an advisory role and having no command powers, provided mobile training teams and instructors. In August 1962, a group of Australian military experts in jungle fighting arrived in SVN.

During 1962, the VC extended their hold on other parts of the Delta, but did not do so well in the Central Highlands, where they were generally short of food and medicines. During the year, to the 5,800 reinforcements which arrived by way of the Ho Chi Minh Trail, were added volunteers enrolled in SVN, until the strength of the Main Force rose to the 20,000 mark. The regular battalions took shape, being about 450-strong, each with four companies, while in February three such NLA battalions in Zone D, the 4,500 square miles forested area about 40 miles to the north of Saigon that was a large VC stronghold, were brought together to form the first NLA Regiment, or brigade, known as the Main Force Liberation Regiment.

The NLF began serious administration of the territory under its control; their political cadres toured the villages preaching a Ten-Point Programme and a policy of helping and identifying themselves with the peasants was adopted. In secure hard-core VC areas, cottage industries were established to help provide the needs of war, such as cartridge-filling factories, workshops for repairing weapons and making mines and grenades, clothing factories to make uniforms, and printing presses were set up to print propaganda material. Also ammunition and food were hidden in secret caches for emergencies.

The NLF's own radio station, Radio Liberation, began broadcasting on February 1st, 1962, from somewhere inside Liberated Vietnam. Starting with about 90 minutes broadcasting daily in several languages it worked up to over nine hours in the ensuing months. There had also been a clandestine 'Voice of Liberation' which had faded out.†

ARVN troops remained road-bound, and in any case they usually patrolled only in daylight, but even so the VC occasionally fell into ambush and NLA casualties remained heavy as overwhelming ARVN

* There were 14 US military personnel killed in SVN in 1961, 109 in 1962 and 489 in 1963.
† According to Douglas Pike it was thought to have been on a boat in the Delta, that was sunk when the tail-end of a typhoon hit that area in late 1961.

43

fire-power told whenever they clashed. In March 1962, the NLA changed tactics (which so far had been basically those of hit-and-run) to concentrating larger numbers to attack defended posts and villages. On April 13th, the GRVN claimed that in six weeks' fighting the VC had lost 2,030 killed, as against 540 ARVN dead. On April 6th, for example three Main Force battalions assaulted the town of Tra Bong, in Kontum province, and other posts in the area, but were repulsed, losing 45 killed.

By the end of March 1962, over 60 US helicopters mostly CH-21s, the "work-horse" of the army, had arrived in SVN, being allocated out to each of the three Corps HQs. These gave the ARVN a degree of instant mobility and surprise, which so far had solely been VC advantages, and the expression 'vertical envelopment' came into military use.

Other incidents illustrative of the pattern of action occurred on June 5th, when the VC ambushed two food trains between Saigon and Hue. Attacks on trains became more frequent, and they now only ran in daylight, with a heavy escort. On July 2nd, the NLA captured two posts near Quang Ngai in the north, killing 24 soldiers and capturing arms; on the 14th the VC ambushed a convoy some 40 miles north of Saigon, killing an American officer and 22 ARVN soldiers; on the 20th on the Plain of Reeds, some 85 VC were killed and quantities of arms seized by ARVN troops; on August 2nd, the VC raided the coastal town of Ham Tan in Binh Tuy province, capturing more weapons; on September 18th, again on the Plain of Reeds, another successful ARVN action resulted in the deaths of 153 VC and the capture of another 38. Generally, during 1962, the NLA policy of attacking defended positions was not very successful, and this despite the fact that the morale of the ARVN was not good at this stage. The GRVN claimed that during the year some 26,500 VC were killed or captured, which indicated the intensity of the silent war.

1963 was a good year for the NLF, whose NLA Main Force strength rose to about 25,000, and was backed by an 80,000-strong Regional and Village Militia, the additional numbers still being obtained mainly from local volunteers, only about 4,200 coming down the Ho Chi Minh Trail from NVN. Against this, up to 400 were killed each month and there were many defections, the GRVN claiming that about 25,000 VC were killed and captured during the year. The NLA was still very short of arms, although by this time quantities were growing in volume, but were slow coming down the Ho Chi Minh Trail. These were mostly modern Chinese weapons that included 75 mm recoilless guns and 90 mm rockets.

In NVN there was still some controversy within the Politburo over whether or not to fight a political or a military battle in SVN, but the scales were decisively tipped in favour of the military in the late summer of 1963. In the first week of September, two senior VPA generals convened a meeting of senior PRP and NLA members, just inside Cambodia, near the Dar Lac Plateau, after which NLA units were reorganised and their development accelerated. The following month, October, short training courses were run in all the 'liberated areas' to teach minor tactics, anti-aircraft defence, sabotage and weapon training. Despite this there was still a feeling of over-confidence, and later it was admitted by both the GDRV and the NLF that they had taken the decision too lightly, believing that only a slight military push would cause the collapse of the GRVN. On September 11th, the NLF issued a Three-Point Peace Plan, the conditions being an end to the American military assistance, withdrawal of American Forces and a coalition government of political and religious organisations.

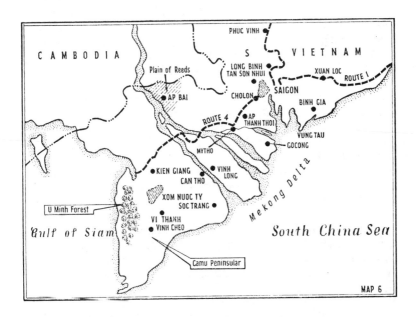

The year of 1963 began badly for the ARVN, when on January 2nd, at Ap Bac, in the Plain of Reeds, a NLA Main Force battalion defeated an ARVN regiment. In the fighting five helicopters were shot down, another eleven damaged, and 65 ARVN soldiers killed, as well as three US Advisers. The US Advisers with the regiment were outspoken in their criticism; the distinct lack of spirit which existed amongst the

45

ARVN troops, who would not obey orders in battle. The US Advisers had been advocating more operations by smaller units, and also operations at night, but President Diem would not agree, as he thought this would simply result in more casualties (already beginning to run at over 1,000 a month), which would be politically disadvantageous to him. Diem had become impatient with the US Advisers, and suspicious of them, wanting to reduce their numbers. This difference of opinions, together with American talk of withdrawing from SVN in 1965, tended to affect the morale of the ARVN and stimulate that of the NLF. On October 2nd, Defence Secretary McNamara stated that "the major part of the US military task can be completed by the end of 1965", and on the 31st, General Harkins said that 1,000 US troops were to be withdrawn by December 31st.

The Americans had long been trying to persuade Diem to grant an amnesty to the VC, but he had always refused. An unofficial one, in February 1963, which had brought in 2,700 defectors in three months, caused him to partially change his mind, and so in April, he offered a Chieu Hoi (Open Arms) Amnesty, but only to VC sympathisers and not to hard-core Communists, whom he declared were incurable. It was later claimed (on August 25th) to have brought in 9,355 individuals.

In the latter part of April, the NLA took the offensive, concentrating upon the Delta, the Central Highlands and the coastal plain of Quang Ngai, commencing on the 25th, when six villages near Quang Ngai were assaulted. A week later the ARVN launched a counter-offensive, in which it claimed to have killed 300 VC, but the NLA had other successes, capturing at least six other army posts within a week, scattered about the country, inflicting heavy losses. In one of these, a surprise attack, some 40 miles north of Kontum, the ARVN lost 40 dead. This provoked a month-long operation in the Kontum area, involving over 10,000 ARVN troops and aircraft, against six Main Force battalions, which generally evaded contact, although on one occasion the VC lost 53 dead, but killed 21 ARVN soldiers. In the Central Highlands, the NLA was still generally on the defensive, and did less well than in the Delta, where on May 18th, 40 VC were killed in an engagement in the Plain of Reeds. On June 29th, near the Cambodian border another 110 VC were killed; on July 20th, in the Delta area, at least 58 were killed in one clash, and on the 30th, in a four-hour battle, 90 VC were killed. The NLA developed a new tactic, making a series of feint attacks on army posts and then withdrawing to tempt the defenders to follow, only to fall into ambushes, which made ARVN soldiers wary of pursuing the enemy. This became known as the 'mouse-trap' tactic.

August was a comparatively quiet month in the field. Although a number of ARVN troops were withdrawn into cities, as the Government was involved in a religious dispute, instead of taking advantage of this, the NLF seemed to concentrate upon propaganda and consolidation, rather than offensive military operations. In the latter part of 1963, both the NLA and ARVN troops had successes and failures, with the ARVN trying to put into practice 'Search and Hold' tactics, which it had agreed to try as a long-term plan to isolate the VC and drive them from SVN.

The general intensity of the fighting continued; for example, in the first week of September, the ARVN troops made 55 separate ground attacks, but in the same period the NLA made over 400, although generally in much lesser strength. On the 9th, the NLA attacked army posts near the town of Gocong, in the Delta, and ambushed a relief column, which, supported by aircraft, stood and fought back for the first time: at least 83 VC were killed. Also on the 10th, the NLA raided the town of Cai Nuoc on the Camu Peninsula, which they occupied for several hours, taking prisoners and arms when they evacuated and leaving over 50 mutilated bodies behind them. The same day the VC carried out a similar raid on the town of Tam Doi, also in the Camu Peninsula, but this time they stayed too long, being caught by ARVN troops. In the fighting 48 ARVN soldiers were killed, but the VC left over 60 dead on the field. On the 16th, ARVN forces attacked a NLA Main Force battalion and killed 122 VC only 15 miles from Saigon, the nearest a VC unit of this size had come to the Capital up to this time. On October 19th, the NLA attacked two ARVN battalions in a village in the Delta, and although the assault was repulsed with the aid of air support, the VC withdrew in darkness. This time the ARVN lost 42 dead and 100 wounded; 13 US Advisers were also wounded.

Impressed by the British success in Malaya with separating the Malayan people outside the towns from the Chinese Terrorists, by putting the peasants and Chinese squatters into defended villages to deprive the guerrillas of food, information, recruits and the weapon of terrorism, the GRVN decided to try this method when the extent of the VC hold on the countryside was realised. Experiments were made, beginning in 1959, in moving groups of peasants into fortified 'agrovilles', each with its own clinic, school and home-guard detachment, where they would be safe at night and divorced from the VC. The GRVN originally used undeveloped land in rural areas and formed the agrovilles on a somewhat socialistic pattern with some economic incentive. In theory the movement into them was voluntary, but in practice most of the peasants had been forcibly removed from their villages, compelled to work for nothing while building the agrovilles and their defences. Their old huts were burnt so the VC could not use them, and the peasants who were deeply attached to their land, either had to walk long distances to their old fields, or abandon them and cultivate fresh land. Accordingly, many slipped away from the agrovilles and walked into the arms of the VC, who promised to help them recover their land and villages.

The agroville project flagged, but was re-launched by President Diem on February 3rd, 1962 as the Strategic Hamlet programme, which was to be something between an agroville and a military village. The project was run by Ngo Dinh Nhu, the unpopular brother-in-law of Diem, the cost being met by the USA. In April, under the codename of Operation Sunrise, a military thrust by the ARVN was made into VC-held territory some 27 miles north of Saigon, in the district of Ben Cat, the NLF fading away as the advance was made. Peasants in the area were forcibly rounded-up and moved into a new Strategic Hamlet, named Ben Thuong, where they had to work on its fortifications. In this showpiece operation, which was well covered by the Press, weaknesses which were highlighted included the discontent of the peasants at being uprooted, their reluctance to become unpaid labourers, their lack of confidence in the ARVN and their apprehension of the VC.

Two types of defended villages came into being: one was the Strategic Hamlet, into which it was planned eventually to move practically the whole rural population, each Hamlet being defended by the villagers themselves, in the form of detachments of the Popular Force. The other type was the Defended Hamlet, usually of some tactical importance, manned by members of the Regional Force of the ARVN. A complaint was that ARVN units frequently failed to respond to calls for assistance at night, when Strategic Hamlets were attacked. Despite confused direction, caused by two separate committees between which there was no liaison, the project was pushed forward; in May it was announced that 8 million people were living in some 6,000 newly-built Strategic Hamlets, and in October 1963, Diem boasted that of the 11,864 Strategic Hamlets planned, 8,600 had been built and that 10 million were grouped into them – but these figures were highly suspect.

We now come to another section of the population of SVN, the primitive hill tribesmen, called Montagnards (mountain-men) by the French. Numbering somewhere between 500,000 and one million, they had been neglected by the French and contemptuously ignored by the SVN, and in fact, in 1958, President Diem had formally dispossessed them of their traditional tribal lands. When the VC originally moved into the Central Highlands, where the Montagnards mainly lived, they were met with hostility, and subsequent VC terrorism caused many of the tribesmen to turn to the Government that despised them, although many served with the NLA elements. On May 26th, 1963, Diem refused to allow US aid to be given directly to them, being forever suspicious that they might become more loyal and attached to the Americans than to himself.

Despite discouragement, the Americans had gone ahead and members of the US Special Forces, the Green Berets, had successfully moved into the Central Highlands, and by August 1962 had trained an irregular force of about 5,000 Montagnards. A few defected, but not so many, and this body developed into a larger semi-military guerrilla force, which became known as the Civil Irregular Defence Group (the CIDG) whose presence handicapped the VC expansion in the Central Highlands.

In adjacent Laos, three rival armies still growled at each other, but during the first half of 1963 there was a split within the Neutralist Forces on the Plain of Jars, and by the end of March fighting had broken out between Kong Le's troops and a dissident left-wing group, supported by the Pathet Lao. Kong Le asked for help from the right-wing general, Nosavan, and sporadic hostilities ensued that spread to central and southern Laos, the results being generally to the advantage of the Communists, thus making the now busy Ho Chi Minh Trail even more secure from any potential threat from the Royal Laotian Government. American aircraft ferried supplies into Laos, and on August 15th, 1962, one had been shot down over that country when carrying food to anti-Communist refugees; another carrying supplies to Kong Le's force had been brought down on November 28th, and a third plane was shot down by the Pathet Lao on January 5th, 1963.

In NVN, the Government had given up hope of a swift victory in the South, and was resigned to "out-waiting the Americans". In addition to its military direction and clandestine support, it also added its voice to the propaganda war whenever it could, and on February 22nd, 1963, the Foreign Minister, Ung Van Khiem, complained to Britain and the Soviet Union about American use of toxic elements.* On March 15th, General Giap stated that 5,000 people had been killed, injured or blinded, between January 14th and February 15th, by chemicals dropped on 41 villages in SVN. On October 5th Radio Hanoi said that a letter had been sent to the United Nations (the UN) proposing the withdrawal of all American aid to Diem, negotiations with all parties without foreign intervention, free elections and a coalition government.

Turning briefly to the domestic scene in SVN, since an assassination attempt made upon him in 1957, President Diem had become aloof and remote from the people, developing a one-man rule through his family, which concentrated power in its own hands and was impatient of

* On January 19th, 1961, the US State Department confirmed that chemical compounds were dropped along the edges of roadways to destroy cover that might be used by the VC, but denied they were dangerous to humans, animals or crops. This tended to indicate American pilots may have been involved, but this was officially denied.

criticism. This had occurred most probably because Diem felt there were so few he could trust, and he certainly had many enemies. His chief adviser and influence, was his brother, Ngo Dinh Nhu, who held no official state appointment, but was head of the powerful Can Lao Khan Vi (Revolutionary Labour Party), which had about 700,000 members, many underground, who collected and passed information on to him. The Can Lao was sometimes referred to as the 'invisible government'. Nhu was also in charge of the National Police and the Special Force. The latter was a section of the National Police, about 6,000-strong, which formed the Presidential Guard and was used for strong-arm political purposes. Through his influence on the President, Nhu seemed to have a big say in government appointments, army promotions and business concessions. His wife, Mme Nhu, the formidable champion of women's rights and a member of the National Assembly, also had assumed great political power. Another brother of the President was Ngo Dinh Can, the political overlord of Central SVN, another was Ngo Dinh Thuc who became Archbishop of Hue. Yet another was the SVN Ambassador to Britain, while Mme Nhu's father was the SVN Ambassador to the USA. The Viet Minh had captured and shot Diem's elder brother, Ngo Dinh Koi in 1945, and later when he unsuccessfully sought Diem's co-operation, Ho Chi Minh brushed it off as "an unfortunate incident".

Diem's restrictive form of government became increasingly unpopular, and on April 30th, 1960, a group of 18 notables, including ten former Ministers, petitioned the President to liberalise his regime. Diem's reply had been to arrest them and others, sending them to join the some 30,000 people in his 'political re-education camps'. His policy remained that of "Security before Liberty".

On November 11th, 1960, there was an attempted military coup against Diem. Paratroops, later joined by armoured troops and marines, occupied certain key buildings and besieged the Presidential Palace, but were held off by the Presidential Guard. The ARVN Chief of Staff was taken as hostage, but released a few hours later. Diem was able to call up other loyal troops and the following day the rebels were forced back into their barracks, where they eventually surrendered without resistance. Apart from a few student demonstrations, the population had remained passive. In 48 hours, about 300 had been killed and wounded, including 45 paratroops. The rebel leaders, who had formed the short-lived Revolutionary Committee of Progress and Liberty, and others prominently involved, escaped to Cambodia, where they were interned. After this attempt on his life, Diem became even more remote, and although on February 6th, 1961, he announced a few minor reforms, these did not amount to much. At the general election, held on

April 9th, Diem was returned as President for another term of five years, with an overwhelming 88 per cent of the poll. There were mutterings of rigged elections, but the indication was that although his regime did not please many, the majority thought he was the only man capable of governing the country.

On February 27th, 1962, two SVN aircraft attacked the Presidential Palace in the early hours of the morning with rocket and machine-gun fire, the assault lasting 25 minutes. Damage was done to the building, but the President and his entourage escaped injury (with the exception of Mme Nhu who fell down stairs and was badly bruised). One of the planes was shot down and the pilot arrested, while the other escaped to Cambodia. This indicated serious military discontent within the ARVN, in which at least half the generals, and many other senior officers, were Diem's own political appointees. In 1962 and 1963, there was a growing feeling of doubt in America as to whether Diem was the best man to win the war against the VC, and the slogan "Can we win with Diem" was frequently uttered. Large discrepancies and differences were obvious between the official reports from SVN and MACV, which were confident and optimistic as to the progress of the war, and those of the Press from the field, which gave a far more pessimistic account. Diem, and indeed those in Saigon, were divorced from the countryside, neither comprehending, nor appearing to care or want to know about the true situation. General Harkins was at loggerheads with the Press over this credibility gap, and there was also friction between himself and some of his officers in the field on the same subject.

In mid-1963, a long smouldering dispute between Diem and the Buddhists literally burst into flames, when on June 11th, a Buddhist monk publicly burnt himself to death in Saigon, which caused riots in the Capital. Just previously, on the 3rd, there had been Buddhist disturbances in Hue, a Buddhist stronghold and the ancient Capital of Annam, because they were not allowed to fly their flags on Buddha's Birthday. These had been harshly repressed, nine people being killed in the process. The Buddhists formed about 80 per cent of the population, although by no means all practised their belief. They felt they were treated as second-class citizens by the Ngo family, and complained of discrimination against them in the government, the armed services and commerce generally. The leaders felt that Diem was trying to make Catholicism the official state religion, but Diem's answer was always that the Catholics on the whole were far better educated and better adapted to modern times than Buddhists, and so inevitably gained a high proportion of the better positions and jobs.

Further Buddhist protest riots occurred in Saigon on July 17th, and tension developed because Diem would not consider their grievances.

Things came to a head during the month of August, when army units had to be drawn into the capital and other cities to maintain order. On August 2nd, a second Buddhist monk immolated himself and more demonstrations followed. On the 22nd, Nhu's Special Force, commanded by Colonel Le Quang Tung, raided the Xa Loi Pagoda in Saigon, causing damage and arresting many Buddhists. Martial law was declared and harsh police action was taken, which did not ease friction. The ARVN soldiers patrolling the streets took care to disassociate themselves from the Special Force police actions against monks and pagodas.

American advisers urged Diem to relax the pressure on the Buddhists, but he would not. Henry Cabot Lodge, the new US Ambassador to SVN, suggested that Nhu and his wife should leave the country, but Diem was outraged at the suggestion. Later, in October, Nhu alleged that the CIA was provoking the Buddhists to overthrow Diem. As the conflict rumbled on many more Buddhists were arrested. On the 8th, a UN Enquiry Mission arrived in Saigon, and on the 23rd, the seventh Buddhist monk immolated himself. Diem would not compromise, as the Americans would have liked him to have done, and certain US financial aid was terminated. This included funds which supported the separate Special Force, in the hope that it would cause Diem to relax his clamp down. Throughout, the Diem family remained adamant and took a hard-line against the Buddhists, Mme Nhu being alleged to have made her notorious derogatory remark about "putting on a barbecue show" after a monk had burnt himself to death. The Buddhist crisis shuddered on.

On November 1st, 1963, Ngo Dinh Diem was overthrown by a military coup, organised by a group of generals, led by General Duong Van Minh, usually known as Big Minh because of his size.* Both Diem and his brother Nhu escaped from the Presidential Palace through a secret tunnel, and then went to a house in Cholon, where they remained in touch with the rebel generals. It is believed that they were offered – and accepted – a safe-conduct pass, but when they gave themselves up the following day, both were shot and killed by an army officer, on the orders of the rebel generals, when being taken in a vehicle to the ARVN HQ. At first it was given out they had committed "accidental suicide", but this was doubtfully received, and later it became obvious that they had been deliberately shot while under arrest. Mme Nhu was in America at the time, Archbishop Thuc was in Rome on a visit, while Ngo Dinh Can sought refuge in the American Consulate in Hue, but was handed

* The Pentagon Papers allege that this coup was planned with the full knowledge and support of Henry Cabot Lodge, the US Ambassador to SVN, and with US Government approval.

over to the new authorities, and eventually brought to trial and shot. And so the power of the Ngo family passed from SVN.

President Diem had made SVN what it was, and although far from perfect, he had given it a form of cohesion and pulled it up by its own boot-straps, contrary to the predictions of most experts at the time. But his later tendency towards dictatorial rule, and the malign influence of his family, alienated practically all sections of the population. The American Government had been unhappy with him for some time, realising that it could neither influence nor control him, but he was the only available leader to back. Diem's clash with the Buddhists was one of the last straws, but it was the dissatisfied ARVN that finally eliminated him. Had he been a Buddhist instead of a Catholic, the story might have had a different ending. Another Catholic, President Kennedy, only survived him by three weeks, being assassinated on November 23rd: both deaths had their effect on SVN.

Development of the NLA–1964   4

"There are two Vietnams, one fighting in the countryside, the other in Saigon, feasting every night" Premier Nguyen Khanh – March 27th, 1964.

With President Diem removed, a Revolutionary Military Committee was formed, immediately composed of the senior plotters, which in turn on November 6th, 1963, formed a Central Executive Committee of 12 generals. General Duong Van Minh became Chief of State,* there was a re-shuffle of all senior military appointments and on the 15th America resumed full aid to SVN. So began a period of confused military, and semi-military, government by the junta, with generals switching posts, ousting each other from power, and then returning again, like a power-crazy game of musical chairs. All this was obviously to the detriment of stable government, the economy of the country and the prosecution of the war against the VC. There were mass demonstrations in support of the new Government in Saigon and other population centres, and many political prisoners were freed.

The first of these musical chair-type moves occurred on January 30th, 1964, when General Minh was ousted from power by his fellow generals in a bloodless coup. General Nguyen Khanh became Premier but such was the unreality of the situation that on February 8th, General Minh agreed to remain on as Chief of State, while the Central Executive Committee was dissolved. The stated object of this coup was to prevent General Minh from pursuing a 'neutralist' policy such as that currently being advocated by President de Gaulle, of France, and he was

---

* Major-General Duong Van Minh, a Buddhist, had directed the campaigns to crush the Hoa Hao Sect and the Binh Xuyen in 1955 and 1956, and was appointed to a field command in 1959. But in 1962, Diem became suspicious of his popularity and he was removed from command of troops and brought into Saigon, being given the empty appointment of Chief Military Adviser.

also criticised for "weeks of indecision and inaction". This was the first of seven changes of Government in SVN in 1964.

Apart from political instability, 1964 was also a year of internal stress, punctuated with terrorism and demonstrations. For example, in February, the COSVN ordered a campaign of terrorism against US personnel, and VC execution groups were sent into Saigon to kill Americans indiscriminately. On the 7th, a bomb in a bar wounded six, on the 9th an explosion in a baseball stadium killed two and wounded 23, and on the 16th a bomb in a cinema killed three and injured 50. On May 2nd, a US transport ship was sunk in Saigon harbour by a mine, and the next day, a bomb, thrown as US servicemen were looking at the wreck, injured eight of them. On the 9th, three men were arrested for laying an explosive device, believed to have been intended for Defence Secretary McNamara (who was to visit on the 12th) one of whom was later shot (on October 15th). This pattern of terrorism ended abruptly, it being thought the COSVN had acted without the approval of the NVN Politburo.

There was growing political action by the Buddhists during the spring and summer, which caused uneasiness amongst the Catholics, and provoked counter-demonstrations. The Buddhists began to demonstrate in provincial towns, and to develop an anti-American attitude. August was a bad month, when students became active in Saigon: the radio station was sacked and the Catholics burnt the HQ of the Buddhist students. In October there were Buddhist demonstrations against the Americans in Danang, an area where the Buddhists hated the Catholics far more than either did the VC. Generally the police and ARVN troops did little to interfere in these disturbances. In October the women at Cantho, in the Delta, had demonstrated demanding the ARVN cease using artillery and aircraft in operations against the VC, as they caused so many civilian casualties. There was another spate of Buddhist demonstrations in Saigon in November. Later official SVN figures stated that 1,350 civilians had been killed in SVN by bombing and acts of sabotage in 1964, altogether an unsettling year in the civil sense.

Political parties were again permitted to operate openly, except those of a Communist nature, and soon there were over 30 active, diverse and mostly small in size. The most effective was the Dai Viet Quoc Dan Dong (Nationalist Party of Vietnam), which had about 2,000 members, and had representation in the successive Governments, until it disagreed too violently with official policies. The Dai Viet, formed in 1941, was an authoritarian, right-wing party, which had collaborated with the Occupying Japanese, the Viet Minh and Bao Dai, and had been driven underground by Diem. It began to struggle to establish a power base within the ARVN, but was not very successful.

55

Heavy disillusionment came in an official report, published in January 1964, which revealed the failure of the Strategic Hamlet project. It admitted that ARVN troops stole livestock from the peasants who were being moved from their old villages into the Strategic Hamlets and extorted money from them. About 45 per cent of those Strategic Hamlets established had been abandoned, and the remainder had been infiltrated by VC agents. The hamlets had been a prime target for the NLA because they had weapons, ammunition and medicine. Many were subjected to mortar fire before being assaulted and overrun, but many had been taken by someone on the inside secretly opening the gates to the VC at night. Poor recruiting for the part-time Popular Force, responsible for defending the Strategic Hamlets, from which there were many defections, usually with weapons, was another reason for the failure.

Great hopes had initially been placed on the Strategic Hamlet scheme, but it had been a half-hearted effort at best, and many senior officers both SVN and American, were still either thinking in terms of a Korean-like invasion from NVN or of deep-penetration tactics. General Harkins was luke-warm towards the project, feeling that it would be better to try and bring the VC to battle and destroy them, and he was in favour of 'Clear and Hold' tactics. Others disliked the idea of uprooting the peasants in mass and imprisoning them in 'concentration camps' as NLF propaganda alleged, while outsiders commented that the political arena was always more important than the military one in SVN. In March, General Khanh said the Government would concentrate upon those Strategic Hamlets that were safe, and expand outwards, a policy that became known as the 'oil spot', that seeped outwards engulfing surrounding territory, which had been the basis of the old French Colonial conquest techniques. The Strategic Hamlets became known as New Life Hamlets, and the name was changed again later to that of the Revolutionary Development Programme, the plan being to 'Clear and Hold' secure small areas and then win over the peasants in them, but the initial round of the battle for the villages in SVN had been lost by President Diem.

McNamara remained on as Defence Secretary under President Johnson, and as he turned his attention increasingly to the war in SVN, it became known as 'McNamara's War' as he tried to bring analytic thinking, logic and cost-effectiveness to bear on it. In February, he established a US Task Force to co-ordinate US policy on Vietnam, but as the months went by, the 'credibility gap' increased as Press reports so often belied official statements. On May 13th, McNamara reiterated that the war in SVN would last another five years. In April, a start was made in re-organising the US military command structure in SVN, so that the training of ARVN forces, command of all US personnel in the field, and control of all US aircraft used in SVN, including those operating from US aircraft carriers, came under one US general.

On June 20th, 1964, General William C. Westmoreland took over as Commander of MACV, with these enlarged powers. Originally an artillery officer, who knew little about basic infantry jungle fighting or guerrilla warfare, he had been picked by General Taylor, who wanted a loyal, conventionally-minded subordinate.* General Harkins's tour of duty in SVN had been marred by his differences with President Diem, the Press and his officers in the field, and he did not seem to have the confidence of all sections of his own Government. For example, it was said that the CIA, the US ambassador and others knew of the impending coup against Diem, but not Harkins. He could not be persuaded by the Press to don combat fatigues and go out to visit the troops in the jungle as his successor frequently did.

We now come to the good work done by the Green Berets. On May 11th, 1961, President Kennedy had approved proposals for "unconventional warfare" against NVN, which included counter-intelligence, sabotage and 'over-flying' missions. Some 400 Special Forces, with over 100 other US Advisers were sent to SVN, and a study instituted on how to increase their scope and strength. While the countryside was being steadily lost by the ARVN, valiant efforts were made to stem the VC tide by the US Special Forces, the Green Berets, which from 1962 until the spring of 1965, were virtually the only serious resistance to the NLF along the SVN borders and in the Central Highlands. Unknown or unpopular with American senior generals, who only understood conventional warfare, they had been pushed into SVN against their wishes, by President Kennedy, whose brother, Senator Robert Kennedy had been impressed with their dedication, toughness and capabilities. They were a counter-insurgency force, taught to live in the mountains and jungle, and to use unconventional methods of fighting.

Officially the tasks of the Green Berets in SVN were border control, surveillance, pacification in NLF areas and to block "logistic corridors", such as the exits from the Ho Chi Minh Trail. Technically their role was a training one, and a training centre was established at Nha Trang on the coast, where a number of SVN Ranger units were formed. The Green Berets were particularly successful in recruiting and training the CIDG, and by mid-1964 had enlisted some 20,000 hill tribesmen, which in 150-man groups prowled the frontier areas from about 50 base camps. They† took into service the Armelite 233 rifle (the M-15), twice

* David Halberstam.
† On July 23rd, 1973, the US Defence Department admitted that Americans had led scout intelligence operations into Cambodia and Laos throughout the war, and the 81 US personnel who had died on such missions had been listed as having been killed in action in SVN.

rejected by the US Army, which was light in weight and had a high velocity at short range. Soon both the ARVN and the US combat troops in SVN adopted the Armelite rifle. In September, it was announced that the US Special Forces in SVN, already 1,000 strong, would be increased by 300 men by the following January (1965).

The bellicose attitude and statements of certain SVN leaders worried the US Government. For example, on July 19th, Premier Nguyen Khanh called for a counter-attack against NVN, which alarmed the Americans, who were not quite sure how the Chinese would react to such a statement, let alone such an action: in any case the ARVN was not in a fit state to tackle such a campaign. On the 26th, at a Press Conference, General Nguyen Cao Ky, commander of the SVN air force, stated that SVN combat teams had been sent on sabotage missions into NVN, having entered NVN by air and land, that his pilots had been trained to fly over NVN to blow up bridges and harbour installations, and that he himself in 1961, had dropped Special Forces into NVN. General Ky added that he had asked America for medium-range bombers for this purpose, but had been refused. He also said that the sabotage missions into NVN had commenced under the Diem regime, and were carried out with US approval. All this was highly embarrassing internationally to America. Radio Hanoi had repeatedly spoken of SVN sabotage operations in NVN, and as recently as July 2nd, had complained to the ICC of an incident that was alleged to have happened on June 30th, when SVN naval craft landed commandos on the coast of Quang Binh province. On July 23rd, the *New York Times* stated that the sabotage raids spoken of by General Ky had little success, some 80 per cent of the personnel involved being captured before carrying out their missions. The GDRV also alleged other incidents of ships shelling its coastline and of violation of air space. On July 31st, General Ky claimed that 30 of his pilots were receiving jet aircraft training (so far he had no jet aircraft), and it was later admitted that SVN pilots were training with the USAF.

It was later revealed* that a three-part operational plan, known as 34A, had been put into operation on February 1st, 1964, which involved kidnapping NVN personnel to gain information, parachuting commando and psychological warfare teams into NVN, and commando raids from the sea to blow up coastal installations, bridges and roads, all to be carried out by SVN or Nationalist Chinese volunteers†; also there were to be US U-2 reconnaissance flights over NVN. This plan was under the operational direction of General Harkins. The second part of the

* The Pentagon Papers.

† The GRVN stated on August 22nd, 1965, that it had rejected an offer of Chinese Nationalist troops by Chiang Kai-Shek, in case such acceptance would re-open the Chinese Civil War.

58

plan was to take place in Laos, where a force of 25 to 40 bombers, with Royal Laotian markings, were to be flown by pilots of Air America (an airline run by the CIA) and Thailand pilots. The third part consisted of US destroyers gathering intelligence in the Gulf of Tongking.

The SVN Air Force, under General Nguyen Cao Ky, had been brought up to a comparatively high state of efficiency and morale, and by the end of 1964, numbered about 12,500 personnel, who had been carefully selected. It had about 350 strike aircraft, organised into about 16 squadrons, which gave ground support to the ARVN. In contrast to sections of the ground element of the ARVN, the air pilots were eager and aggressive to attack the VC, and even to attack NVN. The aircraft included A-1 Skyraiders, a close support attack-bomber which in the following year began to replace the T-28s, and a squadron of A-6 strike aircraft; and by July, some F-100s, Super Sabres, had also been received. There were also about 70 T-28 trainers, 32 C-47 transport aircraft, 25 F-84 fighters, and a few helicopters, mainly Huey CH-34 (Choctaws).* On March 29th, after the production of a photograph of a burnt child, the US Government admitted it supplied napalm to SVN Air Force, but claimed that US personnel had no control over its use.

On April 5th, the GRVN announced that all men between the ages of 20 and 45 were liable to full, or part-time, service, as manpower was short. Re-organising into four Corps, the regular army element of the ARVN amounted to about 210,000, in conventional formations on the US pattern, mainly infantry, armed with AR-15 (Armelite) rifles, 105 mm field guns, and equipped with the M-113 and M-114 armoured personnel carriers, and included six battalions of paratroops. The 6,000-strong Special Force of the National Police, used by Diem as his Presidential Guard, was shaken up, but retained for political and security tasks. The auxiliary forces amounted now to about 186,000, there being 83,000 in the Regional Force, and 103,000 in the Popular Force, both of which had recruiting, morale and desertion problems. On July 27th, Premier Khanh announced US approval of substantial increases in US military and civilian personnel in SVN, who were additional military advisers for the ARVN, including the SVN Rangers, Regional and Popular Forces, and the CIDG; civil advisers for the

* The designation of aircraft and helicopters tends to become confusing, partly because there were so many different types in SVN simply for battle evaluation purposes, and partly because the different US Services, such as the Army, Navy, Air Force and Marine Corps, often had different designations for what was basically the same aircraft. For example, the widely known helicopter, the Sikorsky S-58 was designated the LH-34 and SH-34 Seabat by the US Navy; the CH-34 Choctaw by the US Army; and the UH-34 and VH-34 Seahorse by the US Marine Corps, while as a matter of interest the same helicopter was known as the Wessex in Britain.

police, local government and administration. By the end of the year there were over 23,300 US personnel in SVN. The US involvement in SVN was deepening considerably.

US Advisers were now distributed within the ARVN down to company level, but their role was still only advisory, they had no command power, and this caused frictions and frustrations as their advice was not always asked for, was rejected or was not acted upon. Young US officers, in SVN for a one-year tour of duty, and who were anxious to make their mark and accomplish something, had all too often to work with half-hearted, disillusioned or inefficient SVN officers and administrators with similar outlook and lack of drive.

On the other side, the NLF set out to produce a rival government to that of the GRVN, and the Second Congress of the NLF was held from January 1st to the 8th, 1964, in a 'liberated area', actually somewhere in Tay Ninh province, and Radio Hanoi boasted that it was attended by 150 delegates. The NLF announced that it would observe a five-day ceasefire during the Tet Period, the Vietnamese Lunar New Year celebrations. Later, on July 21st, President Nguyen Huu Tho stated that the NLF was in favour of a suggestion put forward by Prince Sihanouk of Cambodia, that a neutral zone should be formed, to include SVN, Cambodia and Laos.

On the death of Diem, the NLA held at least one-third of SVN and had a varying degree of influence over another third, its fighters lapping at the outskirts of Saigon, which was almost enveloped. A six-battalion Main Force Regiment, known as the 'Capital Liberation Regiment' gradually surrounded Saigon and remained in position, mounting ambushes, mining roads and disrupting traffic. The dozen or so 'liberated areas', were each now controlled by a Provisional Committee, and in these areas, the NLF openly flew its flag, levied taxes, circulated its own currency, ran its own postal system and governed the people.

Situated in Tay Ninh province, the COSVN, protected by a maze of jungle fortifications and tunnels, and defended by three of the best regiments of the Main Force, seemed to develop a new sense of dedication and professionalism. For some months there had been reports of poor march discipline in the NLA, a reluctance to kill, a lack of toughness and many defections. Strong central control by the COSVN caused standards to be raised, discipline to be tightened and training to become more rigorous. For example, the NLA soldier had to be conditioned to remain half-buried in sand, or up to his nose in water, for hours at a time by day, especially when low flying helicopters appeared. This capability contributed greatly to NLA successes in the Delta area, where the ARVN was extremely short of rivercraft.

Political agitation was the first priority of the NLF, and its two primary tasks were the removal of all local government officials and all other strong anti-Communist influences, and then to indoctrinate the population. In 1964, it was estimated the COSVN had over 4,000 small propaganda squads at work, the personnel being southerners, most of whom had been to NVN for training, who could speak to the villagers in their own dialects to influence them. Villagers and NLA members alike were subjected to compulsory periods of daily indoctrination, which were enlivened by songs and sketches with a suitable moral and rousing theme, to give all a sense of mission and togetherness in their struggles.

The weapon of terror continued to be used, but in a more calculating manner and official SVN figures showed that 436 'hamlet chiefs' were killed and 131 'kidnapped' during 1964, bringing the total of government officials of one sort or another killed since 1954 to well over 10,000. This had the effect that it was only extremely brave and dedicated officials who would voluntarily take up a post outside the major population centres, and there were not so many of these. The NLF immediately killed any informers or non-collaborators, sometimes by beheading, after which the corpse and severed head were put on show in the village square as an object lesson. On orders from Hanoi, as far back as 1962, a number of three-man cells of the "specialised units and clandestine forces" were set up in SVN as professional executioners, travelling from one assignment to another through the country, usually pinning a note on the victim's chest to indicate why he had been killed. These executioners were quick to deny any murders for which they were not responsible, such as individuals paying off old scores, or pure criminal acts. A number of US Servicemen were captured, some of whom were killed, and their bodies mutilated before being exhibited, as were many ARVN soldiers and any defectors who were caught. On the other hand the NLF new policy was now modified to identifying with, and being more considerate and helpful towards the peasants, especially in the 'liberated areas'. Unlike the ARVN soldiers, many of whom were from towns and looked down on the villagers, the NLA personnel lived simply, respected village property, crops and livestock, took no more food than was absolutely necessary and frequently helped them with their daily work in the fields.

The strength of the Main Force in SVN remained at about the 30,000 mark, and that of the Regional Militia at about 80,000, while the strength of the Village Militia could only be guessed at. The casualty rate was certainly high, but the official SVN figures of over 26,000 VC killed in 1963 and 21,000 killed in 1964 did not indicate what proportions were Main Force or of which Militia, or indeed how many innocent peasants were caught up in the turmoil, of whom there must have been many unfortunates. About 7,400 VC arrived along the Ho Chi Minh

Trail in 1964, which was not enough to replace casualties, and so the numbers had to be kept up by local recruitment. But the pool of volunteers was drying up, and during this year for the first time, the NLF had to resort to conscription, it being estimated of the '8,400 civilians kidnapped', the majority would be NLF draftees. Previously the NLA had only accepted volunteers, who were of course, carefully screened, as it suspected all others, and felt it might be drafting subversive elements and traitors into its ranks if it enforced conscription. The NLA now had to change its policy in this respect, owing to its manpower requirements; but also it probably felt sufficiently strong and secure not to have to worry too much about potentially unreliable recruits. Radio Liberation boasted the NLF was winning the minds of the people, but US estimates were that only 10 per cent willingly collaborated.

The Main Force now consisted of about 50 regular battalions, and as the policy of moving over to larger formations was adopted, five regimental HQs appeared during the year. The Regional Militia was formed into about 140 regional companies, many of which were over 200-strong. On July 12th, Premier Khanh stated that regular units of the VPA had been identified from prisoners taken as being in SVN, but this was doubtfully received, and was formally denied two days later by the MACV, which stated there was no positive evidence of this. There were units of the VPA in Laos, but none as yet in SVN. The uniform of the NLA remained that of the 'black pyjamas', which enabled them to merge quickly into the background of the people whose customary dress it was, the men wearing either a floppy straw hat or colonial-style pith helmet, decorated with foliage as camouflage, and rubber-soled sandals, often cut from old motor tyres, each carrying a field-pack containing a water-proof sheet, mosquito net and a ration of rice.

NLF expansion was hampered by lack of arms, and it had to rely, especially in its early years on what it could capture or obtain by illegal means, and the arms used included a few US Garrand rifles, 30 mm machine-guns and 82 mm mortars. These together with a small, but steady, influx of arms along the Ho Chi Minh Trail, had enabled the whole of the Main Force to be armed, and for the Regional Militia to be partly armed. Arms for the Regional Militia and ammunition for the Main Force were often hidden in caches for use in operations as required, and occasionally these caches were discovered by searching ARVN troops, or their whereabouts revealed by defectors or agents, which caused the NLA to be chronically short of ammunition. On the whole the VC captured more arms than they lost, but they still did not have sufficient.

In 1963 Ho Chi Minh had been faced with the choice of signing the

Nuclear Defence Treaty, as the Soviet Union had done, and so qualifying for more Soviet military aid by accepting the Soviet line in this matter, or of following the Chinese example, and refusing to sign it. He chose the Chinese line and did not sign, but the friction between the two Communist Powers was such that Soviet military aid was temporarily terminated, while that from the Chinese was increased. This enabled Ho Chi Minh to re-equip most of his VPA with new Chinese-made infantry weapons, most manufactured in 1962, and he was then able to send quantities of his cast-off arms down the Ho Chi Minh Trail to the NLA. In December 1963, for example, a large cache of arms, discovered by the ARVN in Dinh Tuong province, were found to be similar to those in use by the VPA. It was not until late in 1964 that Chinese arms began to reach the VC in SVN, and the first were not captured by the ARVN until December, by which time the Main Force had numbers of the Chinese standard 7·62 series of semi-automatic carbines, assault rifles and light machine-guns, 57 mm and 75 mm recoilless rifles, large mortars, dual-purpose machine guns (ground and anti-aircraft), and anti-tank mines. The US MACV estimated that the NLA possessed at least 130 82 mm and over 300 61 mm mortars, the favourite VC attacking weapons. At this stage both China and NVN had many common interests, the main one being to combat what they considered to be 'US Imperialism'.

Although the NLF had made much of their ability to capture arms from the ARVN they did not do quite so well as they would like us to believe. In the period 1960–1965 the VC captured about 39,000 weapons, but in the same period they lost about 25,000, and so the net gain was only about 14,000, to add to the 10,000 usable ones left in SVN in 1954. This meant that the VC only had about 24,000 arms for about 110,000 Main Force and Regional Militia.*

The slow reaction of the road-bound ARVN played into the hands of the NLA which based its operations upon mobility, speed and surprise, as the VC escalated from terrorism to small engagements and now was moving into larger battles, which were to culminate eventually in the vital all-out Dien Bien Phu-type mass attack that would militarily overwhelm the enemy. In preparation, they developed a 'slash and grind' tactic, of cutting into sections of the countryside, by seizing a small strong point and then dominating the surrounding villages and area, progressively bringing them under firm control. This was successful, in that by the end of 1964 less than half the 12,000 miles of main roadways were open to normal traffic.

Although the NLA still preferred to gain an objective by collusion, and to have the gates of the New Life Hamlets secretly opened for them

* Douglas Pike.

63

at night, they nevertheless carried out offensive action whenever necessary, but tried to ensure that they never assaulted unless confident of success by thorough and careful reconnaissance, preparation, rehearsal, determined action and speedy withdrawal. First of all a replica of the target, be it a New Life Hamlet or a defended post, was constructed in the jungle, and the operation rehearsed until every single man knew his task perfectly. While this was being carried out the Village Militia, aided by children, watched the objective to gather intimate details of the routine, sentries, arms and defences, while VC arms and any essential equipment were placed in pre-arranged caches, ready for the Regional Militia to use.

In darkness, early on the day of the operation, the Regional Militia would collect its arms and silently move into positions along the approach roads to set up ambush positions. Just before dawn a blast on a bugle or the beating of a bamboo drum was the signal for mortar fire to be opened up on the target, under cover of which the assault force – usually Main Force troops – moved in towards the objective from a different direction, blasting its way through the outer wire with explosives fixed on the end of long poles, to swarm over the defences, firing as it advanced. The VC would then kill selected officials, release prisoners, seize hostages, arms, ammunition and medical supplies, burn or demolish buildings and then quickly fade away into the jungle, the Regional Militia remaining in ambush positions long enough to ensure safe withdrawal. If it was intended to stay and hold the position, more Main Force troops would be quickly moved into it, and stronger ambush positions established on all routes leading to it. The pattern of this careful preparation was similar for any ambush, or indeed any type of operation, no matter how small, but there was no flexibility – except cancellation which was frequently done when last minute changes to the defences were observed. The VC attacks were not always successful; sometimes the defenders fought back in desperation knowing perhaps that death or torture might be their lot if overwhelmed and this caused the weapon of terror to backfire at times.

The VC became expert, not only at laying home-made mines, but also booby traps. These included the 'shoe mine', which consisted of razor-sharp slivers of bamboo set sideways along narrow jungle paths intended to cut the ankles and skin, and miniature 'man-traps' with bamboo spikes at the bottom, and also set in the side at an angle, so that when the foot and leg dropped in, they prevented the limb from being freely withdrawn. These bamboo spikes were covered with human excrement so the wounds would fester. Fear of such booby-traps often made the ARVN reluctant to rush to the aid of beleaguered posts, or to pursue the VC into the forests.

64

The COSVN established the Central Research Agency (CRA) to collect and collate information dealing with espionage, communication, research, distribution of information and political re-education. Government defectors were put into special re-education camps, and dependent upon the outcome, the individual was either taken into the employment of the CRA in some suitable task, or was killed if suspected of being a double-agent. The standard of intelligence gathering was high for the NLF had agents in practically all Government departments and branches of the ARVN. It was estimated that details of any ARVN operation were known at least eight hours before it commenced, enabling the VC to either withdraw in time or to set ambushes. But at times the information was slow in reaching the field units and so this did not always happen.

Aerial assaults caused the VC to go underground and construct a maze of tunnels so they could live out of sight of the ever-present reconnaissance aircraft. A special form of defence was developed, especially on the outskirts of the 'liberated areas', in three lines; the outer one consisted of foxholes, the second of bunkers and the third of deep tunnels, with many escape holes, the whole being mainly underground, or extremely well camouflaged. When attacked by aircraft, the VC stayed in their fox-holes while the aircraft dived at them, popping up to fire at it immediately it began to pull away and in this way several were brought down. When ammunition became more plentiful, the NLA was able to put up a solid curtain of fire from every available weapon, whenever a plane attacked, the swarms of bullets being effective in mass.

At first the US helicopters worried the VC in SVN, who tended to run away in a panic as the machines swooped down low and the crew plastered the positions with 'Madame Nhu Cocktails' (a mixture of napalm and charcoal), but they soon found it was better to stay in their foxholes and shoot back at the unarmed helicopters. In mid-1963, the US introduced larger helicopters, which although not armoured, mounted rockets and machine-guns, enabling them to fire at ground troops as they landed or flew low. But again, generally the VC stood and fired back with whatever weapons they had, even when the newer CH-47s appeared. Indeed, in the period 1962–1963, the main effort of the US Army in SVN centred on aviation.

Friction arose between SVN and Cambodia, as the NLF used the port of Sihanoukville to land weapons and stores, which were transported by jungle paths to VC areas in Cambodia near the SVN border. This clandestine route became known as the Sihanouk Trail, and later it was extended to join up with the Ho Chi Minh Trail. Of the many VC encampments near the SVN border, the three main ones were known as the Fish Hook, a piece of Cambodian territory which jutted into

SVN to the east of Kompong Cham; the Parrot's Beak, another piece of Cambodian territory jutting into SVN and pointing at Saigon; and the Bulge, to the east and south of Neak Long, bulging away from the Delta. The Sihanouk Trail linked and supplied these three NLF base areas. The VC in Cambodia were well behaved and kept away from villages.

A serious rupture occurred on March 19th, 1964, when SVN aircraft attacked the village of Chantes, four miles inside the Cambodian border. Using rockets and machine-guns and dropping napalm they set the village on fire, killing 16 people and wounding 14. At first denied by the GRVN, it was later admitted on the 22nd, when it was described as "an error in mapping and location". After this US pilots were ordered not to fly within three miles of the Cambodian border, which made the Sihanouk Trail and the main FLN base areas even more secure. On the ground, on April 4th, in a two-day battle for a village on the Cambodian border, the NLF were driven out by the ARVN, losing 43 killed and 60 wounded. In May the GRVN complained that the VC had caches of arms and supplies hidden in Cambodia, up to 30 miles from the frontier, and that the Cambodian Army and police were unable to cope with the situation, while Prince Sihanouk counter-complained of ARVN troops crossing his frontier.

Inside SVN, against the background of the constant myriads of small actions, the NLF, using Main Force troops, began to mount larger operations, some succeeding and others failing. A five-day battle began on April 12th, when two Main Force battalions overran the town of Kien Long, in the Delta, and were then joined by a third battalion. After a fierce struggle with the ARVN, in which the VC lost 175 killed and the ARVN 55 dead, the VC were eventually driven out by air attacks. This was the first time the NLA had fought such a lengthy pitched battle; previously it had always withdrawn, as it was against its principles to fight an equally-matched contest.

In early June, the VC badly mauled an ARVN battalion in ambush near Ben Cat. On the 4th, they attacked a Special Forces camp near Kontum, killing over 40 defenders, part of the garrison defecting, and the VC making off with arms and ammunition. On the 6th, an attack on another similar camp was beaten off, the VC losing 49 killed, and the defenders 60 (including the first Australian soldier to be killed in SVN). A three-day battle, commencing on July 12th, ended in one of the worst Government defeats of the year, when the NLA attacked the village of Vinh Chee, in Chuong Thien province in the Delta. Five Regional Force companies were sent to its aid, but were driven back, and eventually two regular ARVN battalions reached the village to find it in ruins; over 100 weapons were lost. In another three-day operation, beginning on July 28th, when about 4,000 ARVN troops surrounded a Main Force

66

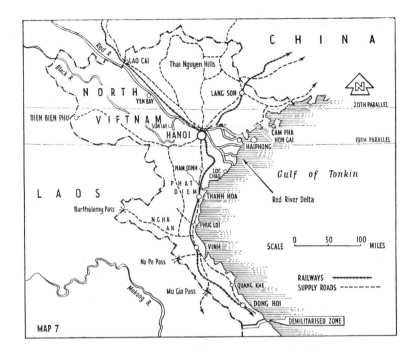

MAP 7

regik near Ben Cat, helicopters flew in 1,000 assault soldiers, only to find the VC had slipped away. On August 20th, an ARVN battalion was ambushed some 45 miles south-west of Saigon in the Delta, losing 60 killed and 135 missing.

On September 15th, the COSVN ordered a general offensive and incidents increased in volume; for example, in that week 975 were recorded, as compared with 580 the previous week, and during the second week of October, ARVN casualties amounted to 260 killed, 440 wounded, and 225 missing, with 545 weapons lost, including 30 guns: the highest so far in the war, while the VC lost 275 dead, 50 captured and lost 100 weapons. Two Main Force battalions attacked an ARVN force of the same size, about 12 miles west of Saigon, on October 7th, shooting down a helicopter and killing 33 soldiers, but on the 11th, in an attack on posts some 30 miles north-west of Saigon, they were forced to withdraw, leaving 55 dead on the field behind them.

Generally, the ARVN troops did not look for trouble, more often than not simply running into it, but there were exceptions, especially when more helicopters enabled men to be quickly airlifted across country. One of the first ARVN successes of this nature occurred on

67

April 27th, when 5,000 ARVN paratroops captured the NLF Inter-Zone HQ for the Central Highlands, at Do Xa, near the border of Quang Ngai and Kontum provinces, in almost inaccessible mountainous terrain which had been in VC hands since 1954. Another successful battle by an ARVN paratroop battalion against a NLA platoon, was on July 21st and 22nd, in the Plain of Reeds, when the VC uncharacteristically stood fast and fought back to the last man killed.

A most spectacular NLA action occurred on the night of October 31st, when the US airfield at Bien Hoa, only 12 miles from Saigon, was bombarded by mortars for almost half an hour from less than a mile away. Five jet bombers were destroyed and 22 other aircraft damaged, four US personnel were killed and another 72 wounded. A few days later, about 1,000 ARVN troops, lifted in 115 helicopters, the largest armada to take off so far, raided the Boi Loi Forest area in Binh Duong province, where it was suspected the Bien Hoa raiders had come from, while 6,000 more ARVN troops in armoured personnel carriers, attempted to surround parts of the area. Again, VC intelligence was good and timely: all had disappeared. The Forest was found to be a honeycomb of tunnels, ten ARVN soldiers being killed searching them, some by booby-traps, and another 11 when a helicopter was shot down.

1964 ended on a triumphant note for the NLA, when a Main Force regiment, 1,500-strong, occupied the Catholic refugee village of Binh Gia, in Phuoc Tuy province, on December 28th. An ARVN battalion, being flown in, lost three helicopters shot down and three more damaged by machine-gun fire. The next day a Regional Force company nearby was overrun by the VC and its 175 men scattered. On the 30th, the airlift continued until the ARVN had three battalions on the battlefield, but a fourth helicopter was shot down. That night the NLA withdrew from Binh Gia, and it was occupied by ARVN troops, but fighting continued on the 31st, as ARVN soldiers tried to retrieve bodies of the dead and badly wounded from the open. Twice they were caught in ambush, and each time had to retire. On January 1st, 1965, helicopters flew in another two ARVN battalions, but they were too late as by this time the NLA had gone.

This was the third time in three weeks that the NLA Main Force – which at Binh Gia appeared for the first time in khaki uniforms, gradually replacing the 'black pyjamas' – stood and fought back for a short while against equal, or even greater strength, and it demonstrated the NLA's capability of operating in regimental strength and fighting protracted battles without air cover, or even equal fire power. It was feared they were nearing the final phase of a gigantic conventional offensive. The NLF now claimed, and was probably largely correct, to control three-quarters of SVN, and eight million of the 13 million people. This was causing population movement; on December 7th, for example, about 16,000 Catholics took refuge in Qui Nhon, as the VC strengthened their grip on the Binh Dinh province. The isolation of Saigon, which was almost surrounded, was becoming so painfully obvious. As the year drew to a close the intensity of the fighting continued, and casualty figures for the last month were given as 990 killed, 2,070 wounded and 980 missing, with 2,050 weapons lost, on the SVN Government side while it claimed the NLA lost 1,890 killed and 680 weapons. The straight human toll for the year of 1964 was given as 29,500 Government casualties, 1,172 American and 21,000 VC.

US Direct Ground
Intervention   5

"I want a joint attack, I want it to be prompt, I want it to be appropriate" President Johnson – February 7th, 1965.

On August 2nd, 1964, the destroyer USS *Maddox*, of the 125-ship US Seventh Fleet, steaming in the Gulf of Tongking, was attacked by three NVN Patrol-Torpedo (PT) ships, of the Soviet Swatow Class mounting 37 mm and 28 mm guns and carrying torpedos. Guns were fired and torpedoes launched by the PT ships, which were driven off by the destroyer's gunfire, there being no US casualties. The Gulf of Tongking was surrounded by Communist territory, and two days previously, SVN Marines had raided the NVN coast about 200 miles north of the DMZ. A second attack was made on the 4th, by six NVN PT ships, on the destroyers USS *Maddox* and *Turner Joy*, and in a four-hour action in which American aircraft and guns took part, two PT ships were sunk and two others damaged. Previously, in January 1964, US warships had been ordered not to approach closer than 15 nautical miles to the Chinese coast and eight nautical miles to the NVN coast.

The NVN Navy was small, consisting of about 15,000 men, which included a marine brigade of about 5,000, and having about 24 small coastal craft, 24 landing craft and about 500 other small craft, mainly armed junks and boats for patrolling rivers. In 1961, the Soviet Union had transferred over 16 PT ships. In February 1964, the US and SVN had established a naval force for raiding operations along the NVN coast, the Americans providing the ships, training and advice, although the ships and men were nominally under SVN command, which was part of *Operation 34A*.

On the 5th, in operations lasting five hours, US aircraft, including Skyhawks, Skyraiders and Phantoms from the aircraft carriers *Constellation* and *Ticonderoga*, hit back at NVN, striking at the naval bases at Hon Gay, Loc Chao, Phuc Loi and Quang Khe, destroying 25 PT ships and MTBs, and also hitting the oil storage tanks at Vinh, 14 being set on fire, thus destroying 90 per cent of the plant. Heavy anti-aircraft fire was encountered in the 64 sorties carried out: two American planes were lost and two more were badly damaged, but no NVN aircraft ventured into the sky.

There was some apprehension in Saigon in case of retaliation and plans were made to evacuate the population and to dig air raid shelters. On the 7th, a State of Emergency was declared, amid rumours of VPA troops massing just north of the DMZ and of Chinese troop movements, but there was no immediate Communist reaction, so anxieties cooled. However, it caused strong American reaction, which produced the famous South East Asia (Gulf of Tongking) Resolution, pledging full support to SVN, which became law when President Johnson signed it on August 11th, 1964. On September 18th, there was another incident in the Gulf of Tongking, when two US destroyers were approached by four NVN PT ships. The destroyers fired their guns and the PT ships went away, there being no damage or casualties. The US authorities suppressed news of this incident, which happened at a time when the USA was not quite sure how China and the Soviet Union would react, but it leaked out afterwards and was admitted.

On July 2nd, 1964, General Maxwell Taylor, smooth and polished, the thinker rather than the rough fighting general, had taken up his post in Saigon as US Ambassador to SVN, taking over from Henry Cabot Lodge, and he became briefly a key figure in SVN events. On September 11th, he put pressure on the SVN generals to reinstate General Khanh as Premier (who had been pushed out by his colleagues) feeling that he was the best man for the job. Taylor generally tended to play the heavy Proconsul, lecturing and talking down to SVN senior officers. Later in the year Taylor fell out with Khanh and a feud developed between them which did not make for happy relations between their two countries. After the November 1st raid on the US airfield at Bien Hoa, General Taylor recommended reprisal raids on NVN, but President Johnson rejected the idea, insisting that the first priority in SVN was a stable government. Ambassador Taylor seemed to be constantly surprised and overtaken by events. Later, on August 20th, 1965, he resigned, and in a US musical chair move, he was succeeded by his predecessor, Henry Cabot Lodge.

During November and December 1964, the SVN Air Force bombed the Ho Chi Minh Trail, SVN ships bombarded the NVN coast, and sabotage operations were mounted against that country. In December, it was admitted that over 100 air raids had been made over north-east Laos, while Tchepone in Laos, an important VC supply centre on the Ho Chi Minh Trail, was bombed and machine-gunned on the 21st of that month. No particular bellicose reaction came from China, but the Soviet Union issued a warning on November 26th, that it might assist NVN against such further attacks (although they took place in Laos). The Soviet Union was getting over its huff because Ho Chi Minh did not sign the Nuclear Disarmament Treaty, and on December 30th, called for the evacuation of US troops from SVN, stating the the NLF would have a permanent representative in Moscow in the New Year. The NLF already had political representatives in Algeria, China, Cuba, Czechoslovakia, East Germany and Indonesia.

After the death of Diem, censorship on reporting was relaxed and more accurate Press accounts came out from SVN, causing the US Administration to be amazed at the many facts that Diem had covered up; they were appalled, for example, to know there was not, and never had been, any positive and successful Strategic Hamlet programme. The credibility gap was wide, and American eyes were opened to just how badly the war in SVN was going; the MACV and SVN reports were mild and optimistic, and the accuracy of some of them was now doubted. An example occurred during an action in the An Lao Valley, just north of Bong Son on the coast, from December 7th–9th, 1964, when an ARVN company was overrun, losing a number of mortars. Eventually a five-battalion offensive was launched to try and clear the valley, which failed. The ARVN report stated that only five of its own troops were killed and another 26 missing, and claiming that 300 VC had been killed. US Observers estimated the Government forces lost at least 500 killed in the battle, while the VC claimed to have received 420 defectors.

Alarmed at the new picture that was emerging from SVN, so contrary to official reports, Defence Secretary McNamara visited that country from December 19th–20th, on a fact-finding mission. Although, on November 15th, MACV had announced that the first 1,000 US servicemen would begin leaving SVN on December 3rd, McNamara stated that US military aid would be continued as long as it was needed or desired. He was convinced that the ARVN simply needed a little more aid to tilt the scales in the favour of SVN: he constantly underrated the stability, staying power and determination of the VC.

On January 3rd, 1965, Secretary of State Dean Rusk had ruled out enlarging the war, and it was known that President Johnson was resisting pressure from the Joint Chiefs of Staff, who felt that a NLF victory could only be prevented by the dispatch of an American Expeditionary Force and destruction bombing of NVN. There were contrary arguments and indecision as to whether it would be better to attack NVN or whether to concentrate first on the war inside SVN. The trend of US strategic thought was changing: Eisenhower had been in favour of "massive retali',tion", but General Taylor, favouring the "flexible response", had persuaded President Kennedy to adopt it in 1961. Taylor also thought that more US aid would enable the war to be won in SVN.

Beginning in January 1965, the Buddhists renewed their agitation against the GRVN, and on the 7th, their strike brought Hue to a standstill; the VC taking advantage of the confusion raided the suburbs. There were more strikes at intervals over the ensuing months at Dalat, Danang and Quang Tri, some with an anti-American bias, and they did not subside until June. Government musical chairs continued, and a military coup on January 27th brought General Khanh briefly back into power, but he was elbowed out again a few days later. There were differences between the right-wing Catholic generals, who wanted to halt the drift towards neutralism, and the Buddhist generals, who favoured it.

Despite this unstable background, January was a fairly successful month for the ARVN, on paper at least, it being claimed the VC lost 2,210 killed and 455 captured, for only 975 soldiers killed. The NLF counter-claimed it had killed 1,547 ARVN troops, wounded 896 and captured 340, and seized 1,038 weapons. The truth was, as usual, somewhere within these wide brackets. ARVN successes in the field included

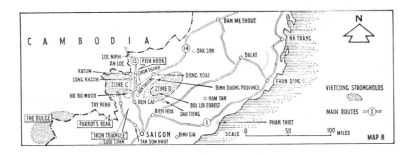

on the 21st, a four-hour battle in Hau Nghai province, in which the NLA lost 72 killed and was believed to have taken away about 130 dead and badly wounded, while on the same day in coastal Kien Hoa province ARVN soldiers landed by helicopter for an operation, killing 54 VC and capturing another 61, but two helicopters were lost; and on the 26th, in an operation at Ap Thanh Thoi, 40 miles south-west of Saigon, ARVN troops successfully encircled a NLA formation, killing 152 VC for the

73

loss of only 18 dead, and capturing large stocks of arms, including guns, and ammunition; the NLA was again believed to have carried away 300 dead and badly wounded.

There was almost a complete NLF cease-fire during the Tet Lunar New Year period from February 1st to 6th, and then suddenly on the 7th the NLA launched a major offensive in the Central Highlands, with the object of cutting the region in two parts along Route 19, from Pleiku to Qui Nhon, which succeeded in severing road and rail communications. Early on this day the VC attacked the US airfield at Pleiku, using 82 mm mortars, destroying six helicopters and damaging 15 other aircraft. The US billet area was also hit, killing two and wounding 126 US personnel. The following day two ARVN companies were overrun just north of the coastal town of Phumy, in Binh Dinh province, and an ARVN battalion sent to their assistance was ambushed on Route 1. Later the GRVN admitted 300 casualties, but it was thought the true figure exceeded 450 killed.

When he heard of the Pleiku raid, President Johnson was reported to have become angry, and to have said "I want a joint attack, I want it to be prompt, I want it to be appropriate".* It was – and later that day, the 7th, both US and SVN aircraft struck at targets in NVN, mainly around the NLA staging area at Dong Hoi. Some planes from an aircraft carrier were not able to complete their mission owing to bad weather. The MACV admitted losing one aircraft in these raids, described as a "defensive one", while the NVN claim four brought down by anti-aircraft fire. On March 17th, 1964, President Johnson had approved planning for an air strike on NVN. On the 17th of the following month a plan was produced by the Joint Chiefs of Staff, known as Operational Plan 34–64, which listed 94 strategic and industrial targets.†

On February 8th, a force of SVN fighter-bombers, led by General Nguyen Cao Ky, head of the Air Force, and escorted by US jet aircraft, raided the Vinh area in NVN near the DMZ. On the 11th there was a "reprisal air raid" against VC staging points in NVN for the NLA assault on US billets in Qui Nhon on the 10th, when 23 US personnel had been killed and 20 wounded. Other raids followed on the Ho Chi Minh Trail and other parts of NLF-held territory in SVN. For example on February 18th, the SVN claimed to have killed 220 VC in an air raid near Danang. Air action was temporarily suspended on the 19th, for about a fortnight, owing to the chaotic political situation in SVN, following an attempted coup. Four air raids had been scheduled for the period February 20th–26th, but three were cancelled for the same reason; and the raids were not resumed until March 2nd, when it can

* *Time*, February 19th, 1965.   † The Pentagon Papers.

74

be said the air campaign against NVN really began.* On February 24th, it had been admitted officially for the first time that US pilots were flying aircraft in action against the VC: so far it had only been confirmed they were acting as co-pilots, observers or instructors.

President Johnson ordered dependents of US personnel in SVN to be evacuated, declared his "continued intention to back up SVN", and ordered a HAWK missile unit to SVN for defence against possible NVN counter air raids. The HAWK, Homing All-the Way Killer, was a surface-to-air missile, with a slant range of about 22 miles, and a ceiling of about 38,000 feet, being designed to bring down high-flying aircraft, although it could operate against aircraft almost as low as 100 feet. The missile used an advanced continuous wave radar homing guidance system. Each unit had about 54 missile launchers.

The restraints and restrictions on bombing NVN were slipping away fast, and on March 2nd, when SVN air activity was resumed, a 160-plane raid was made on various targets in NVN including naval bases; six aircraft were shot down. This was the first "non-reprisal raid"; the original Flaming Dart programme of reprisal was being superseded by that of Rolling Thunder, which was one of graduated bombing. The momentum of these raids increased, both in the number of the aircraft involved and the weight of bombs dropped, and for example, on April 15th, 230 aircraft dropped over 1,000 tons of bombs over NVN. On April 3rd, US and SVN aircraft began striking at non-military targets, which included bridges and ferries. On May 4th an ammunition train was hit, and on the 6th an ammunition dump was bombed. Raids on NVN, now including those of "armed reconnaissance" which meant shooting at opportunity targets, continued until May 13th, when they were suspended by President Johnson, who hoped the NVN would reciprocate. On raids over NVN aircraft had encountered ground fire, but the NVN aircraft did not take to the air to intercept, although on April 9th, US aircraft had clashed with unidentified MiGs near Hainan Island, which were alleged to be Chinese, even though this was never positively confirmed, the Americans claiming to have shot down one. Tragic mistakes occasionally happened; on March 17th, SVN aircraft had accidentally bombed a village only five miles from Danang, thought to be occupied by the VC, only to hit the school, killing 45 children. To the south, on May 1st, US planes had bombed villages in the Parrot's Beak area of Cambodia.

Despite air activity, the NLA continued to win on the ground, and February and March were bad months for the ARVN. On February 21st, a two-battalion NLA operation pinned down an ARVN unit in the Mang Yang Pass, on Route 19, and it was only extricated on the 24th,

* Pentagon Papers.

when US B-52 bombers and Super Sabre F-100 fighters assaulted the attacking formations. On the 26th, the ARVN broke off all engagements in this region, leaving the NLA in control of a large section of Route 19, cutting off Pleiku, which had to be supplied by air. It was not until March 10th, that the road was temporarily opened again and on the 15th Quang Ngai had also be be supplied by air. By mid-March, the NLA had gained control of two-thirds of the some 800,000 population of Binh Dinh province, while in the south, the VC crept nearer to throttle Saigon, where on February 23rd, Cholon had been mortared.

The ARVN did have successes as well as failures, and on February 9th, its troops were flown into action by helicopter near Binh Gia, in Phuoc Tuy province, killing 82 VC for the lost of 21 dead, although three helicopters were shot down. In a three-day attack on the 10th, in the Delta, the NLA lost at least 42 dead; on March 8th, when a NLA Main Force battalion attacked a Special Forces camp in Binh Dinh province, it was beaten back after a six-hour battle, losing over 100 dead. The next day, ARVN Marines, with air support, fought their way through an ambush to relieve the besieged town of Hoai An in Binh Dinh province, and in heavy fighting some 35 miles south of Danang on the 31st, the VC lost over 300 killed. Many of the VC casualties were, of course, due to air attacks. One GRVN success occurred on February 18th, when the Navy captured a Chinese-built ship off the coast of Phu Yen, carrying thousands of weapons, almost all of Communist origin, mainly of Chinese and Czechoslovakian manufacture. Generally, during the months of March and April, there was a comparative lull in the ground fighting, as it was nearing the end of the dry season when movement could be more easily spotted from aircraft.

The tempo of the moment was such that the stage was set for the next escalation of American involvement, that quickly led to all-out combat against the NLF. On March 8th, 1965, a force of 3,500 US Marines, the first combat units to land in SVN, came ashore at Danang. Their mission was to defend the US air base there; in theory they were not there to fight the NLA, but it was stated they would shoot back if attacked. The Marines were followed by other US combat troops, assigned to defend the US air bases at Bien Hoa and Vung Tau. Soon US combat troops were carrying out "offensive patrolling" and frequently came into contact with the VC. On June 8th, General Westmoreland announced that he was authorised to use his troops in offensive operations against the NLA, in co-operation with the ARVN, if requested by the GRVN. On the same day, a detachment of 800 Australian soldiers began to land in SVN, being sent to the Bien Hoa area, where they were later joined by a New Zealand artillery battery, the two becoming known as the ANZ Force. On the 15th, MACV stated that a

US paratroop battalion had gone into action at the request of the GRVN.

On June 26th, General Westmoreland was authorised to commit US troops into battle if necessary, and on the 28th, US, ANZ Force and ARVN soldiers took part in their first joint Search and Destroy operation in the rain forest in Zone D, but made little contact with the NLA. On July 12th, the first US infantry combat troops began to arrive (the 1st Infantry Division, usually known as the Big Red One). Defence Secretary McNamara again visited SVN from July 16th–20th and concluded that the military situation had deteriorated. On the 28th, President Johnson ordered the newly formed 1st (Air Mobile) Cavalry Division, which liked to be known as the First Team, to SVN, and by September it had set up its HQ at An Khe. Already, the US Marines had taken part in the first purely US operation on August 18th, when about 4,000 were landed by sea and air, near Van Tuong, about 16 miles south of Chu Lai, where a Main Force regiment was entrenched. Bombed and napalmed from the air and shelled from the sea, the NLA fought back strongly for a while before withdrawing, when many of the sampans used by the VC to escape were sunk by naval gunfire. NLA losses were estimated to be 599 dead and 122 prisoners captured, while US Marine losses were 50 killed and 150 wounded. America was now fully enmeshed in the war in Vietnam.

US strategy in SVN emerged, with Saigon becoming the base to be strongly defended. Haunted by the ghost of the French defeat at Dien Bien Phu, General Westmoreland concentrated upon establishing a series of coastal enclaves which could be supplied by sea in an emergency if they were besieged, and the unspoken thought was that they could also be evacuated by sea if necessary. These were at Phu Bai, Danang, Chu Lai, Qui Nhon and Cam Ranh Bay, and into these baskets the USA put many eggs. One exception was the US base at Bien Hoa, it being hoped the surrounding area would be soon 'pacified' and the 12 miles of territory between it and Saigon made safe. Another was the base of the 1st (Air Mobile) Cavalry Division at inland An Khe; the military thought in this instance that with over 500 helicopters at its disposal, it could not be trapped like the French had been at Dien Bien Phu. Almost at once these bases became besieged islands in a stormy NLF sea, the VC seeping closer and closer to their outer defences, and to prove they were not inviolate, on the night of August 23–24th, the Bien Hoa base was mortared and 49 aircraft damaged, while on October 28th, both Danang and Chu Lai were attacked in a similar manner, when a total of 47 aircraft were damaged.

While a few Clear and Hold operations were launched in 1965, when US combat troops entered the fray, generally Search and Destroy tactics superseded them, the Americans not being keen to 'hold' on to any piece of inland territory. The Ho Chi Minh Trail remained a point of military controversy; the Americans hesitated to do anything other than bomb it, which they had been doing since December 14th, 1964, although this was not yet admitted, as they calculated it would need at least three infantry divisions to block it, and two more to hold the DMZ.

By July 1965 the ARVN, including the National Police, had risen in numbers to about 545,000, and on the 15th a general mobilisation was ordered, it being planned to increase it further to about 565,000. In June, a Women's Armed Forces Corps, with an establishment of about 1,800, was formed, mainly for clerical duties. A drive on draft evasion was made, and it was claimed on October 6th, that over 8,000 deserters and draft evaders had been rounded up in Saigon alone in four months. The main drawback of the ARVN was its leadership problem, there being still too few officers selected for ability and courage, and too many by family or political influence. Even the more capable officers were cautious as they feared they might become scapegoats for their superiors, as there were deep divisions within the officer corps, such as between the young and the older (the latter having served under the French), Northerners versus the Southerners, and Buddhists against the Catholics.

The soldiers were tired with the strain of constant warfare, and many had been in action for years without a break or hope of early release to civilian life. When the air strikes on NVN began, there was a flood of desertions, especially from the Regional and Popular Forces, which took some 65 per cent of the ARVN casualties, as it was thought that air power would win the war for them. There were times when the ARVN had more deserters than soldiers killed in combat, and one report* stated that 160,000 soldiers had deserted in the past two years.

Morale in the ARVN remained uncertain, the quality of the units depending very much on the capability of the commanding officer, and so varied considerably. Conduct in most actions was mediocre, but at times was good, and at others bad. For example on April 4th, in a three-day operation in Chuong Thien province in the Delta, ARVN troops killed 121 VC; on the 22nd a four-day offensive south of Danang ended in a rout when six ARVN battalions broke and fled before a smaller NLA force; but the next day, some 60 miles south of Saigon, the ARVN killed 152 VC and captured a huge store of arms and ammunition. On May 8th–9th, in an operation on the borders of Binh Dinh and Hau Nghai provinces, ARVN troops panicked and at least 175 were mown down by the NLA; on the 13th the ARVN killed 215 VC in Ba Xuyen province, but on the 30th two ARVN battalions were ambushed some

* *Le Monde* of June 6th, 1966.

15 miles west of Quang Ngai, suffering some 300 killed and 300 wounded or missing, and on June 3rd, twice in one day, a battalion was ambushed by the NLA in Phu Bon province, incurring some 300 casualties.

Great emphasis was now placed on air power to disrupt the NLA and to turn the tables in the GRVN's favour, and in addition to conventional bombs, rockets, cannon-fire and napalm, other devices were brought into operation. These included anti-personnel bombs, some of which were enclosed in a larger casing that opened to release a string of small bombs on a 100 foot line; Lazy Dogs that exploded about 30 yards above the ground, spewing out tiny steel darts; cluster bombs again in cases loaded with small bombs, a small charge exploding to eject them after penetrating the upper jungle canopy; and Snake-eye bombs with an umbrella-like apparatus that retarded the rate of fall to allow aircraft to come in low and avoid the effects of the detonation. The aircraft used the Shrike and Bull-Pup air-to-ground missiles.

The National Police, or the Can Sat, now came more into the picture as they ringed Saigon thickly with road-blocks, check points and patrols, and it was mainly due to them that terrorism in the capital was kept so low, they claiming to have established an almost impenetrable belt seven miles thick. This had not always been so, and the National Police under Diem had been political pawns, and were played off against the army. After his overthrow, they were neglected and distrusted, until it was decided in May 1964, to use them in a counter-insurgency role, on Malayan lines, to deny the VC food, supplies, medicines and information. Early in November 1965, the first class of the new field force element, who wore combat uniforms and carried automatic weapons, graduated: the police in the cities wore white uniforms. US policemen were seconded to train men to move into 'pacified areas' and to police them, and the strength of the National Police was increased from 22,000 to 53,000 during the year. They began to regain confidence, and during 1965, they detected 4,813 VC and apprehended 1,733 deserters in Saigon, everyone over the age of 18 years having to carry an identity card.

On June 19th, 1965, General Nguyen Cao Ky became Premier, but retained direct command of the Air Force. This small, dynamic airman, a Buddhist, had achieved political prominence for his part in suppressing the attempted coup of September 13th, 1964. One of his first acts was to order the first public execution of a VC terrorist. Two days later a US prisoner was shot by the NLF, which said that other similar executions would follow in reprisal. On the 25th, an explosion in a floating restaurant in Saigon killed 23 people, mainly US personnel. Terrorist acts had continued at intervals, and for example, on March 30th, an explosion outside the US Embassy in Saigon killed 16 people and injured many more; on April 7th, the NLF warned that it would shoot a US prisoner if the VC charged with the crime were executed, and on June 16th, an explosion at Saigon airport injured 46 people.* On September 22nd, three civilians were executed in Danang for organising anti-American demonstrations in that city two days previously, and on the 26th, in reprisal, the NLF executed two American prisoners. Premier Ky insisted that more executions for terrorist acts would continue – but without publicity.

Meanwhile, the bombing of NVN caused people in Hanoi (population about 1,200,000) and Haiphong (population about 400,000), the only two cities of any size, to indulge in a flurry of digging air raid trenches and shelters. The initial bombing had taken place when Kosygin, the Soviet Premier, had been visiting Hanoi (from February 6th–10th), and one of the subjects discussed must have been the NVN need for more sophisticated weapons, such as aircraft, radar-controlled anti-aircraft guns and surface-to-air missiles (SAM): America's action had in fact made Ho Chi Minh's point for him. China had supplied infantry weapons, but could not produce sufficient weaponry of this nature. Soviet military aid was dispatched, although it was not until April that it became obvious that SAM sites were being prepared in NVN – but a quarrel arose between China and the Soviet Union over means of delivery.

On March 29th, 1965, the Soviet Union complained that the Chinese were delaying delivery of military material to the NLF, refusing facilities for air transit so it all had to go by slow goods train, and making close and unnecessarily lengthy inspections of Soviet equipment. The following day an agreement was signed between the two countries providing for free transport of all Soviet military aid to the NLF, and denials were made that payment in US dollars had been demanded for this service. By April 6th, it was reported that Soviet equipment was again flowing without hindrance. On July 12th, a communiqué issued in Moscow stated that defence aid would be given to NVN, which included SAMs and the construction of SAM sites, and during the summer a small number of Ilyushin-28 transport aircraft were seen on NVN airfields.

Later, an official letter from the Chinese to the Soviet Government† alleged that the Soviet Union had attempted to obtain Chinese and NVN support in the early months of 1965, for NVN to negotiate with America on the condition that USA stopped the bombing of NVN, and had also proposed to send Soviet troops to NVN as a guarantee against

* On May 16th, 1965, a series of explosions at the US air base at Bien Hoa, killed 16 US personnel and injured 116, destroying or damaging over 40 aircraft. The American authorities stated this was due to an accidental explosion of a bomb, but the NLF claimed responsibility.
† *Observer* of November 14th, 1965.

invasion. An interesting quote from the letter reads, "You wanted to send via China a regular army formation of 4,000 men to be stationed in Vietnam, without first obtaining her consent. Under the pretext of defending the territorial air of Vietnam, you wanted to occupy and use one or two airfields in south-western China and to station a Soviet armed force of 500 men there. You also wanted to open an air corridor in China and obtain for Soviet aeroplanes the privilege of free traffic in her airspace". On December 20th, Chou En-lai accused the Soviet Union of attempting to undermine the NVN unity against the USA, indicating that the NLF leadership was divided into a pro-Soviet element wanting to negotiate with the USA, and a pro-Chinese one, that opposed such negotiations. On the 25th, the Chinese *People's Daily* newspaper alleged that a large part of the Soviet equipment in NVN was obsolescent or in bad condition. Through all this, Ho Chi Minh, who had strengthened his paramount position at the elections in NVN held in April 1964, kept his own counsel, confiding in no one.

On the political front, on March 24th, 1965, the Politburo of the NLF stated it would appeal for volunteers from other countries to fight for it, and by this time there were large numbers of VPA personnel in SVN, but they retained their separate and direct line of command back to Hanoi. On April 13th, Premier Pham Van Dong, speaking to the National Assembly in Hanoi, said that in reply to President Johnson's offer of unconditional discussions, made on the 7th, his Government offered a Four-Point Programme, the points being, recognition of Vietnamese sovereignty and unity and the withdrawal of US Forces; no military alliances with foreign countries by either NVN or SVN; settlements of Vietnam's affairs in accordance with the programme of the NLF; and achievement of re-unification by Vietnamese people without foreign interference. On August 3rd, a NLF broadcast over Radio Hanoi called upon NVN to actively help the female element in the NLF, which was extremely small, women being employed mainly on political and logistical tasks. Wives of NLA soldiers could accompany their husbands, and a number did, but few were involved in combat roles, although the body of a female NLA-lieutenant was found in June, on the battlefield at Dong Xoai. A NLF Women's Liberation Association was active in some villages, whether under NLF control or not, the members writing to ARVN local soldiers urging them to defect, or harassing SVN Government officials. Towards the end of August, the NLF declared the People's Revolutionary Party to be the only "correct leadership", thus removing the fiction that the NLF was a coalition of patriots and democrats.

During the year the VC strength in SVN was increased to about 230,000, by infiltration and local conscription, and on November 30th,

Defence Secretary McNamara said that during the summer rainy season, NPA troops entered at the rate of 1,500 a month, and there were now nine regiments, each about 2,000 strong, operating mainly in the provinces of Kontum, Pleiku and Binh Dinh – some 18,000 regular soldiers. The VC in SVN were now generally adopting an olive-green uniform, the brief khaki phase having faded out.

In the air, as there was no response from Hanoi, after a five-day bombing pause, air raids on NVN were resumed on May 18th. The next day, four US planes were lost, and another on June 7th. By the 22nd, the bombers had passed above the 'Hanoi Line', but still industrial targets were spared, and by July 14th, targets only 30 miles from the Chinese frontier were being hit. China accused both the USA and SVN of violating its air space. On July 23rd, there was a clash with five NVN MiGs, which were shot down for the loss of two US aircraft, after which the NVN Air Force remained passive for a long period.

On June 17th, a force of 30 B-52s, from Guam, some 2,500 miles away, had dropped 300 tons of bombs on the Boi Loi Forest, but although substantial damage was claimed, no VC bodies were found. From this date onwards the B-52s, based in Guam and in Thailand were used to make "mass saturation" raids. Designed and built to carry two H-Bombs, and converted to carry conventional 1,000 lb and 500 lb bombs, the B-52 Stratocruiser had eight jet engines and could fly extremely high, so high that often they could not be heard, even when directly overhead.

The first US plane brought down by a SAM was on July 24th, and the second on August 12th. By September, SAM sites became priority targets, and of the known 22 sites, at least 13 were claimed to have been destroyed by the end of the year, but there were yet others in "semi-mobile" sites, well camouflaged around target areas, and it was not really known exactly how many there were in NVN. Initially the US VCA-4E Pathfinders, with Electronic Counter Measures (ECM) pods, led the way on raids, and the SAMs did not worry the pilots so much, as they received warning of them and were usually able to take evading action, and in fact, only 10 planes were lost by SAM action up until December 24th, when another bombing pause commenced. Anti-aircraft fire was a greater worry to attacking pilots, as there were at least 2,000 radar-controlled Soviet anti-aircraft guns in position by the end of the year. To appreciate the tempo of aerial action, during the period from February 7th until December 24th, the US and SVN Air Forces flew over 12,000 bombing sorties over NVN and over 60,000 strike sorties in SVN, in which 81,000 tons of bombs were dropped. The US Navy and Marine Corps made an additional 6,000 sorties, in the course of which a total of 160 aircraft were lost, of which 80 were brought down over SVN – all except ten by anti-aircraft fire.

Coming now to the war on the ground, generally the NLA had successes in the spring and summer in the Central Highlands and around Saigon, and in the autumn in the Delta, where the VC tried to seize as much of the rice harvest as possible. From August onwards, ARVN, US and ANZ Troops launched a series of counter-offensives and the MACV estimated that in each of the 28 battles, the NLA lost more than 200 killed, US aircraft and fire power being the vital advantage. In October and November, there was again heavy fighting in the Central Highlands. Of the many actions fought, typical examples were the NLA success at Dong Xoai, the siege of Pleiku, the successful defence of the Special Forces camp at Duc Co, the largest and most futile operation so far in the Suoi La Tinh Valley, the NLA failure at Plei Me, the battle at Ia Drang, where US troops encountered the VPA* in action for the first time, and which is regarded by the US as their greatest victory of the year, and the NLA failure at Hoi An.

On June 9th, three Main Force battalions stormed a Special Forces camp at Dong Xoai, in Phuoc Long province, and the casualties included all 20 US Advisers. An ARVN battalion was flown in, but was wiped out on landing; the next day, the 10th, a second unit succeeded in re-occupying the camp and the town, and on the 12th, an ARVN paratroop battalion was ambushed nearby. ARVN casualties amounted to over 700 soldiers and 150 civilians killed – the highest in any battle so far.

After being tightly besieged for six weeks, a strong armoured relief convoy reached Pleiku, after US and ARVN troops forcibly re-opened Route 19, from Qui Nhon, and rebuilt blown bridges. A few days later the troops were withdrawn, and the NLA re-occupied the route again, including the Mang Yang Pass, their favourite ambush spot. After this besieged Pleiku was reinforced and its airstrip developed. Several Special Forces camps in the Central Highlands were besieged for long periods, one of which was at Duc Co, in Kontum province, held by about 400 Montagnards with 20 US Advisers, about seven miles from the Cambodian border, covering a vital cross-road position. From August 1st, the NLA made repeated attacks. On the 3rd, an ARVN battalion of paratroops was dropped, but failed to raise the siege, although in the fighting 158 VC were killed by ground troops, and another 100 from the air. It was not until the 11th, when a strong armoured column from Pleiku, 35 miles away, fought its way through, after having been ambushed the previous day, that the VC withdrew.

* The first regular VPA troops had entered SVN in May 1965 – Pentagon Papers.

In one of the largest operations so far, on October 11th, US and ARVN troops surrounded the Suoi La Tinh Valley, to the north-west of An Khe, and after being held up during the hours of darkness by a Main Force unit, entered the Valley to find the NLA regiment had withdrawn: the VC had known of the operation well in advance. On October 19th, a Main Force regiment made an unsuccessful attack on a Special Forces camp at Plei Me, in northern SVN, losing about 80 dead, but then laid siege. The next day, aircraft including B-52s dropped bombs and napalm. On the 21st, reinforcements were sent by air, and on the 25th, a strong armoured column broke through several ambushes to reach Plei Me. On the 26th, by which time there were three Main Force regiments in the area, a second assault on the camp was repulsed, and the VC started to withdraw towards the Cambodian border. On the 27th, the 1st Cavalry Division successfully ambushed the retreating NLA units. During this battle over 850 VC were killed, and 1,700 wounded, and over 300 Chinese-made arms seized. This was the first instance of the NLA staying and standing up to a prolonged fire-fight, and after it they tended to stay and fight a little longer, instead of immediately withdrawing when they realised they were not going to be instantly successful.

On November 14th, a regiment of the VPA, with NLA support, assaulted an outpost manned by the 1st Cavalry Division, in the Ia Drang Valley, about six miles west of Plei Me, and only five miles from the Cambodian border. US troops counter-attacked, and aircraft were brought into action against the VPA, which on the following day, made five separate determined attacks on the American positions, all of which were beaten back, and after which 869 VPA and NLA dead were left on the battlefield. Although US losses were described as 'heavy',* matched for the first time against the VPA, which had stood, fought and been held, it was regarded as a big victory. The following day, the 17th, a US unit was ambushed, and hand-to-hand fighting ensued, after which there was sporadic fighting until the 23rd, when the defeated VPA and its supporting NLA elements faded away. VC casualties at Ia Drang included at least 1,411 dead.

On December 8th, two Main Force battalions attacked two ARVN battalions in positions near Hoi An, some 20 miles south of Danang, inflicting heavy casualties. Reinforcements, including US Marines, were rushed to Hoi An, and the VC positions shelled by naval guns and bombed by B-52s, but fighting continued until the 18th, when the NLA withdrew, leaving 419 dead behind them.

* Formerly, the exact casualty figures were published for each action, but in July 1965, a restriction was brought in, and instead of precise numbers, US casualties were described as being 'heavy', 'medium' or 'light'.

84

Morale in the US Forces was high; they created a good impression of professionalism in their first year in action in SVN and their operations were well planned and carried out, frustration being felt as the VC invariably, with exceptions, withdrew when they came up against hard opposition. There were occasional setbacks, and for example, on October 15th, a US infantry patrol was wiped out in ambush about 15 miles from Saigon, and on December 5th, an infantry battalion was ambushed in a plantation in Zone D, losing 39 dead and over 100 wounded.

The war in Vietnam was becoming unpopular in America, and when on March 22nd, it was admitted by Defence Secretary McNamara that tear gas had been supplied to the GRVN, there were critical reactions, and on April 17th, 15,000 students from all over America demonstrated in front of the White House. The feeling rose to such proportions in the following months, that in November two pacifists publicly burnt themselves to death, one in front of the Pentagon and the other in front of the UN Building. Neither was American ground intervention popular throughout the world, and an unfriendly Press, American and foreign, made critical comment on alleged indiscriminate bombing, burning of villages and the treatment of the population in SVN, causing General Westmoreland, on September 17th, to issue an order against using unnecessary force which might drive people into the arms of the NLF, to avoid poorly planned "harassment", "reconnaissance by fire" and "preparatory bombing" when villages or villagers were involved or endangered. Areas where the VC grew their own food were sprayed with chemicals from the air, and in December, there was a spate of Press reports alleging the US was pursuing a scorched earth policy in areas controlled by the NLF, that the civilian population were forcibly evacuated by helicopter at times, and their crops and huts destroyed. The rougher side of war was being highlighted.

Although the US Green Berets were having some success in enrolling and training the Montagnards in the CIDG detachments, the SVN Rangers were not always as successful, and for example, there was a revolt in the Dar Lac province of the Central Highlands, where Diem had been settling Catholic refugees from NVN on tribal lands, which broke out on September 20th, 1965, when some 200 Rhade tribesmen training in a camp, mutinied and killed their SVN instructors. They were joined by other tribesmen from adjacent training camps, and all moved into Ban Me Thuot, the provincial capital, where they took over the radio station. The revolt collapsed within a few days when ARVN troops moved into the area, and its cause was wrongly put down to NLF instigation.

Although consisting of some 20 tribes in all, so different in language and culture from the Vietnamese people, the Montagnards, many of them hostile to each other, had been drawn together by the Catholic settlement on their lands, and a number of them, particularly from the powerful Rhade tribe from the Ban Me Thuot district, gave strong support to a movement known as the Unified Front for the Struggle of the Oppressed Races (FULRO),* which demanded autonomy for the 12 northern provinces in SVN. In August, FULRO supporters had surprised a Special Forces camp near Ban Me Thuot, and were joined by many of their fellow tribesmen in training there, carrying off the store of arms and ammunition, but the revolt faded out when ARVN soldiers appeared. Another larger revolt broke out on December 17th, when members of the CIDG seized the town of Phu Tien in Phu Bon province, where 34 people were killed, and Gia Ngia in Quang Duc province, there being also uprisings in three other provinces, which indicated a degree of co-ordination. After some fighting this Montagnard revolt was squashed, and four leaders of it were publicly executed in Pleiku on December 29th.

A Christmas Truce, proposed by the NLF came into effect on December 23rd, and with only minor infringements, lasted until the 26th, when the fighting was resumed with all its petty ferocity. The year of 1965 ended with America fully involved in the war in SVN, determined to pursue it until a military victory was gained; NVN had been bombed and the VPA had been in action in SVN. Visiting SVN on the 28th-29th, McNamara recommended that US Forces, then amounting to almost 180,000 in SVN, should be increased to 300,000. It had been a year in which there had been no major change in the military situation, but the human toll had been high, the US having lost 1,275 killed, 5,466 wounded, 16 captured and 137 missing; the SVN having lost 11,403 killed, 23,196 wounded, and 7,589 missing, while it was claimed the VC had lost 35,382 killed and 5,873 captured.

* Front Unite de la Liberation de Resistance de la Oppressee.

The Air War Continues 6

"The War may last another five, ten, twenty years or longer" Speech by Ho Chi Minh on July 17th, 1966.

When a US Peace Offensive, in which prominent American personalities visited several world capitals, had failed, the bombing of NVN was resumed after a 37-day pause, on January 31st, 1966, during which period the NVN had worked frantically to repair their damaged communications. Just previously, on the 24th, Head of State Nguyen Van Thieu confirmed that SVN aircraft were regularly bombing the Ho Chi Minh Trail, but US spokesmen refused to confirm that it was also being bombed by American aircraft. The radius of the extent of bombing of NVN was gradually extended: on March 4th, heavy raids were made on the railway line from Hanoi to the Chinese border, and two days later many bridges, military stores and barge traffic were included. On April 17th, it was claimed that the main road-rail bridge between Hanoi and Haiphong had been destroyed, and the following day that the Uongbi power plant, only 15 miles from Haiphong, had been hit.

It was found that the US fighter-bomber aircraft were too small to carry enough weight in bombs to completely smash roads and heavy bridges and so B-52s were brought into use. They made their first raid on NVN on April 12th, on the Mu Gia Pass, the main entrance from NVN into the Ho Chi Minh Trail, when many thousands of tons of bombs were dropped. There had been discussion as to whether bombing this pass might widen it or block it – in fact, it tended to widen it, and so made it easier for the VC to use. After this the B-52s were used regularly in raids over NVN, and again on the 27th they hit the Mu Gia Pass.

In April 1966, it was admitted by the US authorities there was a shortage of bombs,* and there was a slackening of tempo for this reason, but this was eventually overcome. The biggest raid of the war took place on May 31st, on the Yen Bay arsenal and munitions stores, on the Red River, some 75 miles north-west of Hanoi. Fires were started and it was claimed that 70 warehouses were destroyed and another 40 damaged. Yen Bay was ringed with about 30 anti-aircraft batteries, comprising several hundred radar-controlled guns, of which the US claimed to have silenced some 25 batteries, but they also admitted the loss of two fighter-bombers.

On June 29th, the US escalated the war by hitting targets in the immediate neighbourhood of Hanoi and Haiphong, prompted by the increased volume of vehicular traffic passing along the Ho Chi Minh Trail. Haiphong was the only NVN port where ocean-going tankers could off-load and so the main targets were oil storage tanks. These raids continued at intervals; the GDRV alleged they caused many civilian casualties and there was also widespread international comment. On July 1st, it was announced in Hanoi that all residents non-essential to the war effort, would be evacuated from the city, and as about 500,000 had already left, the new measures only embraced another 200,000 or so. Government departments moved to their prepared limestone caves in the Thai Nguyen Hills, the old Viet Minh hideout, leaving only skeleton staffs at the Offices of the President, Premier and Foreign Minister. Becoming adept and speedy, the NVN repaired damaged road bridges in a single night, by constructing spans of bamboo and rope, capable of supporting the heaviest trucks.

The first major air battle over NVN occurred on April 23rd, when two MiG-21s (in action for the first time) and 14 MiG-17s engaged 14 US Phantoms: there were irreconcilable claims. Again, on May 11th, MiGs attacked US aircraft; none were hit, but after this they generally kept their distance. The Americans admitted losses, and for example, during the week July 7th–13th, they lost 13 aircraft shot down, and on one day, August 7th, seven more were lost in this way: the NVN made much higher conflicting claims. On September 20th, MACV stated that there were now over 100 MiG-21s and MiG-17s on airfields in NVN, compared with only about 60 six months previously.

The US Phantoms, armed with 'heat-seeking' Sidewinder, and 'radar-guided' Sparrow missiles, with a speed of 1,584 mph were 300 mph faster than the MiG-21s, and although lighter were more powerful,

* The US Defense Department admitted it had to buy back some 5,570 bombs, previously sold as surplus in 1964 to a German firm which planned to extract the nitrates for fertiliser. They had been sold for $1·70 each, and bought back for $21, but were considered a bargain as they now cost $400 to make.

having a faster rate of climb and superior manoeuvrability. The MiG-21, a fighter aircraft, was equipped with a pair of 30 mm cannons, built into the fuselage, while the Phantom only mounted a 20 mm cannon in external wing-pods, which were not as stable or accurate as the fuselage-mounted type. The Phantoms were designed to 'stand-off' some distance, so their missiles could 'zero-in' electronically, but in duels the MiG-21s tried to duck in close, so the missile would be less effective. Both the MiG-21s and MiG-17s were armed with the Atoll (NATO codename) missiles, which were similar to the US Sidewinders.

Raids over NVN continued, and as techniques evolved, by the midsummer, an 'Iron Handle' preceded the bomber aircraft, consisting of four aircraft, one being a pathfinder, able to detect SAM radar signals – the famous SAM Song* – and the three others were armed with rockets, usually the Shrike, which homed in on the SAM radar installation. The SAMS downed 40 US planes during 1966. The US planes carried magnetically-sensitive electronic devices capable of indicating concentrations of VC weapons, and also heat-sensitive detectors, known as 'Eyes in the Sky', which had long been in use over the Ho Chi Minh Trail to detect camp fires at night.

On December 2nd, 4th, 13th and 14th, there was renewed bombing of targets within five miles of Hanoi, causing damage and civilian casualties. On the 23rd, President Johnson, in an effort to salvage the Warsaw Talks, committed the USA not to bomb within a ten mile radius of Hanoi, and an admission was made that occasionally American pilots had accidentally bombed civilian areas. The Christmas Truce was observed from December 24th–26th, 1966, but there were many violations.

The tiny badly battered NVN Navy received more blows during the year, and on July 1st, three MTBs were sunk by US aircraft, two on the 8th, and two more on August 29th, but on July 5th a US Navy fighterbomber had been shot down while attacking two NVN MTBs. On October 25th, US destroyers were authorised to attack NVN shipping up to a distance of 39 miles north of the DMZ, and on November 11th, this was increased to 78 miles. On the 18th, it was stated that two US destroyers in this period had sunk 155 barges and damaged another 144 in about 100 engagements.

In NVN the population prepared against onslaught from the air, and in Hanoi, for example, there were bomb shelters everywhere; deep cylindrical holes on the pavements of the street at ten feet intervals, ready for passers-by to jump into whenever there was an air raid, with a

* The SAM Song was the sudden change in pitch or tune in the ear-phone that indicated to the pilot that a missile was coming towards him, usually enabling him to take evasive action in time.

steel lid to pull across the top like a manhole cover. More children were sent to the country and shops opened only for a couple of hours early in the morning and in the evening, while the decentralisation of industry was providing a rural boom. There was a good harvest in 1966, meaning more food for all, and although there were problems of shortages, prices, inflation and the Black Market, the people generally looked well-fed. Everyone was employed on some task, including the old and the children, and a 225,000-strong conscript labour force was dispersed along the roads and railways to effect instant repairs on bomb damaged communications, which were inevitably completed overnight. Vehicular traffic increased and the Soviet Union was reported to have supplied some 15,000 heavy trucks in the first part of the year, but it was estimated that within months at least 2,000 had been destroyed by aerial action.

During 1966, the GDRV drew nearer to the Soviet Union, and farther away from China. A Soviet delegation visited Hanoi early in January, and increasing numbers of SAMs, a few aircraft – including some MiG-21s – and a great many anti-aircraft weapons were sent to NVN in the ensuing months. On July 31st, it was revealed that two Soviet officers were training the NVN Border Police and although previously the presence of Soviet technicians had been admitted, this was the first time a Soviet military presence was acknowledged. On 28th August, the Soviet Union also admitted it was training NVN pilots: on 2nd October, the Soviet Press revealed that Soviet instructors were training NVN SAM crews, and had been present at a number of engagements, but had not taken part in them; and the following day, the Soviet Union announced a new economic and military aid agreement with NVN.

Allegations that the Chinese were hindering Soviet aid to NVN came up again, being made by Marshal Malinovsky, the Defence Minister, on April 21st. But they were denied by China on May 3rd, which claimed that it had transported 43,000 tons of Soviet military material to NVN at speed and free of charge, adding that the Soviet arms were either old or out of date. On June 19th, the GDRV came into the argument, weakly denying that Soviet aid was encountering any transport difficulties across China.

However, differences between NVN and China were obvious mainly because some Ministers of the DRV wanted to negotiate with America, a policy favoured by the Soviet Union but not by China. But Ho Chi Minh was not prepared to accept Chinese guidance or bow to Chinese pressure in this matter. Also, he wanted SAMs, anti-aircraft guns, aircraft and vehicles, which he could not obtain from China. General Giap wrote* that the "war was taking place on a small territory, where it

* The NVN periodical *Hoc Tap* of June 17th, 1966.

was impossible to apply tactics possible in China, with its vast area", and he was echoed by Le Duan, the First Secretary of the Lao Dong Party, who said "We cannot automatically apply the raw experience of other countries in our own country". Giap wrote other articles in a similar vein about this period. In August, Premier Pham Van Dong and Giap made a secret trip to both Moscow and Peking to try and allay the fears and suspicions of both and to obtain material from both. The Great Cultural Revolution in China began on the 18th, which threw that country into a heaving paroxysm of bloodshed and destruction, and during the latter part of the year, large numbers of the Chinese instructors and technicians in NVN returned, or were recalled, home.

There were notable increases in the strength of the VPA and its auxiliaries in NVN in 1966, a year in which whole divisions penetrated into SVN. The VPA, which for some years had remained at an almost constant strength of about 325,000, formed basically into 15 infantry divisions, had increased to about 450,000 and new divisions were formed. The Militia had risen from the conventional 200,000 to over 500,000, and was frequently called out for periods of military duty. The' Militia was backed by the 'Three Readies Movement', some 1·5 million strong, consisting mainly of those who had not yet received any military training, but were waiting – Ready to Fight, Ready to Join the Army, and Ready to go Anywhere. The previous year, in June, the GDRV ordered some 2·5 million young men and women into the Brigade of Young Volunteers to Fight US Aggression for National Salvation, a grand title for a work force that was used to replace the Militia personnel in the fields and factories, when they were called out for duty.

VPA troops began to take a more active part in the war, and during the year there tended to be more infiltration across the DMZ, and correspondingly less down the Ho Chi Minh Trail, which was increasingly used for munitions and supplies (up to 150 tons a day moving along it) rather than personnel, especially in the latter part of the year. A massive saturation invasion of Quang Tri province, immediately south of the DMZ, was organised, and in July the 324B Infantry Division became the first complete VPA division to infiltrate en bloc through the DMZ. In September, a newly formed division, the 341st, followed and by October, four regular VPA divisions* were in position in the DMZ area.

In mid-1966, the US estimated the total VC strength in SVN as being about 302,000, being made up of about 30,000 VPA regulars, 67,000 NLA Main Force, 150,000 Regional Militia and 55,000 support troops, responsible for transport, administration and medical, and political cadres. By conscription and infiltration an extra 15 battalions for the NLA Main Force were formed during the first eight months of the

* Identified by the US as being the 324B, 325, 341 and 610 Infantry Divisions.

year. SVN troop strengths were about 327,000 in the ARVN, only a proportion of which were available for combat duty, and about 423,000 in the Regional and Popular Forces. US Forces in SVN also increased in strength, and on April 20th, Defence Secretary McNamara stated they amounted to 245,000, plus some 50,000 in the US Naval forces in the area, but of this number only about 100,000 were available for active combat, the remainder being absorbed in the technical and administrative services and in guarding installations. By December 31st, 1966, the US Forces had increased to 389,000.

On the ground in SVN, in the Iron Triangle, the area wedged between the Parrot's Beak, and Zones C* and D in Hau Nghai province, in the 60 square mile forest known as Ho Bo Wood (the HQ of the Saigon-Cholon-Gia Dinh province Special Zone), the largest offensive of the war took place between January 8th and 19th. After intensive preliminary bombing by B-52s, some 8,000 ARVN, US and ANZ soldiers were flown in by about 200 helicopters. A huge network of tunnels was found, some extending to 30 miles and being as deep down as 35 feet, having been started by the Viet Minh years before, and systematically enlarged since. Tear gas was used to clear the tunnels, but few VC were found.

In the Allied "Search and Clear" Operations they had begun to use, the new pattern was that first of all the B-52s made tandem runs over the VC target areas; on the first run they dropped heavy deep-penetration bombs, almost block-busters, and on the second, conventional bombs to catch the surfaced VCs. Then ground troops moved in, using flame-throwers, explosives and tear gas to clear the tunnels, and also levelling the forest terrain to eliminate tree-top snipers. Initially, the US and ARVN troops blew up or caved in the tunnels, but it was soon realised what a mine of information about the NLF they contained, and so instead they were cleared with CS gas and carefully searched. For example, when searching a 14-mile long tunnel in the Ho Bo Wood, they found over 60,000 vital documents that produced much information about the NLF that was not previously known. Listed, amongst other things were the names and locations of VC terrorists in Saigon, as well as a full list of all US officers and their billets.

Tunnelling had become almost a way of life for the NLA, and there were soon untold miles of intricate tunnels surrounding the cities, the 'liberated areas' and ARVN and US installations. Every single VC, no matter what his rank or status dug for at least one hour each day, but generally most of the serious tunnelling was carried out by three-men (or women) teams of 'volunteers', who were actually conscripted from the local villages, and were expected to dig three yards of tunnel a day.

* Zone C was in Tay Ninh province near the Fish Hook.

The tunnels were shored up with bamboo, and there was a right-angle turn every ten yards or so, as protection against blast. Electricity and running water were often laid on, and the larger systems included underground hospitals, stores, barracks, command posts and armouries. When constructing tunnels they used rabbits and gophers (a type of rodent), which bored 'breathing holes' to the surface for them. When clearing and tracing the pattern of the tunnels, the troops used coloured smoke to detect these air-outlets.* Another NLF innovation that was often included was an elementary 'early warning system', made by digging a conical pit, five yards deep, in the shape of a man's ear, when a VC at the bottom of it could hear the noise of aircraft miles away, a distinct advantage as generally the B-52s flew so high they could not always be heard on the ground below.

By 1966, the pattern of US weapons was beginning to change due to war experience in SVN, and for example, the soldiers liked the light, fast-firing M-16, which could spray short burts at a rapid rate, the muzzle velocity being so great at 100 yeards – the estimated average range of most fire-fights – that the bullet generated super-shock waves as it entered the body, that could shatter bone and collapse internal organs. The drawbacks were that its light-weight butt was inclined to shatter if used as a club, and that the sights were so set that a dug-in rifleman had to expose his head and shoulders to aim properly. Another favourite US weapon was the M-79 grenade-launcher, which could project a 40 mm spring-loaded grenade, packed with half-inch steel barbs, into a VC position up to 375 yards distant. They also used Canister mines, that cut down everything within a 20 ft radius, and Claymore mines as booby-traps which ejected hundreds of steel darts. The M-60 light machine-gun was popular, as it was able to form a low silhouette, traverse quickly and fire 550 rounds a minute. The NLA eagerly used captured Claymore mines, whenever they could obtain them, and during November 1966, US troops were hit by VC gas grenades, which helped to nullify the criticism of US use of CS and toxic tear gas.

During 1966, the main areas of military activity were the usual ones, such as the province of Quang Tri south of the DMZ, the coastal provinces of Quang Ngai, Binh Dinh and Phu Yen, those of Kontum and Pleiku in the Central Highlands, in Zone D, in Tay Ninh province, and of course, in the Delta. Just a few of the many actions can be mentioned to give an indication of the trend of the war in this year.

An operation involving some 25,000 ARVN, US and South Korean troops began on January 25th in the area of Bong Son, in Binh Dinh

* Another interesting US device tried out with moderate success, was the ordinary bed-bug, which being blood-seeking, could react to men lurking in ambush, this reaction being amplified into earphones.

province, and continued until March 7th. Four VPA and NLA regiments generally evaded contact, but the MACV claimed they killed 2,084 VC for 'heavy loss', but no further details were given. The GRVN claimed the operation freed 140,000 people from NLF domination, but it had to admit later that five days after the evacuation of this area, the NLA resumed control of it.

A three-day battle in Quang Ngai province began on March 4th, when 7,000 US Marines and ARVN paratroops attacked a VPA regiment. The VPA stood and fought back, but lost 596 men killed, while US casualties were described as 'light'. In further fighting in this province, beginning on April 21st and lasting for three days, the VC lost 320 dead, and on May 4th in another three-day offensive in the Bong Son area, they lost 362 killed. Beginning on June 20th, the NLA attacked US airborne troops near Tuy Hoa, in Phu Yen province, losing 395 dead in seven days.

After a summer lull in Binh Dinh province, fighting flared up again in September, and continued until the end of the year, and on December 17th, MACV claimed that 620 VC had been killed in an operation that had been in progress since October 25th, to the north-west of Qui Nhon.

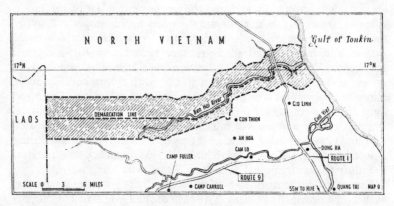

On July 7th, about 8,000 US Marines and 3,000 ARVN troops launched an operation in Quang Tri province against the first VPA Division (the 324th) which had entered through the DMZ. Contact was not established until the 15th, after which fighting continued until the 25th, by which time the VPA had lost 883 dead, and US casualties were 'moderate'. On the 30th, US aircraft bombed the DMZ for the first time,* and frequent raids were then made on it until September 27th, when they were suspended to enable an ICC team to inspect the coastal

* Three earlier raids had been described as mistakes.

94

section of the DMZ, but it would not do so as it doubted its own security, so bombing was resumed on October 18th. US Marines had resumed the offensive on August 3rd in Quang Tri province, gradually driving the VPA from the coastal areas back into the mountains on the Laos border, although the VC remained active in the lowlands and originated many incidents. MACV claimed that by August 16th, 1,227 VC had been killed, but during the week September 18th–24th, the US Forces lost 970 killed, mostly in Quang Tri province.

During the summer and autumn there was sporadic fighting in Kontum and Pleiku, where regiments of the NLA Main Force and units of the VPA had become firmly entrenched. In May, a 15,000-strong joint ARVN, US and South Korean offensive in the Ia Drang Valley, a VC infiltration route from the Ho Chi Minh Trail towards the Qui Nhon area, and the adjacent Chu Pong Mountain range, was mounted against two VPA regiments, and by the end of July, it was claimed that 648 VC had been killed. On June 3rd, in Kontum province, US troops launched an offensive that by the 21st, claimed to have killed 570 VC. A series of engagements in the first half of August in this area resulted in another 540 VC dead, and further battles, beginning on November 19th, cost the VPA 166 killed. But on the 21st, a US platoon was wiped out, while on December 17th, the VPA lost another 65 dead.

On June 2nd, a large operation began against the COSVN, which was in Zone C, in Tay Ninh province. By July 10th, 788 VC had been killed and large quantities of stores captured, including 1,400 tons of rice, but the COSVN had faded backwards into Cambodia. A second operation with a similar objective in Zone C, started on October 15th, in which 25,000 US troops were involved, terminating on November 16th, it being claimed that 965 VC had been killed, but Radio Liberation said there had been heavy US casualties. The COSVN and its protective regiments were forced again backwards into Cambodia, but during December, they all filtered back again, and on the 11th, ambushed a US platoon, causing 'heavy' casualties.

Relations between Cambodia and SVN had been strained for some time, as the Cambodian Government continually accused both the US and the GRVN of bombing its territory, and already on October 18th, 1965, had alleged they had bombed the Cambodian village of Bathu, three days previously. On December 15th, 1965, Prince Sihanouk said that China had offered to assist Cambodia if attacked, but this statement was given little credence. Then on the 20th, US field commanders were authorised to cross the Cambodian border in 'hot pursuit' of the NLA, which brought sharp protest. It was not until April 1966, that Sihanouk admitted that NLA troops were using Cambodia for "rest and refreshment", and on one occasion he had publicly presented them with seven tons of dried fish. At the same time the immensity of the Sihanouk Trail from the port of Sihanoukville, suddenly became apparent, revealed by aerial reconnaissance to be a complex of roads, bicycle tracks, footpaths and waterways. Incidents along the Cambodian-SVN border became more frequent. But the power structure in Cambodia was changing, and in October the right-wing Government of General Lon Nol took office, but Sihanouk remained as Head of State.

In the Saigon area on March 28th, 1966, as a counter to numerous VC attacks on shipping in the Saigon River, a large US force made a landing on the bank about 18 miles below the capital, destroying a small complex of VC camps, but in the following months the VC succeeded in sinking or damaging a number of ships, including on August 28th a SVN mine-sweeper, and on November 1st, a US minesweeper. On April 13th, the US air-base at Tan Son Nhut, just east of Saigon, had been hit by mortar fire, 33 aircraft being destroyed or damaged: this base was later bombarded on December 4th, while at the US ammunition store at Long Binh, 13 miles from Saigon – the largest in SVN – explosions occurred on October 28th, November 18th and December 10th. On August 18th, ANZ troops were involved in their fiercest fighting so far when they clashed with a NLA Main Force battalion in the Vung Tau area, about 40 miles to the south-west of Saigon, the ANZ Force losing 17 killed, but claiming to have killed 245 VC.

In the Mekong Delta, still the main source of NLA food and recruits, the VC were able to prevent the movement of rice to Saigon, the Plain of Reeds and the Camu Peninsula for example being completely under NLF control, and so Saigon had to import its rice from abroad. On July 4th in An Xuyen province, the leading elements of an ARVN force were ambushed by the NLA, who put on dead soldier's uniforms to surprise the main body, being able to open fire at point-blank range. No details of casualties were issued, but they were thought to be heavy. A SVN success occurred on September 4th, when ARVN troops en-circled a NLA Main Force battalion, and claimed to kill 276 VC. From September onwards US ground troops took part in operations in the Delta. Previously, only ARVN troops had been employed there with, of course, US and SVN air support.

Psychological warfare was developed in 1966, when in February, Political Action Teams (PATs) were formed to go into the villages and talk to the villagers. Previously, in November 1964, a small ARVN psychological warfare branch had been formed, and this blossomed in 1965, when MACV formed a joint US Public Affairs Office (JUSPAO). Commencing in April 1965, aircraft began dropping leaflets on NLF territory, soon to number three million or more a week. These leaflets included subversive messages urging surrender, false information and safe-conduct passes. Many devices were experimented with, such as enlisting the aid of local fortune-tellers to advise the VC to defect or they would incur bad luck, producing horrifying noises at night that reminded the VC of their dreaded forest demons and spirits, and using 'voice aircraft' that flew low to broadcast propaganda messages through a loud-speaker or microphone. Armed propaganda teams entered NLF-influenced territory to talk to the people, while the Biet Kich, or Strike Force, composed of hardened VC defectors who had been converted, became irregulars who hunted the NLA by night, ambushing and shooting them in the back. It was said that about a quarter of the defectors were influenced in their decision to some degree by the psychological techniques. The Tet Period was found to be a good time for psychological pressure, and the Hoi Chanh ('returnees') were sent back into NLF territory, taking gifts for their families and to talk to them, and a special broadcasting campaign was aimed on the theme of re-uniting the family.

The Open Arms, or Chieu Hoi Amnesty, programme continued, and during 1966, for example, a total of 20,242 VC officially defected,* but there were comments voiced that these figures were misleading and included many Hoi Chanh, 'returnees', that is peasants who had fled into the arms of the GRVN to escape from the war as they thought, or even NLA personnel who wanted a brief respite from battle. The Hoi Chieu, or "returnees to the true national cause", usually spent eight weeks in a Chieu Hoi centre – there were just over 40 of them – where they were fed, rested, entertained, indoctrinated and sometimes re-warded, after which they were either sent back to their own villages if this were possible, or if not to a Chieu Hoi hamlet. Some volunteered as scouts for the US Forces, or to join one of the SVN propaganda teams that toured the countryside; about half were drafted into the ARVN after six months, when they eventually found themselves back in the jungle again – but fighting on the other side. The Hoi Chieu were not completely trusted, nor were they popular, and consequently they found it difficult to fit into the SVN social structure again, or to get employment. A few VPA defected under this scheme, who by the end of the year amounted to about 200.

Fleeing villagers became a NLF problem, as both their labour and taxes were lost, so the extra burden fell on those who remained in the villages, the burden becoming heavier as the number of VC of all types in SVN increased. Captured diaries told harrowing stories of the Long March to the south down the Ho Chi Minh Trail, of death, starvation, malaria, snake-bites and mud, the men each carrying a 70 lb load, in addition to their own personal equipment, of either ammunition, stores

* The figure rose to 83,000 by August 1968.

or supplies. For example, every pair of mortar bombs fired by the NLA in SVN represented one man's probable 800 mile march carrying them, which perhaps took him three months. The Ho Chi Minh Trail, as a logistic line, was long and slow.

Prisoners now became a factor in the war, and by this time many were held by both NVN and SVN, and the NLF, although NVN would not officially admit any involvement in the war. NVN prisoners taken by the US Forces were handed over the the GRVN authorities, although 19 NVN sailors taken in a naval action on June 19th, were retained in the hope of a possible exchange for captured American pilots, who were having a rough time. Ho Chi Minh had changed his mind about putting US pilots on trial for war crimes. On the 22nd, the GRVN stated that it held "several hundred" NVN prisoners, but there was little real prospect of any exchanges, as the GDRV persistently denied there were any VPA troops fighting in SVN. On the 29th an American pilot who had been shot down was publicly paraded through the streets of Hanoi and shown to the Press, while on July 6th, 50 captured American pilots were marched through Hanoi under military guard, both for purposes of world propaganda and to boost home morale. On June 27th, the first American prisoner, a naval pilot, had escaped from NLF custody, but his unsuccessful companion, caught in the act, was instantly beheaded.

Following the breakdown of negotiations in Paris between the three political factions in Laos – the Royalists, the Neutralists and the Pathet Lao – fighting had been resumed in October 1964, and continued spasmodically, while US and SVN aircraft frequently raided areas controlled by the Pathet Lao and the Ho Chin Minh Trail. The 6,000 strong Neutralist army, commanded by Kong Le, was pushed from the Plain of Jars, but managed to stabilise itself in a position covering a vital cross-roads at Vang Vieng. The 35,000-strong Pathet Lao army, supported by at least 10,000 VPA, were both conventional armies, with motor transport, which bogged down when the rains came, and brought them to a halt. The 70,000-strong Royalist army was weakened by rivalries between its generals, which culminated in an attempted right-wing coup by General Nosavan. After four days' fighting, which began on January 31st, 1965, Nosavan was forced into exile.

This made the broadening Ho Chi Minh Trail in Laos even more secure for the VC, and during 1965 there was a large influx of NVN personnel, Prince Souvanna alleging as many as 24,000. More than one-third of the Trail in Laos was made dual-track, along which trucks moved at night, as did heavily laden elephants, bicycles and coolies with carrying poles or shoulder packs. Many miles of the Trail were completely hidden from the air by good camouflage. Almost daily the 35

T-28 Trainer aircraft possessed by the Royal Laotian Government bombed it, while on the ground there were occasional skirmishes, and in early December 1965 14 VPA prisoners were put on display to the Press in Vientiane.

In February 1966,* there was fighting on the Plain of Jars, and on the 23rd the Royal Laotian Government accused NVN of repeated aggression, claiming there were 20,000 VPA troops in Laos. This was denied by the GDRV on the 25th. The Pathet Lao strength dropped to 30,000, there being at least 3,000 deserters and defectors within a year, and the Royal Laotian army increasingly found itself fighting the VPA, instead of the Pathet Lao, although the latter still controlled about 35 per cent of Laos.

In mid-1966, the US authorities estimated there might be as many as 70,000 NVN personnel in Laos, including soldiers, either supporting the Pathet Lao, guarding or working on the Ho Chi Minh Trail; construction workers improving it, and coolies permanently employed carrying supplies along it. A communiqué issued from Vientiane on September 26th, claimed there were six VPA battalions in the Nakhand area, two battalions facing the Neutralist positions at Muong Soui, and two whole VPA divisions in central Laos, near the DMZ. On October 21st, 1966, General Thao Ma, the air force commander, attempted a coup, by mustering all his aircraft (by this time reduced to only ten machines) and bombing military installations in Vientiane, in the course of which 36 people were killed. The army would not rally to his support as he had apparently expected, so with his group of air force officers involved in the plot, taking the ten aircraft, he flew off into exile to Thailand, leaving the Royal Laotian Government without any effective air force. In November, Kong Le became immersed in a power struggle and resigned the command of his Neutralist force, but retained his title of its commander-in-chief. Later, on March 23rd, 1967, when he was in Hong Kong, his dismissal from that post too was announced.

Early in February 1966, President Johnson gave strong support for Premier Nguyen Cao Ky, and indirectly to the ruling generals, known as the Committee for the Direction of the State, or more usually the Directory. The GRVN remained belligerent, and in early July General Nguyen Van Thieu, Chairman of the Directory, called for an invasion and unrestricted bombing of NVN, which was echoed by Premier Ky on the 27th at a Press Conference. On August 21st, President Johnson stated that the GDRV had been informed the US would

* The Soviet Army periodical *Red Star* on January 18th, 1966 alleged that two battalions of Thai soldiers had assisted the Royal Laotian Army in the battle for Thakhet, on the Thailand-Laos border – but this was denied by both Thailand and Laos.

stop bombing the north if the GDRV would stop sending troops to the south, but this was a sterile suggestion, while the Manila Conference, held on October 24th and 25th, merely suggested that each side withdraw, a course to which neither was prepared to agree. President Johnson on leaving Manila paid a surprise visit to US troops at Cam Ranh Bay* where he promised to support them.

Aside from the war, the domestic scene in SVN was not a happy one in 1966. When on March 10th, Premier Ky relieved General Nguyen Chanh Chi, commander of the 1st Corps (that embraced the five northern provinces) on the grounds that he was acting too independently and replaced him with one of Ky's own loyal Air Force Colonels, he stirred up a hornet's nest of Buddhist demonstrations and protests. General Chi had a strong personal following, which Premier Ky viewed suspiciously, and he also had good relations with the Buddhists, especially their leader, Tich Tri Quang, who was loath to see the General removed.

On March 16th there were Buddhist demonstrations in Saigon; on the 23rd general strikes occurred in both Danang and Hue, and on the 25th, there was another in Nha Trang, which spread to other towns. By April 1st there was almost open Buddhist revolt in the central provinces and many soldiers in uniform took part in the demonstrations. On the 4th and 5th two battalions of SVN Marines were flown to Danang, where open fighting against the authorities was narrowly averted.

In Saigon, from May 20th onwards there were repeated clashes between the Buddhists and the police, and the wave of agitation did not die down until June 23rd, when troops occupied the main pagoda from where the disturbances were directed. In Danang, where a self-styled Revolutionary Struggle Committee had established its authority over the town, there was fighting from May 15th to 23rd, before the Buddhists backed down; but in Hue, where troops were sent to restore governmental authority, between June 16th and 19th, there was little resistance, after which there arose differences within the Buddhist leadership. During this period, the 1st ARVN Division, loyal to the dismissed General, in the Danang region, almost stopped fighting the VC; it had had a quick succession of commanders, but the ARVN 2nd Division was more stable and continued fighting well in the area of Quang Ngai.

Concurrent with the trouble with the Buddhists, the Catholics put forward demands for the return of civilian government, and they also made protests, which grew after May 7th, when Premier Ky said that

* Where the Czarist Fleet had anchored in 1905 before steaming off to be defeated by the Japanese Imperial Navy.

even after the general election, due in September 1966, he would remain in office for another year. On September 11th there was a large poll, when voters elected a 117-man Constituent Assembly to draft a new constitution and prepare for civil government in 1967, which caused President Johnson to feel that it was the SVN people's seal of approval for US policies. In October, there were splits in Ky's Cabinet, mainly between the northerners and the southerners, and on November 11th, he re-shuffled it. 1966 was not a happy year for Premier Ky's Government.

The Year of the Goat–1967

7

"Be resolute, fear no sacrifice and surmount every difficulty to win victory" Mao Tse-Tung *The Little Red Book.*

Ostensibly US air power continued to dominate the war, tending to overshadow that being fought, often unseen, on the ground, along the rivers and at sea, and which produced such good Communist propaganda material, as during 1967 – the Year of the Goat* – additional types of targets were hit and large sectors of Haiphong, for example, were reduced to ruins. In the first big air battle on January 2nd, after the New Year Truce, US Phantoms shot down seven MiG-21s without loss. On February 8th, a four-day Tet Truce began, on which day, President Johnson sent a letter to Ho Chi Minh offering to cease bombing NVN, if NVN would stop infiltration southwards, but there was no reciprocal action. On the 13th, bombing of NVN was resumed, it having been delayed a day at the request of Britain as the Soviet Premier, Kosygin, was visiting that country. Many targets were still forbidden to US pilots, such as Haiphong port installations, MiG airfields and the dikes in the Red River Delta rice areas, but the restrictions gradually began to ease.

On March 10th, a bombing raid was made on Thai Nguyen about 40 miles north of Hanoi, where there was a steel plant, the first that was not officially declared to be aimed at interdicting men and supplies moving towards SVN. Then on the 24th two airfields used by MiG aircraft were attacked. NVN airfields had not been bombed previously as it was felt that if this step was taken, the MiGs would simply be withdrawn back into the sanctuary of Chinese territory, from where they could still operate freely over NVN, and any attempt to attack them might involve China directly in the shooting war.

* According to the symbols denoting the years from the Chinese Lunar Calendar; the Goat denotes patience and devotion.

The next day, the 25th, air raids were resumed on the Hanoi area, but on May 30th, it was stated by MACV that both Hanoi and Haiphong were removed from the target list for the time being. This was partly due to the crisis building up in the Middle East, but mainly to heavy US aircraft losses, some 38 having been lost in the month of May. It was estimated that NVN now possessed between 7,000 and 10,000 modern anti-aircraft guns, and between 35 and 40 SAM batteries, the bulk of which were deployed round these two major cities.

NVN had developed a considerable air defence capability that surprised the Americans, and it was based on a combination of SAMs, anti-aircraft guns and interceptor aircraft. The SAMs were used primarily to force the attacking aircraft to fly low to avoid them, which made them more vulnerable to ground anti-aircraft fire that accounted for the majority of the US and SVN aircraft losses. The general deduction in this, the first war in which missiles had been used extensively, was that they were far less effective against either aircraft or ground targets than had been predicted or expected. The ECM pods and low-flying had largely nullified their deadliness, while that of conventional anti-aircraft guns had been underestimated and underrated. NVN fighter-aircraft generally avoided combat contact with US aircraft, but took to the air occasionally to force the heavily laden US bombers to jettison their bomb-load before reaching their targets.

By January 1967, the small NVN Air Force had about 3,500 personnel and just over 100 combat aircraft, of which only about 20–25 were the modern MiG-21s, the remainder being MiG-15s and MiG-17s, both being slower and not able to match up to US aircraft, and so were not committed into aerial battles. Most of the MiGs flew from Phuc Yen, which had a long airstrip, and was about 15 miles north-west of Hanoi. MACV claimed to have destroyed about 100 MiGs on the ground during 1967, but at the end of that year, the NVN still seemed to have had about the same number of planes. Certainly, more MiG-21s arrived, and also a few large helicopters, able to carry up to 100 people.

Aircraft from the two US aircraft carriers, *Kitty Hawk* and *Ticonderoga*, mainly Skyhawks and Phantoms, also took full part in the bombing of NVN, and naval pilots began using the new, more accurate air-to-ground missile, the Wall Eye, so named because in shape it resembled a species of fish with protruding eyes.

By August 1967, there was an intensification of bombing of NVN and on the 11th and 12th Hanoi was again hit; on the 13th and 14th targets within ten miles of the Chinese border were struck, the common border with NVN extending about 500 miles, and on the 25th a further evacuation of the population in Hanoi was ordered.

On August 31st, a Senate US sub-committee report, commented that the "civilian authority consistently overruled the unanimous recommendations of the military commanders and Joint Chiefs of Staff, for a systematic, timely and hard-hitting integrated air campaign against the vital NVN targets". It had been known for some time there was dissatisfaction amongst the American military chiefs over the restrictions placed on the bombing of NVN. McNamara, the "civilian authority" referred to, had steadfastly been against such escalation and on February 15th, had declared that the war could not be won by bombing alone, but that it must be won in SVN. McNamara had begun to have severe doubts as to the wisdom of bombing NVN at all, but had not spoken out against its continuation, because he was persuaded that it diverted resources – at least 300,000 people were constantly employed repairing bomb damage – increased the material cost of the war to NVN and boosted the morale of the SVN. After the view of the military commanders had become public restrictions were further relaxed.

From September onwards the US pilots began to use what they called the 'pursuit of a target' system. Previously, they had hit and damaged a bridge, and then waited for it to be repaired, to hit it again; but now instead, whenever they could they scored hits on a series of bridges along a road or a railway line, trapping vehicles in the sections between, the stationary vehicles then being vulnerable to individual aircraft attacks. In this month, the pilots noticed a distinct slackening off of anti-aircraft fire, which was put down to shortage of ammunition. The NVN took to rebuilding their bridges about six inches below the surface of the water, so they would be harder to see from the air, and they also established regular VPA anti-aircraft batteries in the northern part of the Ho Chi Minh Trail. The Soviet Union several times complained of damage to Soviet ships in the port of Haiphong by US bombing, and there were also claims by the Chinese to have shot down American aircraft, one or two of which were admitted by the MACV, being put down to navigational errors, but the Americans firmly denied dropping any bombs on Chinese territory. On March 22nd, US aircraft bombed the Montagnard village of Lang Vei by mistake, killing 95 people and injuring another 200.

The cost of the air war was revealed to the Americans on December 22nd, when it was stated that since the war began 1,833 fixed-wing aircraft had been lost, of which 767 had been brought down over NVN, and 216 over SVN, the remainder being due to accidents, destroyed on the ground and other causes. The NVN in turn claimed to have brought down 2,500 American planes, obviously an inflated figure – a tendency which made all their communiqués automatically suspect. The Americans also said they had lost 1,204 helicopters, and there was no doubt the NLA concentrated upon them whenever possible. For example, concealed, pointed six-foot vertical stakes were stuck in the under-growth to rip open the underside of the helicopters as they came down to land. A conventional barrage of all types of small arms was auto-matically aimed at any helicopter that ventured near a NLA unit.

To the VC a helicopter brought down was a prized capture and high rewards were given, that might include a month's leave, a bicycle, a fountain pen or a watch – all prestige items.

Thailand by now was playing a considerable part in the air war against NVN, by both permitting and encouraging the presence of US troops and allowing them to operate from its territory. At the beginning of 1967, there were some 40,000 US troops in Thailand, known as the US Army 9th Logistical Command, with its HQ at Korat, of whom over 28,000 were Air Force personnel, and the previous year, 1966, about 75 per cent of the sorties over NVN had been mounted from Thailand, averaging about 225 missions weekly. There were 11 fighter-bomber squadrons in Thailand, at Korat, Takhli, Udorn and Uborn (con-fusingly similar names). From Korat, Takhli and Uborn the Phantom and Thunderchief fighter-bombers operated; the RF-101 recon-naissance and fighter planes operated from Udorn, while squeezed right up against the Laotian frontier near the narrow neck, at Nakhon Phanom, were the air-sea rescue teams, where CH-34 helicopters carried out missions to rescue downed pilots either from the sea or the jungle, many being snatched right out of the heart of NVN. From August, the Thailand Government gave increased aid to SVN, which included facilities for training SVN pilots.

On the ground during the early months of 1967, operations were carried out against the NLF areas near Saigon, and in the Tay Ninh and Phu Yen provinces, but the main fighting was in the region just south of the DMZ. Then, after a comparative lull during the summer the NLA launched large scale attacks designed to inflict the maximum US casualties, to strengthen opposition to the war in America and to influence the Presidential election campaign. NLA inactivity during the summer, failure to take full advantage of the rainy season and very heavy casualties gave the somewhat false impression that the SVN and US Forces were doing better than they were, especially as at the year's end it was pointed out by the ARVN that the NLF controlled only 40 per cent of SVN, that being mostly jungle and swamp, as against over 50 per cent the previous year.

The Allied strategy was to concentrate first upon securing a HQ base near provincial population centres and then clearing the NLA Main Force units from the surrounding area, using new techniques of moving and supplying troops by helicopters, and using armoured vehicles in Search and Destroy missions at increasing distances from base, the roadside being cleared of trees and vegetation, which reduced incidents of ambush. This proved successful to a degree around Saigon and in the central provinces, and many NLA Main Force units only escaped destruction by moving temporarily into Cambodia or Laos. The US strategic plan continued to be that of primarily holding on to Saigon, the coastal enclaves and then other population centres; then to build up strength to hit at the VPA and NLA Main Force formations, and to leave the countryside to the ARVN, and the Regional and Popular Forces, which were to hold and pacify it – but there inevitably had to be modifications to the American plan.

Some of the main actions of the year can be briefly mentioned, and we can begin with the region just south of the DMZ. Regular VPA troops were concentrating in the DMZ, turning it into a gigantic staging area and an artillery and mortar fire base against US and ARVN soldiers to the south; on February 5th, US aircraft commenced spraying chemicals in the DMZ to destroy foliage to reveal the VC supply lines, but this was confined to the southern part, which was technically SVN territory anyway, and on the 21st, US artillery fired northwards across it for the first time. In March, after two US artillery positions (one two miles and the other six miles from the DMZ) had been shelled on several occasions, strong US reinforcements were moved up towards the DMZ. On the 13th, US aircraft bombed a VPA battalion, killing at least 200, but on April 6th, the VPA and NLA successfully raided Quang Tri, 15 miles south of the DMZ, killing 126 ARVN troops* and releasing 250 political prisoners, and again on the 13th the VC shelled the town and blew up two bridges on the road from Quang Tri to Danang, thus cutting land communications with the US forward positions. On April 22nd, it was announced that 15,000 troops would be sent into Quang Ngai and Quang Tin provinces to free US units there for duty nearer the DMZ.

A twelve-day battle began on April 24th, over a ridge, some 2,700 ft high, about 14 miles south of the DMZ and some five miles from the Laotian border, which commanded vital VC supply routes, and despite heavy air and artillery support, VPA units in position along the crest repeatedly repulsed US attacks. The fighting centred around two main peaks, known as Hills 881 and 861,† and it was not until May 2nd, that the Americans captured them, and after more fighting gained a third vital peak on the 5th. The Americans lost 160 killed and 746 wounded, while they claimed to have confirmed 570 VC dead, probably with another 589 killed.

* On March 15th, 1967 MACV announced it would resume publication of casualties after each action as the former terms used had been misinterpreted by the Press.
† Measured in metres.

There was a three-hour battle on May 8th, when a VPA formation, about 1,000 strong, attacked the US post at Con Thien, just two miles south of the DMZ, in which 35 US troops and 179 VC were killed. In the following days US posts in the area were repeatedly shelled by VPA artillery. On the 16th, there was more fighting around Con Thien, resulting in 18 American and 96 VPA soldiers being killed, and on the same day US aircraft attacked SAM sites which had moved to just within the northern edge of the DMZ. In the fighting around Con Thien, the VC used flame-throwers for the first time.

On the 18th, a force of some 15,000 US and ARVN troops launched an offensive into the DMZ by land, sea and air, advancing to the Ben Hai River, the actual boundary between NVN and SVN, attacking posts, bunkers and tunnels. On the 21st ARVN soldiers engaged a VPA battalion, and killed 250 VC, and on the 26th US units captured a hilltop fortress position after 36 hours of fighting. The US and ARVN troops on the 18th left the DMZ, after removing about 9,000 peasants into a resettlement camp, burning their villages and laying waste their fields in order to create a 'Free Fire Zone', inside which any movement would be fired upon. In this operation the Americans lost 142 killed and 896 wounded, but claimed that 787 VC were killed.

Throughout June and July, American posts just south of the DMZ were subjected to continual pressure and frequent attacks. These were mainly Con Thien, Gio Linh (two miles south of the DMZ), Dong Ha (eight miles south of it) and Khe Sanh in the hills. Con Thien was particularly singled out by the VC, and on July 2nd and 3rd a VPA attack on it was repulsed by air and off-shore naval support, but the Americans lost 51 dead, 170 wounded and 34 missing, though they killed at least 65 VC. On the 6th, there was a further battle at Con Thien, this time the US claiming to have killed over 150 VC. There were two heavy assaults in September, one on the 11th and the other on the 24th, but the position was held. Later, General Westmoreland was to say that the battle for Con Thien was a "Dien Bien Phu in reverse", claiming victory in the biggest artillery battle in the war so far. In October and November, large numbers of contact-detonating mines were laid in the Ben Hai River, either by low-flying aircraft or by the ARVN. On November 14th, Major-General Hochmuth, GOC 3rd Marine Division, which was operating in the area of the DMZ, was killed in a helicopter crash about 40 miles south of the DMZ, being the most senior US officer killed in the war so far. On December 26th, ARVN troops surprised a VPA battalion near Quang Tri, killing 203 for the loss of 15 dead.

Just to the south, throughout the year the VC maintained strong pressure on Danang, and on February 27th assaulted the US base with 140 mm rockets – the most destructive weapon they possessed – from a distance of five miles, killing 42 people. They repeated the attack on May 14th, when they destroyed 12 anti-aircraft missiles. On the 13th and 14th, US troops, in a two-day battle some 30 miles south of Danang, killed 351 VC. A ten-day operation began on May 28th in Quang Tin province to the south of Danang, in which, although the American forces claimed to have killed 701 NLA soldiers, they lost 110 dead and suffered 241 wounded.

On July 15th Danang camp was again bombarded by NLA rockets, at least 19 aircraft being destroyed or damaged, an ammunition dump hit and 12 Americans killed. On the same day, the NLA raided Hoi An in Quang Nam province (as was Danang itself), freeing 860 political prisoners. On the night of August 28th/29th, the NLA blew eight road bridges, temporarily isolating Danang. The Americans lost 54 dead fighting in the Que Son Valley about 25 miles south of Danang on September 4th and 5th, and on the 6th a strong NLA attack on Tam Ky in Quang Tin province was repulsed with air support, the attackers losing 219 dead and the ARVN only nine men.

Looking southwards towards Kontum province, one of the fiercest battles of the war was fought around the American base at Dak To, near the junction of the SVN-Laotian-Cambodian frontiers, beginning on November 1st and lasting nearly the whole month, as control of a series of forested ridges, running somewhat parallel to the Cambodian border, was contested. On the 13th, a whole VPA division and NLA Main Force troops made a direct attack on the base, only to be driven back by artillery fire. Two days later a heavy VC shelling from a nearby hill destroyed the airfield, ammunition dumps, two transport aircraft and the militia camp. On the 17th, the hill was stormed by US infantry, but it was not until the 19th that ARVN troops overran the VC outpost at the top.

On the 19th heavy fighting began around Hill 875, only two miles from the Cambodian border. A US battalion attacked, but soon found itself surrounded; eight helicopters trying to evacuate the wounded were hit by fire and 22 soldiers were killed when a US aircraft accidentally dropped a bomb near them. On the 20th a second battalion succeeded in breaking through to the first one, and the attack was renewed. Although for three days tons of bombs and napalm were dropped on Hill 875, on the 22nd the attackers were forced back again after almost reaching the crest. The next day, in a renewed advance it was found the VPA had evacuated the previous night under cover of darkness. In this 23-day battle, the Americans had lost 281 dead, but claimed to have killed at least 1,400 VC. On December 3rd, the Americans abandoned Hill 875 after blowing up the fortifications on it.

Near the coast to the east, in the central provinces, a South Korean division began an operation on January 3rd to clear an area of some 270 square miles in Phu Yen province, which had been under guerrilla control for several years. While the NLA was pursued into the central hills, special Korean units surrounded each village to isolate it; over 16,000 inhabitants were screened and temporarily evacuated, but were later allowed to resettle in their villages after the operation was concluded on March 5th. The South Koreans claimed they had killed 221 VC and captured 403, detaining another 673 suspects.

On February 15th, South Korean troops repelled an attack by a NLA Main Force regiment in a three-hour battle near Quang Ngai, the retreating VC being heavily bombarded by artillery and from the air, losing 242 dead. Two days later South Korean troops launched an offensive in the same area, and on February 19th, in a ten-hour battle with the ARVN, it was reported that 746 NLA troops were killed. The NLA raided Quang Ngai on August 30th, and under cover of a mortar barrage, released over 1,000 political prisoners. At the year's end, on December 6th, US and ARVN troops began a six-day operation in the Bong Son area in Binh Dinh province, which concentrated upon locating the NLA and blocking escape routes while aircraft and artillery fire attacked them and although the Americans lost 33 dead, they killed 471 VC. On the 16th and 17th, there was further fighting in the same area in which 104 VC were killed, for the loss of 22 US dead.

On January 8th, a combined US and ARVN force, about 15,000 strong, began a Search and Destroy operation in the Iron Triangle against the Ho Bo Wood, now the NLF HQ of its 4th Region, responsible for conducting operations against Saigon. As the troops advanced into the massive complex honeycomb of tunnels, bunkers and underground living and working rooms, they demolished more than 500 tunnels and scores of bunkers, and seized huge stocks of rice, weapons, uniforms and ammunition, and a printing press. Also discovered was a 60-bed underground hospital. The aim was to convert the Ho Bo Wood into a Free Fire Zone, and by means of loud-speakers affixed to helicopters the inhabitants were ordered to leave their villages, which were then destroyed by bombing or were flattened by bulldozers. About 6,000 people were evacuated, and an American spokesman later admitted that some who had refused to move might have been killed. The operation ended on January 26th, but on February 2nd, MACV admitted the VC had returned to the Iron Triangle.

Beginning on February 22nd, a combined US and ARVN force launched the largest offensive of the war against the COSVN in Tay Ninh province, employing over 25,000 troops. It opened with the first parachute drop of the war; some 750 paratroops were detailed to open an airhead at Katum, thus enabling other troops to be flown in by helicopter and deployed along the Cambodian border. During the first few days there was little contact with the NLA, which had advance warning of the operation.* There was no serious fighting until the 28th, when a NLA Main Force battalion lost 150 killed, and a US company was badly mauled. The COSVN simply withdrew temporarily into Cambodia. In this operation the US tried the new tactics of deep penetration with massive air and artillery fire power on instant call. So far US patrols had been used for reconnaissance and intelligence gathering, and it was not until 1967 that US air mobility and fire power allowed these tactics to be tried out, with helicopters standing by making it possible to support particular bodies of troops.

On March 2nd, a NLA Main Force regiment attacked US positions, but was compelled to fall back under heavy air and artillery bombardment, leaving 423 dead on the field. Still in the same area on the 21st, a NLA regiment attacked an American battalion, the assault being held off for four hours, until the arrival of an armoured relief column. US casualties were 31 killed and 109 wounded, while the VC left 596 dead on the field, and were believed to have suffered at least 200 more killed. In an engagement on March 31st and April 1st, the NLA lost 591 killed, the majority by aerial action, as against only ten US dead. After this the US and ARVN troops withdrew from Zone C, the main area of operation at the time. They had not succeeded in penetrating far into the Ho Bo Wood.

Just to the north of Zone C, in Binh Long province, the NLA suffered one of its most costly defeats when, on October 29th, it attempted to seize the town of Loc Ninh and the adjacent Special Forces and Regional Force camps. A VPA and a NLA Main Force regiment made repeated mass assaults against the two camps, initially penetrating the outer defences of the Regional Force camp, part of which was overrun, but all other assaults were held off. The next day strong US and ARVN reinforcements were flown in by helicopter, as the airstrip was under heavy fire, in time to beat back further mass attacks on the 31st. More mass attacks were made on November 2nd, but all were unsuccessful, and during the night the VPA and NLA faded away. This action was considered to be of special significance as the VC had been told to take the positions 'at all cost' – a most unusual order – and two elite regiments had been used for the purpose: it was reminiscent of the human-wave assault tactics used at Dien Bien Phu. In this battle, clearly a VC defeat, they lost over 900 killed, while the Americans suffered 11 dead and the ARVN about 50.

In Saigon and the immediately surrounding provinces, the situation remained uneasily the same in 1967, although MACV claimed a steady

* Known as Operation Junction City: all operations had code names.

improvement and one optimistic report* stated that the "main roads are relatively safe, and commercial vehicles, though subject to VC taxes, go out to all provinces . . . except that of Phuoc Long, on the Cambodian border, which has to be supplied by air". There were repeated attacks on shipping in the Saigon River, and for example, in January, on the 9th, a British tanker was bombarded only 15 miles from the capital; on the same day, 40 miles south of Saigon, the US dredger *Jamaica Bay*, the fourth largest in the world, was sunk by a VC mine. On the 26th, a US minesweeper came under VC machine-gun fire on the river, and on the 30th US minesweepers were again attacked. Other incidents included, on February 8th, a US infantry company being ambushed about 26 miles north of Saigon; on the 12th the VC made a mortar attack on the MACV building in Saigon, killing 12 ARVN soldiers and wounding 40 others, who were in a nearby convoy. On April 4th, disguised as ARVN soldiers and National Police, the VC raided a police station on the outskirts of the capital, which they destroyed; on May 12th the US air base at Binh Hoa was struck by 140 mm rockets, six US personnel being killed and 106 wounded; and on October 31st, the Presidential Palace was hit by mortar fire, from a building about 1,000 yards away, on the occasion of the inauguration of President Thieu at which US Vice President Humphrey was present, but no one was hurt.

During the year, US participation increased south of Saigon in the Mekong Delta and a number of battles took place, of which a few can be briefly mentioned. In one on February 15th, in Chuong Thien province, 225 VC were killed, but the US lost ten helicopters, the largest number in any one day so far. From April 9th–11th, in Long An province, a rich rice growing area which had long been under VC control, US infantry with air and artillery support killed 209 VC for the loss of only one man. On June 14th ARVN troops killed 211 VC in Phong Dinh province, on August 27th the town of Cantho was bombarded by the NLA and 46 people were killed and 222 wounded. On December 4th, 200 VC were killed in a nine-hour battle on the borders of Dinh Tuong and Kien Tung provinces, when a NLA Main Force battalion was surrounded by US infantry and ARVN marines and on the 8th, the GRVN claimed as its greatest victory of the war an engagement in Chuong Thien province when ARVN troops killed 365 VC. As this almost blow-by-blow account of countless actions and incidents is typical of the course of the war, such a long catalogue will not be tediously repeated, as it tends to bore, weary and obscure.

For a long time the NLA had been smuggling in men and arms along the nine tributaries† of the Mekong River, and so far the River Assault

* *Daily Telegraph* of June 11th, 1967.
† Known to the Chinese traditionally as the Nine Dragons.

Groups (RAGs) had to use old French river gunboats manned by SVN personnel. But the US took an increasing participation in the Mekong Delta, a watery maze of swamp, criss-crossed by rivers and canals, which brought problems of movement, both of men and boats. The larger, heavier American soldier sank even deeper into the mud, than his lighter, smaller ARVN comrade, while the conventional western-type rivercraft available were cumbersome and noisy, so the Americans came up with the idea of 'water jet' patrol boats, and by the beginning of 1967, about 120 were operating in the Delta, and more were on order. Known as the Patrol Boat-River (PB-R), they were 31 feet long, had a very shallow draught, were practically unsinkable, and instead of the conventional screw, they were propelled along by twin diesel engines which powered 'water jets', that made them extremely manoeuvrable, enabling them to go anywhere the small Vietnamese sampans could. With no propeller to foul, a particular drawback in the dense reeds and undergrowth infested waters of the Delta, they were a technical break-through. Having a four-man crew, they had two ·50 machine-guns in the bow and one ·30 aft, as well as infra-red sights, radar and a search-light. Additionally, the Americans formed a River Assault Force,* manned by about 3,000 personnel, which consisted of ten Monitors, armoured gunboats small enough to move along the canals to be used to shell NLA positions, and about 50 amphibious armoured personnel carriers, which carried a 107 mm (formerly the 4·2 inch) mortar, a 3·5 inch rocket launcher and two machine-guns one ·30 and the other ·50.

On the naval side of the war, on February 26th, US warships, lifting their guns from coastal targets, shelled targets inland in NVN. The next day, President Johnson announced that mines were being dropped from aircraft into NVN rivers, but said that as they did not float, they could not be washed out to sea and so would not endanger shipping. In March, the Australian destroyer *Hobart* arrived in Vietnamese waters, and on the 15th, US ships destroyed a number of NVN armed trawlers. On May 27th, a US destroyer was hit by shell fire from the NVN coast; on July 15th, more NVN armed trawlers were sunk by US ships; on the 24th, the first joint aircraft-naval gun attack was made on the thermal power station at Vinh; and on August 28th, another US destroyer was hit by shell fire from shore guns. On July 29th, the US aircraft-carrier *Forrestal*, which carried about 4,300 personnel and six squadrons of air-craft, when in Vietnamese waters, was swept by fire, losing 129 dead; the NLF unconvincingly claimed responsibility.

In March, Premier Ky put forward the idea of a "death zone", to be 220 yards wide, that would stretch at least 12 miles from the coast to the

* This was the first force of this type to be formed by the US since the Civil War, when one was used for operations on the Mississipi River.

foothills across the Quang Tri plain. It would be a physical barrier that would block movement southwards from the DMZ, where the build-up of VPA strength had become so obvious,* covered by fire and heavily mined, but at this stage the Americans were not so keen on the idea of constructing a "mini-Maginot Line". However, McNamara, who since October 1966, had been resisting General Westmoreland's request for more US troops, and being opposed to proposals put forward (in April) for an invasion of NVN, Cambodia and Laos,† was now disillusioned with the lack of effect the bombing of NVN had produced and was desperately seeking an alternative to win or end the war, and so began eventually to look favourably at Ky's idea. On September 7th, he said that a physical barrier would be erected along the DMZ. The next day reports confirmed that a strip of land between two US posts, overlooking the DMZ, seven miles long and 600 yards wide, had been cleared. This would be extended to the coast, five miles to the east, and then another four miles west to the foothills of the mountains that formed the Laos frontier. A few watch-towers, 80 feet high, had been built, but almost immediately four of them had been burnt down by the NLA. This scheme seemed unable to get under way to any significant degree, although Defence Secretary McNamara said on the 15th, that an electronic barrier would be erected across the DMZ, which would result in less bombing. He obviously thought this might placate some American critics of the war.

Acts of terrorism had become almost the accepted way of life in SVN and so commonplace that little notice was paid to them, but in fact NLF terrorism took a far greater toll of human life in SVN than did US and SVN bombing of NVN. Terrorist activities were mainly directed against the Americans in the population centres and against Goverment officials in the countryside. On June 27th, for example, 40 civilians were killed when a bus hit a mine near Saigon. But the worst atrocity occurred on December 5th, when the VC killed or burnt to death in their homes at least 114 Montagnards, in revenge for the alleged use of their village – Dak Son in Lam Dong province – for counter-insurgency operations. During 1967 there were campaigns of terrorism to prevent villagers voting in the first local elections held since 1964, and in the village of Suoi Chan, some 40 miles east of Saigon, the VC tied up 18 villagers including three girls, shot them and also burnt others. Official SVN figures indicated that 3,820 civilians were deliberately killed by the VC during 1967.

* An example of the Asian-wall complex, and reminiscent of the two 20 feet high walls at Dong Hoi and Truong Duc, built by the Nguyen dynasty in 1630, just to the north of Hue, in a vain effort to stop the warring Tring Emperors of the north.
† The Pentagon Papers.

It became the policy for US troops to free the ARVN for counter-insurgency work, and in 1967 a gradual change-over took place in the ARVN from Search and Destroy operations to providing security for the SVN Revolutionary Development Teams (RDTs), a role hitherto left to the Regional and Popular forces. This task – to be the shield behind which pacification could be carried out – was only reluctantly taken on by the ARVN, which still tended to have an attitude of indifference towards the peasants, and also felt it was being pushed into the background by the US troops. The Americans were also accused of indifference to the villagers, and on August 16th, after a series of US bombing of villages, mistakenly thought to be harbouring NLA, General Westmoreland ordered his military commanders to review their procedures to "minimise civilian casualties".

The regular element of the ARVN was now basically formed into ten infantry, one airborne and one armoured division, with 20 Ranger battalions, all on the US pattern, every trace of French military influence having completely disappeared. The US installed a data processing system for the ARVN, which gave every soldier a personal number, and this revealed that there were 20,000 men less than the required number. On August 4th, Premier Ky announced that extra men would be called up, of whom 33,000 would join the 142,000 man Regional Force; 17,000 would go to the 171,000 Popular Force, and about 30,000 were destined for the regular element, mostly as replacements for the "20,000 phantom troops".* Morale still varied from formation to formation, and still there were cases of ARVN units being reluctant to go to each other's aid in battle.

In manpower terms the brunt of the war was being borne by the SVN, closely followed by the Americans. Other 'Third Nation' forces were sent to SVN, but perhaps because of their small, and often token, size they did not gain any headlines. Nevertheless they made a practical contribution and a show of solidarity against Communism. In January 1967, there were about 62,000 Third Nation troops in SVN, consisting mainly of some 46,000 South Koreans, 4,500 Australians and 150 New Zealanders, as well as other Third Nation personnel working as non-combatants, such as 2,000 Filipinos. The following year (1968) the South Korean contingent increased to 49,000, and that of the Australians to 8,000.

American prisoners became a source of frustration through lack of contact or knowledge of them and their treatment at the hands of their secretive captors. On May 12th, US pilots were once more paraded through the streets of Hanoi and compelled to give Press Conferences.

* In January 1968, strengths were rather confusingly given as 142,000 in the Regional Force and 143,000 in the Popular Force.

American field engineers preparing to destroy a Viet Cong tunnel in the
Iron Triangle. US Army

Top: General Creighton W. Abrams visits a forward fire base in Quang Nam province. US Army

Left: American troops under fire from the Viet Cong, in Binh Dinh province. US Army

Bottom: American troops reload an AH-1 'Cobra' helicopter 'gunship'. US Army

Top: A CH-47 Chinook helicopter airlifts supplies to a helicopter pad on the Black Virgin Mountain. US Army

An American M-113 armoured personnel carrier. US Army

Top: A view of Cam Ranh Bay. US Army

A UH-1D helicopter being loaded with rations to take to a forward fire base. US Army

Top: American troops examining a captured Chinese 90 mm recoilless rifle.
US Army

An American 4.2 inch mortar in action about 30 miles north-west of
Saigon. US Army

US and ARVN soldiers look at the scene of a Viet Cong massacre in the
hamlet of Phu Lam, in Vinh Long province, about 70 miles south-west of
Saigon. Twenty-five prisoners, including three women, were chained and
padlocked together before being shot by the Viet Cong. US Army

Top: A senior US Special Forces (Green Berets) officer presenting Tet gifts to a Civilian Irregular Defence Group unit. US Army

US Special Services (Green Berets) personnel set up their 60 mm mortar, which they prefer to the larger 81 mm one, normally used by the infantry. US Army

Because America would not officially recognise the NLF, despite a few exchanges arranged by the International Red Cross of sick and badly wounded, the GDRV refused to enter into negotiations for a general exchange. By July, it was estimated that NVN held more than 160 US pilots and 20 soldiers, as well as some US civilians, but there were more than 500 US servicemen listed as missing, some of whom were thought to be prisoners. On November 16th, the NLF threatened to execute three US prisoners if three terrorists condemned to death for bomb-throwing in Saigon were shot, but their death penalties were cancelled.

The main political events in SVN during 1967 included the promulgation of a new Constitution on April 1st, and in the elections held on September 3rd, General Nguyen Van Thieu became President, with General Nguyen Cao Ky as his Vice President. Both took office on October 31st, when Ky resigned as Premier and a Government was formed by Nguyen Van Loc.

The NLF made increasing use of Cambodia to avoid the heavily bombed Ho Chi Minh Trail, but Prince Sihanouk also had other troubles. In April, a revolt said to be Communist-inspired, broke out in Battambang province which lay to the north-west and was adjacent to Thailand, over a land reform measure being enforced by the new Premier, Lon Nol. Lon Nol resigned on April 30th, and on May 2nd Sihanouk formed a new Government, with Penn Nouth as Premier, who attempted to come to terms with the left-wing extremists. By June the revolt had collapsed, but Sihanouk admitted the rebels numbered several thousand, and said on the 21st, that they had laid down their arms and would be pardoned. On August 7th, Sihanouk stated the Communists had refused to come into his Government and the following month he accused the Chinese of fomenting subversive activities in Cambodia.

On December 12th, Cambodia radio stated the NLA had used Cambodia as a "haven", but denied that the Government had permitted the VPA to use its territory for the infiltration of men and supplies. On the 27th, Sihanouk indicated he would not stop US troops from entering Cambodia in "hot pursuit" if the enemy entered illegally and were in remote sections of the country. Early in January (1968) Prince Sihanouk took delivery of 11 Soviet aircraft, including three MiG-17s and about 40–50 guns. He then flew off to confer with the GDRV.

Meanwhile, in NVN, back in the caves of the Thai Nguyen hills, the GDRV was worrying what effect the Chinese Great Cultural Revolution – which was in full swing – would have on war supplies for the NLF. Ho Chi Minh in November (1967) was to decline the proferred Soviet Order of Lenin, until the fight was won, but in fact he did not want to offend the Chinese. War material had been coming in, but losses were high, and for example, of some 14,000 Soviet trucks received in the previous three years, about 9,000 had been put out of action by the enemy by April. Nguyen Duy Trinh, the Foreign Minister, visited Moscow, Peking and Eastern Europe to ask for some assistance. Soviet aid had included, apart from the 8,500 modern anti-aircraft guns and SAM batteries, most of NVN's oil, tractors, trucks, generators and another 20 PT Ships. Chinese aid included infantry weapons (almost 80 per cent of such arms in both the VLA and NLA were of modern Chinese origin) and this year, rice too, because of food shortages in NVN. Aid came from Eastern Europe, and included small arms and flak jackets from Czechoslovakia, field guns from Poland, medicines from Rumania, and bicycles from East Germany and Hungary. Two-thirds of all this material came through the port Haiphong. To supplement this war material, small factories had been started up in NVN and these were producing limited quantities of grenades, mines, and pistols, but in insufficient quantities.

China and the Soviet Union came to a face-saving agreement over their transit problems, by which Soviet material for NVN was formally taken possession of by NVN as soon as it came on to Chinese territory. Although the Red Guards interfered with this traffic, the flow did not stop, but the Soviet Union continued to complain that the Chinese exchanged their old jet fighter aircraft for new ones destined for NVN, and examined the SAMs minutely to obtain their secrets. It was a slow process, made slower by the Red Guards, and the material took weeks to cross the Chinese maze of a railway system to the NVN frontier at Lao Cai, where it had to be transferred to NVN railway rolling stock, as the track gauge was different.

The COSVN had divided SVN into five regions, each having a regional committee directly responsible to it, headed by men with military experience. From these regional committees the chain of command went down vertically from region to province, district to villages, to hamlets; it was all-embracing. Control of the military units and HQs was assured as about one-third of all officers at battalion-level and above, were NVN, and not indigenous SVN. Unlike the GRVN which drew the best officials into Saigon and sent the others out into the provinces where promotion and prospects were slow, the COSVN picked the best men to send out into the field, where the chances of advancement were much better. The regional committees were given four tasks; to organise themselves, to fight, to terrorise, and to govern the peasants under their control. A beaucracy thus developed, in which all were involved – political workers, organisers, administrators, soldiers and militia.

Under the direction of the COSVN many aspects of the NLA were regularised, such as the distribution of arms, which were now more plentiful. Indeed practically all the full-time soldiers were armed with AK-47 rifles, a good, accurate weapon, with a 30-round clip, or the Chinese ones of the 7·62 series, while other weapons included 120 mm mortars, 140 mm rocket-launchers, 12·7 mm machine-guns, rifle-grenades and flame-throwers. The arrival of American combat forces, with their fire power and mobility, had changed the old pattern when the NLA had plenty of time to reconnoitre and rehearse attacks, and had compelled the COSVN, and of course the GDRV, to take steps to modernise the armoury of the NLA and SVN. Conscription had also been regularised, and whereas almost anyone had been taken for the NLA between 1964 and 1966, after that those whose kinsfolk were with, or had been with, the ARVN, those of doubtful political persuasion, Catholics, those having any relatives killed by the VC, amputees, the deformed, those who were unfit physically, and those who were under four feet ten inches in height, were not accepted. On the other hand extreme youth was not objected to and some of those accepted for the NLA were only 14 or 15 years of age.

Great attention was paid to morale, which was not always of the highest, especially amongst those who had just made the dangerous and hair-raising journey along the Ho Chi Minh Trail. One deserter stated that of his 300-strong unit, only 30 survived the march, the losses being mainly due to bombing and defection. The fact that the NLF had openly stated the war would last anything up to 20 years or more, did not help the morale of the battle-weary and disillusioned. Generally the NLA had a bad year in 1967, being weakened by casualties and defections, so much so that Main Force formations had to be strengthened by infusions from the VPA. Material rewards had long been given for bravery in battle, such as a bicycle or fountain pen, but now medals and titles were awarded. The Liberation Medal, in three classes, could be awarded to any officer or soldier, but only if all his comrades openly agreed he deserved it; also a man might be publicly commended for some act on the battlefield, and given the title of "Determined to Win Soldier", or "Valiant Killer of Americans".

Under COSVN direction training was also regularised, together with indoctrination, and to help the illiterates and semi-illiterates, slogans were abundantly employed, such as the Three Firsts, which were First in Combat, First in Indoctrination and First in Observing in Discipline. Others were the Three Defences, against spies, fires and accidents; the Five Togethers, to eat, work, play and sleep together and to help each other; the Five Uniformities, of unified training, equipment, command, organisation and re-organisation: the Five Main Skills of weapon firing, mine detonating, bayonet drill, grenade throwing and armed combat; the Four Quicks, to quickly advance, assault, clear the battlefield and withdraw; the Three Strongs, to attack, assault and pursue strongly; the Three Ravages, to seize, burn and destroy rice and houses; and the one Slow, to prepare slowly. These slogans were drummed into everyone, soldiers, militia, cadre and workers.

Ever-present was the NLF tax collector, and as early as 1965, the VC were forcibly selling Victory Bonds, redeemable after the defeat of the Saigon Government. Vouchers were solemnly given for all taxes taken, which added to the snow-storm of paper that made its way upwards to the regional committees and on to the COSVN. Many villages were taxed twice, by the GRVN and by the NLF, while in Saigon and other large cities 'protection money' was collected, especially in Cholon, the city of prosperous Chinese, who could afford to buy their exemption from military service and to pay the VC and the GRVN to leave them alone. By these untiring methods the VC in SVN were able to pay for about one-third of the cost of the war, the remainder being borne by the GDRV.

As the year 1967 drew to a close, there was, after great argument, only a 24 hour Christmas Truce, and a 36-hour one for the New Year, the latter being punctuated with many violations. As in former years, the cost in blood had been heavy, and in his last annual report to Congress Defence Secretary McNamara, stated that during 1967, the NLA and the VPA had lost about 165,000 effectives, including 88,000 killed in action, 30,000 died or disabled from wounds, 6,000 prisoners, almost 18,000 defectors and about 25,000 lost by desertion or disease. But he admitted these figures should be treated with caution. General Westmoreland and other military chiefs admitted they simply could not understand how the VC could suffer such casualties, and yet return to the battlefield in strength a few weeks later.

The Tet Offensive—
February 1968   8

"We failed to seize a number of primary objectives"   A COSVN statement of April 12th, 1968.

During the first months of 1968, both the VPA and the NLA strongly took the offensive in SVN, and on January 3rd, VPA troops bombarded Danang air base with 120 mm rockets, destroying or damaging 27 aircraft, and also attacked six ARVN posts in the area. On the same day the VPA assaulted two US artillery bases in the Que Son Valley, and it was reported that 329 VPA soldiers were killed in the fighting. That night the NLA struck the Ban Me Thuot airfield, destroying or damaging 15 helicopters, and bombarded An Khe, the HQ of the 1st (Air Mobile) Cavalry Division, also destroying aircraft. This was the pattern of attacks across the length and breadth of SVN, hardly a day passing without one or two serious actions.

Towards the end of the month the focus of the attention of the VPA turned to Khe Sanh, 14 miles south of the DMZ and six miles from Laos, garrisoned by about 3,500 US Marines with artillery support, the main defences being built around the airstrip. US forces held three hills to the west of the base, Hills 881 North, 881 South, and Hill 861, covering Route 9 which led to the coast at Dong Ha. To the south-west lay a Special Forces camp, manned by ARVN and Montagnards, near the village of Lang Vei. Generally, since the fighting in April and May 1967, the area had been comparatively quiet, although in the autumn the VC had destroyed a number of road bridges, isolating Khe Sanh, which had to be supplied by air.

VPA units launched their first attack just before dawn on the 21st, and in the heavy shelling 18 US personnel were killed and 40 wounded, an ammunition dump blown up, a helicopter was destroyed and five others damaged. Concurrently, other VPA units attacked the three hill outposts and the camp at Lang Vei. The next day, the 22nd, the US troops were forced out from the village of Khe Sanh into the defensive perimeter proper, the inhabitants being flown to Danang. Both sides rushed in reinforcements, and during the first three days of what was to develop into a prolonged siege, US transport planes and helicopters flew in troops, until the garrison exceeded 5,000, together with tons of ammunition and supplies. On the other side, the VPA massed about 18,000 regular troops in the area of Khe Sanh, the largest VPA concentration so far. There were the 325C and 304 Divisions besieging Khe Sanh, and the 320 Division near Camp Carroll, 15 miles to the northeast of Khe Sanh.

On the 24th, under cover of fog that prevented air intervention, the VPA shelled the base with 152 mm field guns, the largest employed so far, and although reasonably protected by a good system of bunkers and trenches, the US lost seven killed and 77 wounded. Gradually the VPA crept forward until they were within 1,000 yards of the airstrip, which it bombarded with mortars. On the 26th, all US air missions over NVN were cancelled and their full force directed instead on to the VPA surrounding Khe Sanh, some 480 sorties being flown that day. On the 27th, a unit of ARVN Rangers was flown to Khe Sanh to establish a "suicide line" about 300 yards to the east of the outer defences. There was more shelling by the VPA, and in a clash with the VC, when US troops attempted to open Route 9, the Americans lost 19 dead, but claim to have killed 150 VC. In the ensuing days there was sporadic shelling and patrol action. By this time the US and ARVN were worried by the extent of the VPA build-up, there being another formation, the 324B Division in position near Con Thien and Gio Linh, which brought the estimated VPA strength up to about 40,000 infantry and about 10,000 artillery, engineers and support troops.

The NLF had announced it would observe a seven-day truce during Tet, begining on January 29th, and on the 27th, the GDRV announced it would release three captured US airmen at Tet (it had not released any so far), while going one better the NLF released 14 SVN prisoners on the 28th. On the 28th, VC activity slackened off noticeably throughout SVN, and apart from some shelling of Khe Sanh, the only significant action was an all-day battle near Dong Ha, in which seven US Marines and 53 NVN were reported to have been killed. Just before the Tet Truce was about to start, the GRVN announced it would not be observed in the five northern provinces because of the extensive build-up which conclusively established that the VPA forces were engaged in a massive offensive against the northern part of SVN. Bombing of NVN was also to be continued.

On January 30th, the VC launched the biggest operation of the war, which has since become well known as the Tet Offensive, attacking many towns in the northern and coastal provinces and the Central Highlands, and extending it on the following day to Saigon, Hue and many towns in the Delta. By February 5th, some 30 of the 44 provincial capitals had been assaulted. The COSVN, claiming it was the HQ of the Revolutionary Armed Forces, said it was directing the general offensive, while Radio Liberation announced that the long-awaited final offensive had been launched, and a new organisation formed, called the Alliance of National and Peace Forces, claiming it was supported by many intellectuals and industrialists, but nothing more was heard of it, except for a few dying murmurs in Hue. The VC were driven from most towns within a few days, although in the provinces attacks on towns and bombardment of American installations continued well into February. On the 18th, a new offensive was launched, but it was a much feebler one, the main force having been spent. Fighting continued in Saigon until the 23rd, and in Hue until the 24th. And now for some more detail of the main battles.

Commencing with Saigon, between January 29th and 31st, 1968, the VC infiltrated in small groups and in ones and twos, 17 battalions, amounting to over 5,000 men. Unarmed and unnoticed in the throng of Tet visitors to the city, they came in by bus, motor tricycle, bicycle, pedicab and on foot. Once inside Saigon they made their way to pre-arranged points, where they were issued with arms and rations for 36 hours, the arms and ammunition having been previously smuggled in by trucks and especially in coffins at fake funerals, and hidden to await the signal.

At 0300 hours on the 31st, the VC attack began by launching 'suicide commandos', small squads of about 20 men, in carefully planned and rehearsed raids on selected targets. One such unit, dressed in ARVN uniforms, attacked the Presidential Palace and blew in its gates, but were eventually beaten off, while another similar unit assaulted and partly burned down the Saigon radio station, managing to remain in occupation for 24 hours. Other units attacked the US Navy HQ building, the Philippine Embassy, and three US officers' billets. The main 'suicide' attack however was made against the US Embassy, which had been rebuilt after the bomb explosion in 1965 into a supposedly impregnable fortress, surrounded by a high concrete wall and guarded by US Marines and National Police. VC disguised as civilians blew a hole in the surrounding wall to gain access into the outer compound to aim grenade and mortar fire against the main entrance. They failed to enter the main building, being kept back by rifle fire from a US helicopter. The VC were able to hold out in the outer compound for six hours, until US troops landed on the roof by helicopter and worked their way down the building to close with the attackers of whom 19 were killed, and the other captured for the cost of five US military personnel and one ARVN soldier dead.

Concurrently, other VC units operating from the refugee areas in the suburbs, where they already had an underground network of cells and support groups, were able to seize a number of military and police outposts without difficulty. The VC also openly occupied Cholon, establishing their HQ in the An Quang pagoda, the centre of anti-Government Buddhist agitation, situated on the border of Saigon and Cholon. On the outskirts of the city, the VC attacked the Tan Son Nhut airport, the nearby ARVN General Staff HQ, where both President Thieu and Vice President Ky lived, and the Armoured Command HQ; certain parts of these targets were occupied.

Later that day, the 31st, President Thieu declared martial law, a curfew was imposed in Saigon and Cholon, flights from the Tan Son Nhut airport were suspended, and a number of VC prisoners were summarily shot without trial on capture, as a warning to the people not to collaborate with the NLF. One Press photograph that was shown around the world was of the Saigon Police Chief, Brigadier Nguyen Ngoc Loan, shooting a captured VC with his own pistol. The US Embassy intervened to stop such summary executions, in case the GDRV should take reprisals on US prisoners.

On February 1st, US combat troops were rushed into Saigon, a US general assumed command of the operations against the NLA, and soon the Saigon radio station was re-taken. Next, US soldiers successfully stormed the upper floors of a hotel in which the VC 'suicide commandos', who had attacked the Presidential Palace, had taken refuge, one of whom was a 17 year old girl. In the suburbs, US troops, using armoured personnel carriers and mortars, became heavily involved in street fighting. Where possible the population was evacuated, houses held by the NLA with machine-guns were bombed by US aircraft and rocketed by helicopters, and within a few hours the NLA was on the withdrawing defensive. After NLA strongpoints around the An Quang pagoda had been bombed from the air and some snipers eliminated by mortar fire, ARVN toops and National Police moved in to find that only monks, nuns and children remained.

At the Tan Son Nhut airport, American troops with tanks drove the NLA out from that part of the buildings it had occupied the previous day, and after some 36 hours fighting the VC were cleared from those parts of the ARVN General Staff HQ and the Armoured Command HQ that had been overrun. Fighting continued in Cholon on the 2nd, where gun battles were fought in the forecourt of a children's hospital, in the northern suburbs and around Tan Son Nhut, while thousands of people whose homes had been reduced to ruins, flocked into the centre of Saigon, the police having to erect barricades to prevent them congesting the city.

That night, the main NLA forces withdrew into the northern suburbs of Gia Dinh and Thu Duc, and during the next two days the situation in Saigon eased considerably. On the 3rd, the curfew was partially lifted, and ARVN troops, with only US support personnel and military police, became solely responsible for operations inside the capital, leaving the US combat units to concentrate upon the northern suburbs and the surrounding countryside. On the 5th, it was reported that over 4,000 civilians who had helped the NLA had been detained, but a great many more had known about the offensive and had helped it in many ways. In Saigon on the 5th, the NLA captured a police station, set fire to another police building and in the ensuing fighting a complete district was set on fire, with hundreds of refugees trapped in the cross-fire from both sides. The Tan Son Nhut airport was again closed because of fighting adjacent to it, and the following day, a heavy NLA attack on its entrance was repulsed.

Meanwhile, in Cholon, there were still some 1,600 regular NLA Main Force troops in control of whole blocks of buildings, with their snipers harassing troops and police, and VC reinforcements from the Delta began to filter in. On the 7th, barricades were erected across streets and fighting broke out at the Phu Cho race-course, just west of Cholon, where a NLA Main Force battalion was operating. On the 9th, US troops in helicopters moved against it, but the fighting was inconclusive. During the next few days the situation improved from the GRVN point of view. NLA reinforcements were now moving towards the capital from all sides, and on the 13th, B-52s bombed areas only ten miles from the city, their nearest so far, where NLA troops were concentrating, but two days later MACV admitted that at least 42 people had been killed by their bombs which had fallen outside the target area, and that it was not known whether they were VC or innocent civilians.

As in other areas, on February 18th, the NLA launched a new offensive in and around Saigon, bombarding the National Police HQ, on the boundary between Saigon and Cholon, from the Phu Cho racecourse, in which seven police were killed. Tan Son Nhut airport was also bombarded, when four US aircraft were destroyed, and in the north of the city there was heavy fighting in which a VPA unit took part, this being the first instance of VPA troops being so near the capital. On the 19th, the airport at Tan Son Nhut was subjected to a rocket attack; on the 20th, the NLA overran the village of Tan Thoi, within easy mortar range of the airport; and on the 21st, four US helicopters were shot down only four miles from the city centre. By the 20th, it was estimated that three NLA 'divisions' were surrounding Saigon, and it was known that many of the NLA units were now armed with the new Chinese 140 mm rocket, which had a range of over five miles. That night ARVN soldiers clashed with a strong NLA unit attempting to penetrate Cholon from the Phu Tho racecourse. On the 23rd, it was officially claimed that all the VC troops who had entered Saigon and Cholon in the Tet Offensive, had been driven out, except for a small number who mingled with the thousands of refugees, but fighting continued on the outskirts.

The other important struggle for a city was at Hue, having special significance and status as the former capital. Its predominantly Buddhist population had been hostile to the Saigon Government for some years and it was the scene of many demonstrations of an anti-American character. Buddhist agitation in 1963, which led to the overthrow of Diem, had originated in Hue, and in April 1966 the population, headed by students, had rebelled against the Ky Government, the revolt taking two months to suppress. With a population of about 145,000, Hue comprised two cities, separated by the Perfume (Huong) River; the Old City, with the citadel to the west of it being on the north bank, and the New City, the former French residential, administrative and university area being on the south bank. The Citadel, built by French engineers in 1810, for the Emperor Gia Long, covered a seven square mile rectangular area, having 20 feet high walls which were up to 14 feet thick, and was protected by the river on the south side and moats on the other three. Inside the Citadel was the Imperial City, also surrounded by high strong walls, containing the palaces and elaborate gardens of former Emperors.

At 0300 hours, on January 31st, 1968, VPA and NLA troops entered Hue from the south, seizing six tanks from a post at the entrance to the city and then rapidly overrunning every military and police post within it, except for the HQ of the ARVN 3rd Division. The first VC action was to release some 3,000 political prisoners, but although the VC were joined by a considerable section of the staff and students of the university, there was no mass public support or any instantaneous uprisings.

The battle to recapture Hue lasted three weeks and joint American and ARVN operations concentrated first of all upon regaining the New City, but in the first three days all their attacks were repulsed. More US reinforcements were brought in, many by helicopter, and then a steady advance was maintained, the fighting moving from block to block. On February 7th, the VC blew the bridge over the Perfume River linking the two cities, and both sides tried to prevent the other from obtaining reinforcements and supplies, and for example, armoured convoys from the US base at Phu Bai, ten miles to the south, were shelled, and on one occasion, 20 US personnel were killed and several vehicles destroyed in an ambush. By the 10th, the New City had been completely regained by US and ARVN soldiers.

To the north of the river, the Old City, firmly in VC hands, had been bombed by SVN aircraft on February 3rd, when many houses were destroyed, and on the 5th, the walls of the city had been bombarded in an unsuccessful attempt to open a breach through which an assault might be made. On the 11th, US troops, supported by helicopter 'gun ships', crossed the river in assault boats and penetrated the north-west corner of the Citadel, while other US units took up positions, also on the north-west of the city, to block the VC supply routes. A violent two hour battle erupted some seven miles from Hue, in which US naval guns took part. During the 12th, ARVN troops struggled forward house by house, but the VPA and NLA held on to the southern part of the Citadel, the fighting continuing on the 14th and 15th, when US fighter-bombers gave close ground-support. On the 14th, an assault on the southern ramparts had been repulsed, although US aircraft had dropped bombs, napalm and nausea gas and fired rockets into the Citadel in support.

The VC had received reinforcements through entrances in the west wall, and more fighting occurred on the 15th, when bad weather limited US air support. In the narrow streets US and ARVN troops were often fired on from behind and in the flanks, but using mortars and rockets they forced their way forward over ruins of houses and across courtyards. Heavy fighting continued during the next and subsequent days as US troops, with tanks, tried to breach the southern wall, but the VC held fast, and by the 20th, the US regiment involved had lost half its combat strength in killed and wounded. On that day, a fresh attack by US troops, who sprayed irritant gas ahead of them was again repulsed by VPA soldiers.

Both sides received more reinforcements, the VC through tunnels burrowed under the walls, and the US and ARVN by helicopters. The vital battle began on the 21st, when a break in the weather enabled Allied troops to be given heavy air support, which had not been possible during the previous five days. Under cover of bombs and napalm, US and ARVN troops, some firing nausea gas, renewed the assault and gradually pressed the defenders back. On the following day they succeeded in reaching the southern wall, which enabled them to use the river bridge, soon made serviceable to evacuate wounded. The VC still held out in the south-west corner of the Citadel, against the west wall and in the Imperial Palace. The first two pockets were slowly reduced, but when Allied troops launched an assault on the Imperial Palace area, on the

24th, it was found that the defenders had withdrawn under cover of darkness. The Battle for Hue had been won – but at a terrible cost.

Casualties had been very heavy, but estimates of them varied, the Americans claiming that 119 American, 363 SVN and 4,173 VC had been killed, and 961 Americans and 1,242 SVN had been wounded; the SVN claimed that 2,943 VC had been killed, while the NVN News Agency claimed that over 12,150 US and ARVN troops had been killed or wounded, including 2,223 Americans. A large part of Hue in both cities, had been reduced to ruins; there were over 100,000 homeless refugees, the refugee centres set up were overcrowded and the municipal facilities had broken down. Matters were made worse by the apathy of the refugees, who for example, would not dig their own latrines and bodies lay neglected and rotting on the streets. By the 25th, food reserves in the city had been used up, and the ARVN had to ferry in emergency supplies.

On the 20th, the Mayor of Hue had announced that a number of VC prisoners captured during the siege would be publicly executed within two days, including Nguyen Chi Canh, the former Police Chief who had defected to the NLF after the 1966 Buddhist revolt. He had returned as a leading member of the People's Revolutionary Committee for the Thua Thien province (in which Hue was situated), set up under the leadership of Professor Le Van Hoa on 14th February, in Hue. Hastily, on the following day, the ARVN commander stated that all suspects captured would be tried by a military tribunal, and that none would be executed in public, which provoked the People's Revolutionary Committee to reply that if any such prisoners were executed it reserved the right to take appropriate measures against American prisoners.

After the battle had died down evidence of atrocities by the VC came to light and a later SVN report* stated that the bodies of more than 1,000 civilians shot, beheaded or buried alive during the Hue battle had been discovered in a dozen mass graves in and around the city, and that many of the victims, who included police, politicians, teachers, students and schoolboys, were tied together.

Provincial centres were targets for the VC in the Tet Offensive, and in the northern provinces, for example, Danang was singled out when it was attacked by rocket fire only two hours after the truce was cancelled on January 29th, five aircraft being destroyed. The following day, the VC made their deepest raid into the Danang military complex for three years to attack the HQ of the ARVN 1st Corps. Although they were driven back, there was much house-to-house fighting and sections of the suburbs were devastated. The next day, the 31st, another rocket

* Issued on April 23rd, 1968, and confirmed by the U.S. Embassy on the 30th.

attack on the airfield destroyed or damaged 18 aircraft. Danang, like Hue, had taken part in the 1966 Buddhist revolt, and over 200 people were detained for helping the VC. On the 30th, two NLA Main Force battalions had invaded the town of Hoi An, but were driven out after two day's fighting, while on February 1st, the VC attacked Quang Tri, and occupied the village of Nam O, just outside Danang, French sources reporting that later US aircraft bombed the village, reducing it to ruins and killing 300 civilians.

In the central coastal region the towns of Qui Nhon, Tuy Hoa and Nha Trang were all temporarily occupied by the VC, who destroyed buildings and released hundreds of political prisoners. In the Central Highlands, also on February 1st, Dalat was overrun, and the VC were only driven out after a week's fighting, this being the first time that either Dalat or Nha Trang had been attacked. Kontum, Pleiku and Ban Me Thuot were all occupied by the VC, who were only expelled after several days fighting. Air support was given, and on the 2nd, Kontum and Ban Me Thuot were bombed.

In the Delta area, the Tet Offensive began on January 31st, when 11 out of the 16 provincial capitals were occupied or bombarded; these included Cantho – the largest town and HQ of the ARVN 4th Corps – Mytho, Bentre and Vinh Long. Within four days the NLA were expelled from Cantho, Mytho and Bentre, but the towns suffered heavily from air and artillery bombardment, and on February 2nd, the US were compelled to evacuate their naval base at Vinh Long, after a VC assault. In the fighting for Bentre much of the town was razed and civilian casualties were given as between 500 and 1,000 killed, and about 1,500 wounded. At Cantho 50 civilians were killed and 300 wounded, and at Mytho 63 killed and over 680 wounded. In the provinces the first flush of the Tet Offensive died down early in February, but bombardments and a few sporadic assaults were continued, such as on the town of Xuan Loc in Zone D, in the province of Long Khanh, on the 2nd, Tuy Hoa on the coast on the 5th, and Tan An, 25 miles south of Saigon, on the 11th.

The second phase of the Tet Offensive which began on the 18th, brought a weaker response from the VC in the provinces, being limited generally to mortar and artillery bombardments, some 47 towns and military installations coming under fire. Only a few places were attacked by infantry, and they included Kontum, Dalat, Cantho, Mytho and Vinh Long, the largest NLA success being at the coastal town of Phan Thiet, in Binh Thuan province, which was overrun, the VC releasing over 500 political prisoners before being ejected two days later.

The GRVN stated that between January 30th and February 26th, the period of the Tet Offensive, 2,788 ARVN troops had been killed,

8,299 wounded, and 587 missing; that the US and other Allied troops lost 1,536 killed, 7,764 wounded and 11 missing; that the VPA and NLA lost 38,794 killed and 6,991 captured. The NLF said that the SVN and their Allies lost over 90,000 killed, wounded and captured – which either way, is a lot of casualties for a four-week period. The GRVN also stated that about 7,000 civilians had been killed, that nearly 700,000 had been rendered homeless in this period, that in the fighting some 50,000 houses had been destroyed, and further that insanitary conditions had caused epidemics and outbreaks of bubonic plague.

Under the direction of Nguyen Chi Thanh, who had been in charge of the COSVN and who favoured large scale warfare, the NLA Main Force had been regularised into battalions, which were being grouped into regiments. No doubt he was planning to form the regiments into divisions when he died* in the summer of 1967. Giap who favoured smaller scale, mobile warfare, in spite of the tactics he used at Dien Bien Phu, disagreed with Thanh, who was senior to him in the Politburo of NVN†, on this and other military matters. Thanh had prepared the plan for the Tet Offensive, and with him removed from the scene, it was handed over to Giap to put into operation. Giap correctly estimated that the VC were not yet ready for the final conventional battle, and that the more fluid, mobile phase should be prolonged. However, perhaps due to political pressure, he had to go along with it, and so against his better judgement he launched the Tet Offensive. Already, in September 1967, he was enunciating a new strategy, saying that "Guerrilla activities and large scale combat co-ordinate with each other, help each other and encourage each other to develop", something that had not been said quite that way before, and it was a hindsight indication that Giap had been persuaded to throw the VC into an all-out offensive. General Nguyen Van Vinh, Deputy Chief of Staff of the VPA, succeeded Thanh as Head of the COSVN, and his assessment had been that the US was having difficulty in fighting a 'double war', viz – one against the VC regular formations and a second one to secure the countryside, which he estimated the Americans could not do successfully.

On February 19th, the NLF, over Radio Hanoi, claimed the Tet Offensive to be "our greatest victory ever", but later, on April 12th, the COSVN in an apologia, admitted that "We failed to seize a number of primary objectives, and to destroy mobile and defence units of the

* Thanh was reported to have died of a heart attack, but it was thought he had fallen a victim to US bombing, American pilots at the time referring to his death as being from "B-52-itis".

† Giap, known to his colleagues as the "Volcano and the Snow" (the snow-capped volcano) because his general calm was punctuated with outbursts of temper, was then sixth in the Politburo order of importance.

enemy. We also failed to motivate the people to stage uprisings. The enemy still resisted, and his units were not disrupted into pieces." Giap put down the military failure to poor communications and poor co-ordination, and the fact that he was unable properly to mount the second wave of attacks on February 18th with sufficient momentum, gave this a ring of truth. The VC units around Saigon, for example, had begun to drift away by this time. Later the command structure was shaken up and re-organised, the sub-areas of the city being linked by radio. The political failure, the vital one, was that the people did not rise and rally to the NLF generally; had they done so the outcome might have been different. NLF political cadres produced insufficient 'carrot', still concentrated too much on the 'stick', as evidenced by the fact that political commissars, armed with photographs and dossiers of those to be eliminated, accompanied the VC troops into Hue and elsewhere.

Another cause of the failure of the Tet Offensive was the improved quality of the ARVN. In their initial attacks, the VC bypassed US units and installations and hit directly at the ARVN, accurately calculating that most units would be below strength due to Tet leave, and that they would generally have a relaxed holiday atmosphere. Almost all the regular ARVN battalions were involved in the fighting, yet none broke and ran, and most beat off the VC assaults, which most probably would not have been the case two years previously. As the population centres were attacked, so troops were withdrawn from the countryside to reinforce them, and of some 54 ARVN regular battalions* in support of the Regional and Popular Forces, about 20 were immediately sent into the towns. The other 100 battalions within the 12 ARVN divisions were already there, or adjacent to the population centres, which meant that only about 30 battalions remained in the countryside, and they tended to be understrength. MACV had left the ARVN to control the countryside, and of the nine US combat divisions in SVN, three were in the northern provinces blocking the DMZ, another three were immobilised around Saigon, and the remainder were employed on interception tasks around Hue and Quang Tri. So the countryside was literally denuded of SVN and Allied troops – a situation of which the VC took full advantage. For example, the VC flooded into the provinces of Quang Tri and Thua Thien, leaving Khe Sanh, Camp Carroll, Dong Ha, Gio Linh and Quang Tri as tiny isolated 'islands'.

The Tet Offensive caused the GRVN's pacification programme in the countryside to collapse, leaving it with the immediate dilemma of whether to abandon large sectors of countryside to the NLF and concentrate all available military resources on defending the population centres, or to denude the towns of soldiers and give the troops an

* The ARVN had 154 regular battalions at this stage.

offensive, and more mobile, role. Although on February 2nd, President Johnson at a Press Conference, claimed the Tet Offensive had been a "complete failure" for the VC, and that the purpose of the "general uprising" had failed too, a view echoed later by President Thieu, on the 25th, General Westmoreland admitted that "the enemy had obtained a certain psychological advantage", and that the US "had underestimated the enemy's capacity to employ the tactic of infiltration into inhabited centres". The brief epitaph of the Tet Offensive must be that while the VC narrowly failed to take the cities, they gained considerable territory in the countryside. After the Tet Offensive, the GRVN established, with some 19,000 volunteers, 53 People's Self Defence units in Saigon, and 204 smaller ones in provincial capitals, but this scheme soon foundered.

After the Tet Offensive there was some military re-organisation within the ARVN and certain commanders were replaced, but there was American uneasiness at the corruption revealed in Government circles and the ARVN itself, especially as relief supplies for the Tet refugees were blatantly misapplied. There were probably two million refugees in SVN (although the GRVN insisted the number was only 1·5 million), and only a small percentage said they had fled from the VC, while most had been displaced by the GRVN and the ARVN, the latter becoming anti-US in sentiment. On March 21st, President Thieu warned that penalties for corruption and bribery would be strictly enforced.

The Year of the Monkey–1968

"The monkey symbolises success" Chinese Lunar Calendar.

Meanwhile, besieged Khe Sanh held out, and on February 4th, it was reported that the VPA 308 Division had moved into the area, bringing the number of VPA divisions south of the DMZ up to five. The following day Khe Sanh was heavily shelled, and that night VPA troops made two attacks on Hill 861, both of which were repulsed after hand-to-hand fighting. On the night of February 6th–7th, VPA troops using nine PT-76* light Soviet tanks, attacked the post at Lang Vei, held only by 24 Americans, 400 Montagnards and 500 Laotian troops, the latter having fled across the border into SVN after the VPA had captured their positions a few days previously. In the fighting, the first in which the VPA used armour, four of the tanks were knocked out by the defenders and a fifth by US aircraft, but the post was overrun, only some 12 Americans and 64 Montagnards escaping into Khe Sanh. Between 5,000 and 6,000 SVN, Montagnards and Laotians were refused entry into the Khe Sanh perimeter, and an attempt to evacuate them by air failed when on the 10th, an explosion rendered the airstrip unusable.

A fierce three day battle began on the 8th, when the VPA made ı major assault; the base was heavily shelled and although the B-52s maintained concentrated bombing, the VPA evaded the effects of much of it by moving close into Khe Sanh, in places as near as 100 yards. On the 15th, it was stated that 120 million pounds of napalm had been dropped around Khe Sanh in the past month, but on the 20th, thick fog stopped aerial bombing, preventing supplies being flown into the base and allowing the VC to creep nearer. A heavy artillery bombardment occurred on the 23rd, when a US helicopter was shot down

* A light Soviet amphibious tank, with a 76 mm gun, the chassis being used for a variety of purposes.

as it left Khe Sanh; another helicopter was lost on the 28th, all 19 people on board being killed. After the 26th, on which day a US patrol was ambushed with heavy casualties, the fog lifted and enabled the B-52s to recommence bombing the by now extensive system of bunkers and tunnels which the VC were busily constructing around the base. Meanwhile, VPA pressure was maintained on the other US bases near the DMZ, such as Dong Ha, Camp Carroll, Con Thien and Gio Linh, all being periodically bombarded by artillery and assaulted by infantry. On the 17th, the first VPA PT-76s were reported to the north of the Ben Hai River.

Pressure was maintained by the VC on Khe Sanh during March, with the VPA 325C Division pushing from the north and the VPA 304 Division pushing from the south. After the 6th of that month, when a C-123 transport aircraft was shot down and all 49 on board were killed, accurate VPA fire compelled the Americans to use smaller and faster helicopters to supply the base. On the 17th, the VPA attempted to blow up part of the outer defences, and the next day a VPA battalion launched an assault that took two hours to beat off. On the 23rd and 24th, the VC heavily bombarded Khe Sanh, it being estimated that in these two days some 1,265 shells, bombs and rockets exploded inside the perimeter. During the last week in March, VC troops besieging Khe Sanh were reduced in number from about 12,000 to 10,000 men, although the almost ceaseless bombardments continued.

During March, the other US bases in the north remained under VPA pressure, and for example, on the 7th, in a battle near Dong Ha, 138 VC and 16 Americans were killed; on the 10th, another 102 VC and three Americans were killed, while on the same day in the fighting near Gio Linh, 104 VC and four Americans were killed. This was the violent pattern. A particularly heavy artillery barrage on the night of the 10th destroyed a US ammunition dump at Cua Viet, on the Cua Viet River, along which US supply boats moved up to Dong Ha, the supplies then being dispersed to other US bases in the area, and by the 18th, eleven US supply boats had been sunk in ten days.

An operation for the relief of Khe Sanh began on April 1st, when elements of the US 1st (Air Mobile) Cavalry Division made an airborne landing about ten miles east of the base, which became the HQ for the operation. On the 3rd, a strong, joint US and ARVN force began to advance towards Khe Sanh along Route 9, meeting no resistance except for long-range shelling, but progress was slow as mines had to be cleared and some 15 bridges made passable again. By the 7th, the force entered Khe Sanh unopposed, relieving the 6,000 strong garrison that had withstood a 77 day siege. International negotiations were in progress at the time, and there was speculation as to why the advance was unexpectedly unopposed and whether some secret arrangement had been made with the VC.

On April 10th, the US/ARVN force went on to Lang Vei, which had fallen on February 7th, and which was also entered unopposed, but the force immediately withdrew. During the night the VPA garrison returned, and when this was discovered, three Allied attacks were made on it the following day, all of which were unsuccessful. On the 12th, another attack was mounted on Lang Vei, which found it deserted. US and ARVN troops then remained in Lang Vei until the 17th, when they were withdrawn, and once again the VC took possession.

The pressure on the US northern bases was suddenly renewed, on the 15th, the VPA resumed its bombardment of Khe Sanh, and on the 17th, a US patrol was ambushed, losing 19 killed and 56 wounded. Two days later a supply convoy to Khe Sanh was ambushed on Route 9, when 11 trucks were destroyed. During the five days beginning on April 30th, three VPA regiments launched a series of assaults on the Dong Ha complex of US defences, in which the Americans lost 68 killed and 323 seriously wounded, while VC losses were estimated at between 400 and 570 dead. A series of raids and attacks on Danang and adjacent villages, and VPA reinforcements moving southwards to join the estimated 20 VPA battalions surrounding Hue, caused US troops to mount operations in the coastal sector between Quang Tri and Hue, during the latter part of April.

US attention was then turned on to the A Shau Valley on the Laotian frontier, which had been controlled by the VPA since 1966, and which formed a main artery from the Ho Chi Minh Trail into SVN. Beginning in March, B-52s frequently bombed the 22 mile long valley, along which ran a motor road. This was continued in April, when between the 1st and the 18th, it was stated that B-52s dropped over 9,000 tons of bombs in 61 raids. An offensive that involved over 10,000 US and ARVN troops was mounted on the 19th, the intention being to surround the two VPA divisions in the area (the 304 and 325C), but forewarned, the VC withdrew and managed generally to avoid contact. Although quantities of arms and equipment – including a hospital and a radio station – were captured, bad weather hindered air support, and additionally, the VPA anti-aircraft guns came into effective action, the Americans losing 108 helicopters, the largest number lost in any one operation so far. On May 17th, the operation officially came to an end when the US and ARVN force withdrew, MACV stating that it would not keep a permanent garrison in the A Shau Valley because of its remoteness, the difficult terrain and the bad weather. The casualties were officially given as 139 Americans and SVN killed, for 726 VC dead. On the 24th, MACV admitted the VPA had again occupied the A Shau Valley.

Briefly, elsewhere in SVN after the Tet Offensive only the principal towns and isolated bases remained in Government hands, and periodically these were bombarded and assaulted, being countered by saturation bombing by the B-52s. On March 26th, a VPA regiment, using flame-throwers, attacked a base some 20 miles west of Kontum, but was driven off when US aircraft intervened. In the Saigon sector a series of joint operations was launched to clear the VC from the adjacent provinces and to open the roads to the Delta, while the Delta itself had been almost completely taken over by the VC, only the principal towns holding out.

The VC did suffer a setback, when in mid-March, a fierce fire broke out in the U Minh Forest, the traditional refuge of river pirates and criminals, which had been a VC stronghold since the days of the French. The fire raged on, helped by US ships firing phosphorus shells and air-craft dropping napalm, until the end of April. The U Minh Forest, situated in the extreme south of the Camu Peninsula, was a 1,500 square mile area of tangled swampland, criss-crossed with rivers and canals, where dense foliage resisted all defoliants. ARVN troops surrounded the area to shoot or capture the fleeing VC, and it was estimated that this fire set the NLF back at least two years in this region, as so much equipment and arms were lost.

In May, the VC began an offensive, attacking Saigon and bombarding 119 other population centres and US installations, after which much of Cholon lay in ruins. But from mid-June to mid-August, there was a marked lull in the fighting and although US and ARVN troops carried out offensives in the A Shau Valley area and in the Delta, the VC generally avoided contact, though incidents of terrorism in the towns increased. On June 27th, it was announced by MACV that Khe Sanh was to be abandoned as there were now eight VPA divisions south of the DMZ, which enabled the VC to mount several attacks at the same time, and despite heavy artillery barrages the evacuation was completed by July 5th. VC activity declined in the second half of October, when the secret negotiations were entering a decisive stage.

In the air in the early weeks of 1968, bombing operations over NVN were largely concentrated on its southern areas to counter the threat to Khe Sanh and other US bases. On January 15th, bombing of the Haiphong area was suspended, and on the 18th, this restriction was extended to the Hanoi area, restrictions that were removed after the Tet Offensive. During February, the main targets in NVN were the airfields, and on the 20th, it was announced that the number of B-52s based on Guam and in Thailand, which were mainly employed for pounding the Ho Chi Minh Trail and the area around Khe Sanh, had been increased from 50 to 75.

On March 15th, a US raid on Nam Dinh in NVN, the 201st such raid, hit the cathedral and killed the Vicar-General, but on the 31st, President Johnson broadcast an offer to negotiate with the GDRV, and after that date, bombing of NVN was confined to below the 20th Parallel (225 miles north of the DMZ) and was further restricted to below the 19th Parallel on April 7th. On the 14th, reconnaissance flights over Hanoi were resumed, but on July 31st, the US stated they would not pursue NVN planes north of the 19th Parallel.

On March 17th, six new swing-wing F-111 fighter-bombers, the most modern aircraft the US possessed, each costing $6 million, arrived at the Takhli airbase in Thailand, and made their first raids over NVN, commencing on the 25th. On the 27th, one F-111 was lost, the NVN claiming to have shot it down by ground fire; on the 30th, one crashed in Thailand; and on April 23rd, another F-111 was lost, its wreckage not being found, but the US authorities believed it also crashed in Thailand.

On April 3rd, the GDRV had agreed to accept President Johnson's offer to negotiate (contained in his broadcast of March 31st), and on May 3rd, it was decided the talks would be held in Paris. They began on the 13th, but made little progress. In October, secret negotiations resulted in a compromise suggestion by the GDRV that the VC would greatly reduce its military activity, that a large proportion of the VPA forces would be withdrawn, and that the GRVN could be included in the Paris Talks if the NLF could be represented too. On the 31st, President Johnson agreed, and ordered the bombing of NVN to cease immediately, but a few reconnaissance flights continued, and for example on November 25th, a US reconnaissance plane and one of its accompanying fighter-bombers, were shot down. At the beginning of 1968, the US had about 5,900 aircraft, including helicopters in SVN, but their losses were heavy, it being stated on October 2nd, for example, that 903 US aircraft alone had been lost over NVN. Previously, on June 9th, the US said the total aircraft lost over both NVN and SVN amounted to 2,340 aircraft and 2,103 helicopters. The GDRV claimed the figure was very much higher.

On April 1st, 1968, Clark Clifford had succeeded McNamara as Defence Secretary, and one of his first jobs was to consider General Westmoreland's request for an additional 200,000 US troops, which he rejected. Clifford, an advocate of US disengagement from SVN, was anxious to promote peace talks, and constantly chided the GRVN for its delaying tactics. In May, he announced that the burden of the war would be gradually turned over to the ARVN, a policy to which little

135

more than lip-service had been given so far. For three years the MACV had run the war, consigning the ARVN either to static duties or to countryside pacification, only a small proportion being actually engaged in combat duties, and then usually as auxiliaries to the US forces engaged. However, reinforcements brought the force level of US personnel in SVN by August, up to 540,000 men, and this did not include the 35,000 sailors of the US 7th Fleet.

The strength of the ARVN continued to rise, and in June, President Thieu signed a decree that allowed for an increase in establishment of the ARVN from 775,000 to 910,000 by the end of the year, the minimum age for conscription being lowered from 20 to 18 years, and the liability age raised from 33 to 43 years. When he visited Saigon in July, Defence Secretary Clifford said he wanted to do everything possible to encourage the ARVN to take a larger share in the burden of combat, and stated that the M-16* rifles would be produced at a greater rate and handed over to the ARVN. Previously, on May 18th, the Government of Nguyen Van Loc resigned, being criticised for its ineffectual conduct of the war, although on the 10th, it had passed the General Mobilisation Law widening the conscription liability. On the 25th, Tran Van Huong formed a Government.

The war at sea continued, and on March 1st, four NVN coastal vessels with supplies for the VC were intercepted off the coast of SVN, outside the 12 mile limit; two were destroyed as they exploded when hit by gunfire, a third went aground and was blown up by its crew, and the fourth escaped, which indicated that arms and supplies continued to be moved southwards by the sea route. An unfortunate incident occurred in June, when US aircraft sank a US patrol boat and damaged the USS *Boston* and the Australian ship, *Hobart*, seven personnel being killed and nine wounded; the error was put down to faulty SVN intelligence. The 56,000 ton USS *New Jersey*, the world's only operational battleship, recently recommissioned, came into action for the first time on September 30th, shelling targets in the DMZ; her 16 inch guns, with a range of 23 miles could strike targets well inland, while remaining out of range of the shore batteries. On October 31st, naval bombardment of the NVN coast ceased, as did air bombing of NVN.

In NVN it was estimated that as some 12,000 fit men reached draft age annually the force level of about 480,000 was easily maintained, but the country still had a severe manpower problem, as about 200,000 manned the anti-aircraft defences, another 500,000 worked on repairing roads and bridges, and yet another 200,000 were impressed as labourers. There were also between 30,000 and 50,000 Soviet military personnel in

* The M-15 Armalite had been redesignated.

136

NVN, to help anti-aircraft defences and to maintain Soviet equipment, practically all of which was of a defensive nature, such as SAMs, and to train NVN personnel.

The US estimated that in March, there were between 207,000 and 222,000 VPA and NLA forces in SVN, who included support troops, Main Force and Regional Militia, but excluded political workers and village militia, which showed a decline of between 20,000 and 30,000, caused by heavy casualties during the Tet Offensive. The casualties had been heaviest in the Main Force units, and to compensate for this the VPA regular soldiers were increased from 67,000 to 70,000 almost immediately, and then to over 90,000 by July, after which the infiltration rate dropped to less than 2,500 a month. Of this number about 15,000 VPA soldiers were attached to NLA Main Force formations. About 80 per cent of the VPA troops in SVN were members of the Lao Dong Party, and so were thoroughly indoctrinated and dedicated. The political structure was based on three-man cells, which were as much a prison as a home, all the men eating, sleeping, working and fighting together, and of course watching each other for any signs of political deviation. VPA discipline was strict, the troops for example, being billeted away from the villages to avoid friction with the villagers, and indeed the few VPA deserters often moved over to the NLA, where discipline was more relaxed.

During 1968, the VC became equipped with better weapons and their possession of accurate rockets tended to change the tactics of the war. The Soviet-made self-propelled 122 mm rocket with a 42 lb warhead had a range of up to seven miles, fired from a tripod, and was used against cities and camps, the range being well beyond the radius of action of US and ARVN ground patrols. Their other Soviet-made rocket was the RPG-7 (or B-41), which weighed 20 lb, and could penetrate ten inches of armour up to 550 yards, and had been used by the VC 'suicide squads' which had attacked the US Embassy in Saigon during the Tet Offensive. The VC also had a Chinese-made 107 mm rocket which appeared for the first time in action during the Tet Offensive. This weapon was more powerful and had a larger warhead than the Soviet 122 mm. The VC were fond of the easily portable Chinese 82 mm mortar, which had a range of up to 3,000 yards, and had been used effectively for three years or more. The Soviet AK-47 almost turned a rifleman into a machine-gunner, as the dependable weapon was fast-firing, although it was heavier than the US M-16, which had a tendency to jam.

The other important event of 1968, was that General Westmoreland, after 46 months in command in SVN, became Chief of Staff to the Army and was moved to Washington in March 1968. With his departure the long-term friction between the Army and the Marines* tended to ease, the Marines basically favouring a pacification strategy, while the Army placed its reliance upon weapons and fire-power. An example of this friction occurred at Khe Sanh, where the task of the Special Forces was to block and monitor VC routes into SVN. When it was besieged this task became impossible, but US Marines were still poured into Khe Sanh. They were not keen to hold it, but Westmoreland insisted and the prolonged siege resulted.

The removal of Westmoreland from SVN was taken by some as a Presidential decision against escalation and troop increases, and by others as a result of Westmoreland's failure to predict and prepare for the Tet Offensive. Nevertheless great credit should be given to him for his logistic feats of 1965 and 1966, when the US forces were built up: organisation and management were his strong points. As regards strategy, at first he wanted to bring the VC into set-piece battles, but his idea was politically unwelcome in the USA because of the casualties it would cause; the VC could absorb losses that Western States would find unacceptable. After this his strategy was a compromise between 'Search and Destroy' and 'Holding' operations. This strategy involved the modified 'enclave' theory, by which he kept as many US combat units in, or as near to the populated areas as possible, only sending them out into the countryside to counter serious VC build-ups, such as near Khe Sanh.

General Westmoreland longed to fight a great battle that would forever be told and re-told in military history, and at one Press Conference I attended, he sighed and said that there was he with the greatest, best equipped and trained army the world had ever seen, and he was unable to bring the enemy to battle. He complained he was "over directed" by the Pentagon and the Joint Chiefs of Staff; he was discontented about the lack of support from the Administration and the people back home, and resented the fact that he was expected to fight a war on the cheap. It should be remembered however that in the best General MacArthur tradition on the Korean pattern, he "wore two hats" for he was in charge of MACV but also retained direct control of the US forces in SVN, which gave rise to certain criticism. General Westmoreland could be faulted mainly for his over-optimistic statements, and his lack of perception of VC strategy and tactics, being at times caught by surprise; but his greatest omission was his neglect and relegation of the ARVN.

His successor was General Creighton Abrams, Jnr, an armoured corps officer, who had been Vice Chief of Staff to the Army, before

* Most US soldiers served for 12 months in SVN, while the Marines served for 13.

being sent to SVN in April 1967, as Deputy to General Westmoreland, who detailed him to concentrate upon the ARVN. Abrams got to know the ARVN well, and his efforts improved it so that it performed creditably during the Tet Offensive. Ignored, rather than deliberately neglected, the ARVN had unspokenly been consigned to the seemingly secondary task of pacifying the countryside, while US troops prepared for and fought the big battles, thus gaining glamour; a situation that unconsciously caused the SVN soldiers to be regarded as inferior and unreliable.

General Abrams found the ARVN to be defensive-minded; the main concern of the units in the field was to establish a defensive perimeter, to sit in it and to wait for the VC to attack. Little night patrolling was carried out, and generally there was an atmosphere of a 'five day week', with officers dashing off to Saigon for the week-end. He observed that the ARVN officers were an elite class, removed from the peasants, with whom they had little in common, and there was hardly any chance for the good soldier to rise from the ranks. Abrams insisted that between 4,000 and 6,000 soldiers who had done well during the Tet Offensive should be promoted to commissioned rank. The basic arms of the ARVN which had been the US World War II M-1 rifle and the ·30 calibre Browning machine-gun, were no match for the AK-47s of the VC, and so the ARVN had no incentive to volunteer to take the offensive.

General Abram's ten months with the ARVN had been put to good use, and now with the open backing of the US Defence Secretary, he was able to make further progress, especially in ensuring that better arms (such as the M-16), better communication equipment, armoured personnel carriers and more helicopter support were given to the ARVN. He abandoned the huge, elephant-like sweeps through the country-side – so beloved by General Westmoreland – and instead used smaller units, supported by aircraft and helicopters on a roving basis. But after a while, he too, fell back on larger Search and Destroy operations at times, and on November 21st, for example, a force of 5,000 US and 2,000 ARVN troops moved into the Dien Ban area, about 15 miles south of Danang, which for years had been under VC control and was now held by three VPA regiments, which stood and fought back. By the end of the operation on December 9th, it was claimed that 1,019 VC had been killed and 122 captured. Another large joint operation had been launched on December 7th, to drive back the VC forces threatening the US base at An Hoa, 20 miles south-west of Danang, into the mountains. This became a prolonged operation, which did not terminate until March 10th (1969), when it was claimed that 1,398 VC had been killed. After the evacuation of Khe Sanh, the former static US artillery bases, which made it easy for the VC to seep in and surround them, especially in the northern provinces, were replaced by mobile artillery camps. In accordance with this policy, on December 28th, Base Camp Carroll was abandoned, as others had been, although the static artillery positions at Con Thien and Gio Linh remained in use.

There was considerable controversy over the observance of an alleged unwritten agreement reported to have been part of President Johnson's decision to end the bombing of NVN, which stipulated the VC should refrain from shelling population centres and respect the DMZ. The GRVN lodged repeated complaints about this to the ICC, but on November 24th, Defence Secretary Clifford said that VC infiltration through the DMZ had ceased. On the other hand, the GDRV protested about US reconnaissance flights over its country, and the US methods used to rescue downed pilots, which were usually to move in with fast, low-flying helicopters, guarded by fighter-bombers, and to snatch the pilots from the ground where possible. For example, on November 25th, a US reconnaissance plane and one of its accompanying fighter-bomber escorts were shot down over NVN. Short truces were observed at Christmas and the New Year, in which a few breaches occurred, but none of a major nature.

In adjacent Laos, often referred to as "Hanoi's second front", the main incident of the year was on January 26th, 1968, when two VPA divisions and five units of the Pathet Lao attacked the Royalist-held town of Nam Bac, which had been taken from the VC in 1966. After a two-day battle, the 4,000 defenders were routed. Also in January, the VPA made its first air strike into Laos, hitting the anti-communist Meo town of Muong Yut, in a raid in which two VPA Soviet Antonov An-2 (of 1947 vintage) were shot down.

The Provisional Revolutionary Government–1969   10

"No matter what difficulties may lie ahead, our people are sure to win total victory" Political Testament of Ho Chi Minh – May 10th, 1969.

The year of 1969 saw the establishment of the NLF Provisional Revolutionary Government of SVN, a major change in VC strategy, and the death of Ho Chi Minh, the veteran Communist leader. It was also the first year of the Nixon Administration in America. Since 1966, the official NLF policy had been to break down the Government's "rural administrative councils" in the villages, often controlled by a Saigon nominee, and once this had been done, in 1968, the policy changed. After the Tet Offensive, in June and July, elections were held in villages under NLF control for People's Liberation Councils, each of between 15 and 35 members, depending upon the size of the village. The Councils then elected People's Liberation Committees, of between five and seven members, who took charge of all administrative, political and military matters. This was followed by the election of similar committees in provinces and towns, not all under full NLF control, and culminated in the formation of an underground People's Liberation Committee for Saigon and Cholon on May 30th, 1969. A firm grip on the grass roots of village politics had been gained,

Next came the formation of a Provisional Revolutionary Government of SVN (the PRG), announced on June 10th, 1969. The PRG had been elected on June 6th–8th at a congress of some 88 representatives of political parties – religious, social and other groups – convened jointly by the NLF and the Alliance Forces (the Alliance of National, Democratic and Peace Forces). The Alliance had first appeared during the Tet Offensive, in Hue, and consisted mainly of those with political views of many shades, opposed to the GRVN.

The President (later titled Chairman) was Trinh Dinh Thao, who had been a Vietnamese Minister during the Japanese Occupation. The Premier was Huynh Tan Phat, usually regarded as the theoretician of the NLF. The Deputy Premier was Nguyen Van Kiet, leader of the Alliance, and the Defence Minister was Tran Nam Trung, the Secretary-General of the PRP, and the suspected director of all NLF military forces. The PRG adopted a Twelve-Point Programme, and the first country to recognise it was Cuba, with recognition by other Communist states following.

The next important event was the death of Ho Chi Minh on September 3rd, 1969 (he had been in failing health for some time) at the age of 79, and this was marked by a three-day VC cease-fire. His political testament, dated May 10th, 1969, was read at his funeral on September 8th.* Ho, President of NVN, had developed into the father-figure of his country, respected, revered and the symbol of NVN revolutionary greatness. In his latter years he was depicted as the gentle, kind and solicitous elder statesman, the Uncle Ho, everyone's favourite uncle, whose thoughts were always on the well-being of his people, and he was frequently photographed with children. This picture should not disguise the fact that he was a shrewd, dedicated Communist, determined to get his own way at all costs, and in his early days in his quest for power, and his struggle to retain it, he was single-minded and ruthless in his methods.† In his latter years of power his immense prestige enabled him to keep his Politburo intact and seemingly united. In 1945, he had formed an 11-man Politburo, and since that time every single member had remained with it, although some portfolios were shuffled, and now at his death, in 1969, of the original eleven only Nguyen Chi Thanh, who died in 1967, was missing. With his prestige and masterly touch, Ho had maintained unanimity amongst his Ministers, but on his death there was speculation as to whether there would be an open split, and who might rise to power in his stead.

On September 23rd, Ton Duc Than, the 81 year old Vice President, was elected President of NVN by the National Assembly. The leading personalities in NVN were now Le Duan, First Secretary of the Lao Dong Party, Pham Van Dong, the Premier and Giap, the Defence Minister, all of whom favoured a mixture of guerrilla and conventional warfare in SVN. The other dominant personality, Truong Chinh, Chairman of the National Assembly, advocated a complete return to

* See Appendix B.
† For example, in 1925, he betrayed a rival nationalist leader, who was arrested by the French and executed, and in answer to the 'sentimentalists' who criticised him for this act, Ho justified it by saying that the man was a dangerous rival, that his execution occurred within Vietnam and so created a revolutionary climate, and that in any case the reward he would obtain from the French for this betrayal was needed to finance his own revolutionary organisation. *Time* of September 12th, 1969.

guerrilla warfare in an effort to outlast the US and SVN, while conserving the manpower and other resources of NVN.

The Paris Peace Talks opened on January 25th, 1969, but up until the end of April no progress was made, largely because the US and the SVN wanted to concentrate upon military aspects, while the NVN and PRG wanted to discuss both political and military matters. On May 8th, Tran Buu Kiem, the NLF leader at the Talks put forward a Ten-Point Peace Plan, and this was countered on the 14th, when President Nixon presented an Eight-Point one. Back in SVN, on May 29th, President Thieu said he would never enter into a coalition with the NLF.

In America there was a growing feeling of disillusionment with the war in Vietnam, never popular, which found expression on November 15th, in a mass demonstration, a 'Moratorium' against the war, in Washington and other major American cities, demanding that the US pull out. Aware of the public demand to 'bring the boys home', President Nixon did what he could to terminate the war, but his international politics had become complicated, and he had to take the GRVN along with him, which was not easy. On June 8th, when he met President Thieu on Midway Island, he announced that 25,000 US troops would be withdrawn from SVN.

On July 25th, President Nixon stated that in future the US would avoid situations like that in Vietnam, by limiting any assistance to economic and military aid, rather than active combat involvement, and this became known as the Nixon Doctrine. He then visited SVN on the 30th, to discuss troop withdrawals and future strategy. On September 16th, he said that another 35,000 troops would be brought home by December 15th, on which date he announced yet another withdrawal of 50,000 more US soldiers, to be effective by April (1970). On November 3rd, he had stated that a plan had been adopted for the replacement of all US ground forces in SVN by ARVN troops, according to a timetable, depending upon the Paris Peace Talks, the level of VC activity and the progress in training the ARVN. By the end of the year it was estimated there were still about 479,500 US troops in SVN, of whom about 300,000 were combat soldiers.

In this major change of Allied strategy, US troops were progressively withdrawn from combat areas, and for example, they had completely evacuated the Mekong Delta by September 1st, the ARVN taking on the whole responsibility for that area, although US air support continued to be given. On October 9th, Melvin Laird stated that all US commanders had been instructed to give the highest priority to the 'Vietnamisation of the war', and to make the maximum effort to give actual combat responsibilities to the ARVN as quickly as possible. Large numbers of M-16 rifles, over 50,000 vehicles and 50,000 field radios were handed over to the ARVN during the year. However, there remained an undercurrent feeling among many US generals that the ARVN was hesitant and dubious about taking over the full conduct of the war, and also that it only needed 'just a little bit more US military effort' to tip the scales and bring victory against the VC in the field.

In August, it was officially stated that the strength of the ARVN was 1,045,000 men, there being some 430,000 in the army, 391,000 in the Regional Force, 103,000 in the Popular Force, 79,000 in the National Police, and 21,000 each in both the air force and the navy. It was also stated that plans were laid for increasing the ARVN by the end of the year by another 71,000 soldiers, 8,000 sailors and 10,000 police.

Within SVN, the early months of the year were disturbed by renewed Buddhist agitation, and on February 12th, a monk immolated himself (the 28th person to have done so since 1963). From February to April there were negotiations between political parties that resulted in new groupings. Also in April, there were trials of NVN agents and SVN intellectuals. On August 23rd, Premier Tran Van Huong resigned and was replaced by Tran Thien Khiem to enable a broader based Government to be formed.

Early in 1969, the NLF also decided to change its strategy from intense military activity to political erosion, influenced by the obvious fact that sooner or later American public opinion would force the disengagement of its forces from the war. A COSVN document, known as Resolution 14, ordered all VC to organise and prepare for the US Forces' evacuation from SVN, to step up terrorist activities, and to establish three and five man cells in the population centres to operate 'legally', the lack of which had been a weakness of Tet Offensive. In additional, the NLF decided to step up the infiltration of agents into the various SVN organisations.

By the end of 1969, the NLF had built up an intelligence service; it was later* estimated that a network of at least 30,000 agents was operating inside SVN. About 20,000 agents were thought to be ARVN officers and senior non-commissioned officers who tried to recruit for their cause, carried out assassinations, and generally made arrangements for 'inactivity' on the battlefield. The second group, consisting of about 7,000 agents, concentrated upon sabotage and had infiltrated the police and all government services, as well as the ARVN, while the more selected and highly trained 3,000 had penetrated the intelligence services of the US military forces in SVN, the CIA, the ARVN, police, government, religious and political parties. Despite this information which had been gathered by the CIA, none of these alleged agents had

* *Time* of August 17th, 1970.

been identified, nor had any arrests been made, which indicated a high degree of general SVN tacit complicity, perhaps encouraged and aided by apathy. This vast, all-embracing intelligence network enabled the NLF to have advanced warning of military operations against it, and knowledge of the Allies' strategic thinking and their future intentions.

On the military side, already the large scale conventional VPA attacks of up to regimental strength had been superseded, and the fighting in SVN in 1969 was on a reduced and smaller scale. A number of VPA formations had been withdrawn in the autumn (of 1968), and those remaining in SVN began to operate in smaller units, and with the NLA concentrated upon the bombardment of airfields, military HQs, attacking isolated posts and villages and ambushing convoys. This caused a change in Allied tactics, the forces again operating in smaller formations; a change that was made because the VC troops in the 11 provinces surrounding Saigon had withdrawn from the environs of the population centres, and were concentrating upon selected 'practical targets'. On August 25th, the US Military Command stated that the Allies were fighting "a completely different war" to counter the new VC tactics, and were using small unit attacks against limited objectives. Commencing in July, the US troops had started to use company and platoon-sized formations, aimed at keeping the NLA off balance around key points. Although this was the pattern that developed during the year, there were many exceptions.

During the first two months of 1969, the VC generally avoided action, though the indications were that a VC offensive was in preparation. On January 9th, a large VC HQ complex was discovered in the U Minh Forest. The complex included 180 barrack compounds, a 100-bed hospital, 16 engineering workshops, a printing press, and several tons of paper and documents, as well as some diving suits. On the 13th, the largest amphibious operation of the war so far was launched with 4,000 US and ARVN troops being airlifted in helicopters to a small peninsula in Quang Ngai province, about 65 miles south of Danang, that had been under VC control for years. When the operation was completed on February 8th, it was claimed that over 700 VC had been killed. The civilian population, about 11,500, were rounded up and taken to refugee camps for screening. On January 22nd, US and ARVN troops began an operation in the A Shau Valley, while a US division was moved into Tay Ninh province to counter the VPA which was infiltrating from Cambodia.

Despite the VC change in strategy, there were three VC offensives in SVN in the year, albeit involving multiples of smaller formations. On the night of February 22nd, the VC launched their long-awaited offensive which lasted until early May, by bombarding 115 targets, concentrating in three sectors: near the DMZ, the Central Highlands, and around Saigon. In accordance with the new VC tactics, the attacks were not large ones against major population centres, but small ones against US bases and posts, isolated villages, outposts and small towns. The assaulting units became smaller in size and there was an increased use of sabotage mission squads. The VC had some success in the destruction of US military material, and for example, on the 23rd, they bombarded Danang, when an ammunition dump exploded, and on the 26th, at Cu Chi base, 21 miles north-west of Saigon, by using rockets they destroyed nine large helicopters and damaged three others.

On March 18th an Allied force, with armour, launched an offensive in the Michelin Company's rubber plantation near Dau Tieng, an area of about 30 square miles on the edge of Zone D, which had been a VC stronghold for years, and was a HQ and a rest and assembly centre for VC coming in from Cambodia. It was estimated there were about 7,500 VC in amongst the trees. On the 21st, B-52s bombed areas adjacent, but not the actual plantation, for fear the Company would pull out from SVN and so impair the national economy, if this was done. In Tay Ninh province, where the COSVN, at least two VC Main Force and two VPA divisions were, on April 11th, the town of Tay Ninh was bombarded, buildings set on fire and munition dumps exploded. On May 6th, a VC battalion attacked Camp Carolyn, a US fire base about 12 miles from the Cambodian border, broke through the defences, but was driven out again. The VC aims in this offensive had been to inflict casualties on US personnel to influence American public opinion and so put pressure on the US Government to make concessions at the Paris Peace Talks.

With hardly a pause the VC swung into a second small-unit offensive on the night of May 11th, by bombarding over 100 towns and bases. During the following six weeks, there were never less than 20 nightly bombardments, fighting centring on the A Shau Valley, the Central Highlands and Tay Ninh province. The previous day, the 10th, US and ARVN forces had begun an offensive in the A Shau Valley, and on the 14th unsuccessfully assaulted Hill 937, the Ap Bia Mountain, which became known as Hamburger Hill, being hardly one mile from the Laos border. During the next five days in all another nine unsuccessful assaults were made on this VC-held feature, and despite heavy US air support, the attackers were on each occasion driven back by VC rifle and machine-gun fire. On the 20th, Hamburger Hill was stormed by 1,000 US and 400 ARVN troops, this time successfully, but most of the defenders had withdrawn, only about 250 VC remaining. The execution of this battle prompted Senator Edward Kennedy to comment that the tactics employed "were senseless and irresponsible".

In clashes in the A Shau Valley there had been fairly heavy US casualties, but in June some three VPA regiments were withdrawn from that area, and generally VC infiltration declined. On June 6th, the VC launched yet another unsuccessful assault on Tay Ninh town. During May and June, the majority of the VPA troops, previously in adjacent Cambodia, moved into the provinces of Tay Ninh, and Binh Long, where their respective capitals were besieged by several thousand men. On the 25th, President Thieu said that five of the 15 elite ARVN battalions forming the 'general battle reserve'* had been sent to Tay Ninh province. Extensive use of B-52 bombers was made during the VC offensives. Later, on the 15th, Defence Secretary Melvin Laird said that President Nixon had given specific orders to General Abrams "to keep casualties at the lowest possible rate".

The pause in the fighting, coinciding with the withdrawal of US Forces from the combat areas and the decline of VC infiltration, continued until August 11th, when the VC launched their third small-unit offensive by bombarding 179 targets and launching 44 ground attacks, the fighting being heaviest in the provinces of Tay Ninh, Binh Long and Phuoc Long. On August 17th, a major battle developed in the Que Son Valley, 25 miles south of Danang, when two US companies were encircled by a VPA regiment. On the 19th, a US helicopter was shot down near the fighting, and it took US troops five days to fight their way to it. By September 1st, when the surrounding VC faded away and the operation ended, it was claimed that at least 1,000 VC had been killed, for the loss of 100 US dead and 300 wounded. During September, Allied troops were withdrawn from the A Shau Valley, which was flooded and was declared to be inaccessible as an infiltration route.

During the last three months of 1969, VC operations, again small-unit ones, were directed primarily against the ARVN positions, there being fairly heavy fighting in parts of the Central Highlands and the Delta. The largest battle of the year, from the ARVN point of view, occurred on October 19th, in the U Minh Forest, when 96 VC were killed. A three-day Christmas Truce was observed, but with many small breaches. At the end of the year, according to US estimates, there were about 250,000 VC in SVN, consisting of about 100,000 VPA, 50,000 NLA Main Force, and 100,000 Regional and Village Militia. In total, this was about 50,000 less than in the autumn of 1968. About 115,000 VC had entered SVN in the year, but not all had stayed, as opposed to about 250,000 entering in 1968.

During 1969, 9,249 US personnel were killed, 69,043 wounded and 112 missing, while it was estimated the VC lost 152,842 killed, the

* Eight were guarding key points around Saigon and the other two were in the Delta.

majority by aerial action. In answer to a question as to whether the American claim that the VPA "had lost half-a-million men" was correct, General Giap was reported* to have answered "That's quite exact", although according to the US estimates, VPA battle deaths only numbered about 200,000. On September 25th, the Australian Defence Minister had stated that 350 Australians had been killed in SVN, and over 2,150 wounded since 1963.

* *Time* of April 18th, 1969.

Incursion into Cambodia–1970   11

"We must resolve to fight against the US aggressors until total victory"
Political Testament of Ho Chi Minh.

During 1970, which can be thought of as the year of the incursion into Cambodia, the scale of fighting in SVN generally diminished, largely due to the new VC policy of preparing for the day when US forces would be withdrawn. The VC, whose over-all strength in SVN remained in the region of 250,000 (only some 60,000 infiltrating during the year), generally avoided large scale attacks, concentrating upon attrition. They developed a two point strategy, one in the countryside against the Regional/Popular Militia and the Self Defence Force, and the other aimed at the urban front by setting up subversive cells. Some of the VC divisions and regiments were broken down into battalions, companies and even platoons, in order to operate independently. This made their task of disrupting the GRVN's pacification scheme in the countryside more difficult, but rendered them less vulnerable, especially to bombing by the B-52s. On the Government side a major effort was made to disrupt VC supplies.

After brief New Year and Tet Truces in which there were no major violations, numerous incidents on the ground in SVN continued. The main fighting occurred in the first quarter in the northern provinces, where the VC struggled to keep the supply routes open in areas from which US troops had been withdrawn, or were withdrawing, such as the A Shau Valley, and along the Cambodian border. On February 20th, for example, a US armoured column was ambushed in the Que Son Valley, in the north, losing 14 dead in a five-hour battle. On April 1st, the VC launched an offensive in which 13 US and ARVN positions were attacked and 115 bombarded, the force of which gradually died down, but outbursts of periodic bombardment by artillery, rockets and mortars

149

continued throughout the year. On that day (the 1st), the VC raided Dalat, killing 27 people, when they attacked the military academy and political warfare school.

In the third quarter of the year, after intervention in Cambodia, the scale of fighting declined in central and southern SVN, but continued in the northern provinces around the supply routes from Laos. An American base known as Ripcord, 25 miles west of Hue and 11 miles from the Laotian border, was besieged on July 1st, by the VPA, and after its garrison lost 58 killed and suffered 325 wounded, it was evacuated by air on the 23rd. Another base at Kam Duc, also near the Laotian border, which had been abandoned in 1968, was re-occupied on July 12th, by 2,500 US and ARVN troops, but it came under heavy attack and had to be evacuated again on August 26th. On September 8th, when the VPA attacked the Special Forces camp at Tra Bong in Kontum province, near the Laotian frontier, although the garrison lost 35 dead, the VPA were driven off after a four-hour battle, at least 23 VC being killed. The only really co-ordinated bombardments on bases had occurred on 30th August, probably as a VC reaction to SVN elections that were being held.

In the last quarter of the year, fighting diminished further, the major activity being in the Delta area, where on December 1st, after concentrated bombing by B-52s, ARVN troops opened an offensive (the 11th in two years) on the U Minh Forest, to try and drive some 3,000 VC out from the swamps and bamboo thickets. On the 8th, it was claimed that 144 VC had been killed, but the operation lost impetus and the Forest remained unpenetrated. There were no major violations of the Christmas Truce, and on December 27th, President Nixon ordered the "present herbicide operations" to be phased out quickly, after which only those herbicides permitted in the USA were allowed to be used. Toxic herbicides, which allegedly caused damage to plant and animal life that took years to correct, had been employed and America had been criticised internationally for this. Although the ground fighting was at a lower rate of intensity than in former years, the human toll (also less), continued to be extracted, and in the course of the year the US lost 4,204 killed and had 29,734 wounded. VC infiltration was chiefly into the northern provinces, mainly to tempt ARVN formations from the Delta area.

The war in Vietnam became increasingly unpopular in America; on June 24th, the US Senate repealed the Gulf of Tongking Resolution, which had pledged full support for SVN. There was agitation to bring the American soldiers back home again, causing the US Administration to seek means to disengage, which took the form of even more Vietnamisation, so US troops could be thinned out more quickly. In April 1970, port aircraft, the faster A-7 Corsair jet fighters, F-4 Phantoms and F-105 Thunderchiefs. The GRVN pointed out that the Americans needed about 4,000 helicopters to fight the war, but the Americans were only giving SVN about 500, and that it was probable the NVN were about to move their MiGs nearer to the DMZ.

The transfer of 650 small combat coastal craft from the US to the SVN Navy, spread over two years, was completed on December 29th, during which period it had accumulated about 1,500 coastal, river and sea-going craft, and had an establishment of 40,000 men. Quantities of supplies for the VC continued to be brought into the Delta from the sea, where SVN naval surveillance was reckoned to be less than 50 per cent effective.

During the spring and summer, SVN was again troubled with Buddhist disturbances, the worst since 1966, mainly provoked by rapid inflation, Government measures against opposition movements, and the granting of emergency powers to President Thieu. Many were rallying to General Duong Van Minh (Big Minh), who had been allowed to return to SVN and had announced on November 13th, 1969, that he would oppose Thieu in the 1971 Presidential elections. He declared himself in favour of a middle course, somewhere between that adopted by the President and that of the PRG, which was openly welcomed by Madame Nguyen Thi Binh, the Foreign Minister of the PRG, who suggested that General Minh should confine his policy to the towns.

Throughout 1970, American aircraft, including B-52s, gave ground support to operations in SVN and also took part in raids over NVN. Disagreement and misunderstanding had arisen between the US and the NVN, the Americans insisting that when they discontinued bombing NVN in 1968, they retained the right to continue to make reconnaissance flights over NVN. The NVN would not accept this, and so the USA claimed that when its reconnaissance planes were fired upon they could retaliate. On January 28th, a US reconnaissance plane was fired on when over NVN, and so its escorting fighter-bombers immediately attacked a SAM site 90 miles over the border, but one was shot down, while the US helicopter sent in to rescue the crew, was also shot down by a MiG–23.* This brought the number of US aircraft downed over NVN since the bombing pause to nine. On January 30th, the US Command in Saigon revealed that other NVN anti-aircraft sites had been attacked since the bombing pause, but this fact had not been released as

* The MiG-23 was a high altitude, all weather interceptor, of considerable strike capability and with a speed of Mach-3 was superior to any aircraft possessed by the US. This was the first indication the Allies had that the Soviet Union had supplied any MiG-23s to NVN.

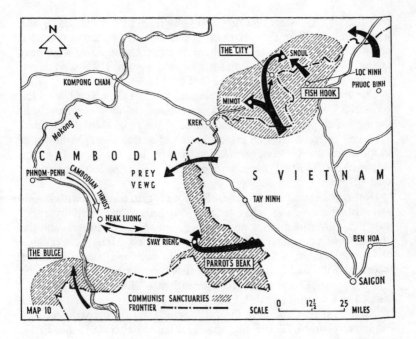

Map with labels:

N

THE "CITY"
SNOUL
LOC NINH
PHUOC BINH
KOMPONG CHAM
FISH HOOK
MIMOT
KREK

Mekong R.

C A M B O D I A
S   V I E T N A M

PHNOM-PENH
CAMBODIAN THRUST
PREY
VEWG
TAY NINH

NEAK LUONG
SVAY RIENG
BEN HOA

THE BULGE
PARROTS BEAK
SAIGON

MAP 10
COMMUNIST SANCTUARIES
FRONTIER
SCALE
0   12½   25   MILES

there were still 429,900 US Servicemen in SVN, and on the 20th, President Nixon said he planned to withdraw another 150,000 during the course of the year. US troops were progressively brought in from combat zones to base camps as the ARVN increasingly assumed responsibility for areas where there had formerly been heavy fighting, such as the supply routes in the north from Laos, the Central Highlands, the border provinces and the Delta.

The SVN also assumed greater responsibility for air and naval operations; on November 4th the SVN Air Force took over the airfield at Soc Trang, in the Delta, the first for which it was solely and completely responsible. At the beginning of 1970, the SVN Air Force had about 400 aircraft (which included 125 helicopters), and the plan was to increase that number to 800 by the end of 1971. There were some 1,30 pilots, and as many more in training. The GRVN felt the Vietnamisati of its Air Force was still not fast enough, pointing out that the Americ had passed on C-119s and C-47s, old transport planes and Cessna A light bombers, when the GRVN really wanted newer C-7 Caribou tr it was not considered to be 'significant'. On February 2nd, US aircraft attacked another SAM site in NVN, and on the 28th, another US fighter-bomber was shot down by a MiG-21. The GDRV claimed that US aircraft had attacked its territory on April 19th and this was admitted.

On May 2nd, in the biggest raid since 1968, some 400 US aircraft struck at targets in NVN, Radio Hanoi claiming that many civilians were killed in the provinces of Quang Binh and Nghe An. A spokesman in Washington stated the raids had been made as "protective reaction", since reconnaissance aircraft had been fired upon; while Defence Secretary Melvin Laird said he would recommend the use of air power in the north, if NVN retaliated against US and ARVN intervention in Cambodia by attacking across the DMZ. On the 4th, a US spokesman said the bombing had been halted after three strikes into NVN, but this was almost immediately amended to four strikes. On that day, the Defence Department said there would be no more large scale air attacks against NVN, but that small raids might be conducted if US reconnaissance planes continued to be attacked. The NVN claimed the US carried out 63 raids during the period May 14th–29th. Nevertheless, NVN anti-aircraft sites were bombed by US planes on July 21st, August 28th and September 5th. On November 13th, a US reconnaissance plane was shot down over NVN, and on December 10th, President Nixon said that if such planes were fired on he would order the military complex responsible to be destroyed.

On November 21st, under cover of diversionary bombing raids on selected NVN targets, a small task force of US service volunteers, who had trained specially for the purpose at Fort Bragg, made a helicopter raid on a POW camp at Son Tay, about 23 miles west of Hanoi, to release American prisoners. The camp was found to be deserted, and the grass in the compound waist-high. The US personnel returned safely but the incident caused uneasy doubts to be raised as to the quality of US intelligence, and especially upon how much reliance could be placed on US information about other NVN targets.

In adjacent Cambodia the VC had struck comparatively close to the SVN border and avoided the towns, although there was much truth in the GRVN claim that there was a "30-mile wide VC belt" along the length of the frontier. The three main 'sanctuaries' – the Fish Hook, the Parrot's Beak and the Bulge – had expanded and were VC defended strongholds, staging camps and springboards for operations into SVN. The VC had avoided clashes with Cambodian troops as far as possible, and the Cambodians had not looked for trouble, with the result that only about 1,000 Cambodian soldiers had been killed or wounded by the VC since 1963. Cambodian relations with the NLF fluctuated, and in May 1969, the NLF diplomatic representation in Phnom Penh was raised to Embassy status. In its search for food, the NLF arranged to buy quantities of rice for US dollars, and General Lon Nol took a large cash advance, but no rice was forthcoming: both the Cambodian Government and the NLF eyed each other warily.

The new VC strategy of preparing for the evacuation of US troops from SVN led them to send personnel into the provinces adjoining SVN, in both Laos and Cambodia, to expand and consolidate the network of communications and supply dumps. At the beginning of March 1970, it was estimated that there were at least 5,000 VPA combat troops, and another 40,000 VC of different types, engaged in organisation, administration and supply in Cambodia, the north-eastern part of which (including both banks of the Mekong River down to a few miles north of Kompong Cham) was in VC hands. Their presence attracted US and ARVN bombers, and in the raids inevitably the villagers suffered.

On March 13th, Prince Sihanouk (who had been in France for some time) went to Moscow to ask the Soviet Government if it would persuade the VC to withdraw their forces from Cambodia. While there, on the 18th, he was formally deposed by the National Assembly, power being assumed by General Lon Nol, who had right-wing views, and who formed a Government far more in sympathy with American policy in South-East Asia than that of Sihanouk.

There then followed a brief period of confused civil war as factions fought each other. One of these factions was the Khmer Serai, the Free Khmers, recruited and trained by the US Special Forces from Cambodians living in SVN and who raided into Cambodia from Thailand. Another was the KKK, Khmers of Kampuchea Krom, a force which had fought for the French as mercenaries. Both rallied to General Lon Nol, while the Khmers Rouge, the Red Khmers, fought against them. Into this confusion advanced the VPA and NLA forces, being opposed by the 38,000 strong Cambodian army, already involved in an attempt to stem insurrection. On March 25th, General Lon Nol said that all NVN and NLF diplomatic representatives were being withdrawn from Cambodia, and the port of Sihanoukville, reverting to its original name of Kompong Som, was now closed to all VC traffic: thus the source of the famous Sihanouk Trail was blocked.

In April, the anti-Lon Nol forces achieved success in southern Cambodia. In other areas anarchy reigned: civilians were massacred and many bodies were seen to be floating down the Mekong River, tied together, after having been killed and mutilated. On the 14th, General Lon Nol appealed to America, SVN and Thailand for arms for his expanding army. SVN sent limited quantities of captured VC weapons, including 1,500 AK-47 rifles, a few were sent by Thailand, but none came from the USA, which was of the opinion that Cambodia was not really in danger of being overrun by the VC. He also asked for the return of 10,000 Cambodians serving in the ARVN, and for 4,000 Special Forces, but neither were forthcoming. Gradually the VC pressed back the Cambodian army, seeping during the next two months into the greater part of the country, harassing towns and taking over the countryside. Phnom Penh became almost isolated, with only Route 1, to Saigon, remaining open.

Although wishing to continue to observe the neutrality* of Cambodia both the SVN and the Americans were concerned about the concentrations of VC in Cambodia so close to the SVN border and also the suspected presence of the 2,400 strong COSVN. It was therefore decided to mount operations against them. The COSVN, the political and military HQ of the PRG, was mobile in the sense that it changed its position to avoid attention by Allied bombers, having moved from its original site in Tay Ninh province to one nearer Saigon in early 1960, before moving back into Tay Ninh province and eventually moving again at the end of 1968 into Cambodia. On April 29th, 12,000 ARVN troops entered the Parrot's Beak sanctuary, the piece of Cambodian territory that projected into SVN, in the Svay Rieng province. From here at least five VPA and NLA Main Force regiments operated into the Delta. The VC avoided contact, and the invasion force linked up with the Cambodian army in the town of Svay Rieng the next day. On May 6th, about 8,000 ARVN soldiers were withdrawn, claiming to have destroyed bases and stores and to have killed 1,197 VC, taken 168 prisoners, for the loss of 66 killed and 320 wounded. The remainder of the ARVN force continued to operate in the Parrot's Beak area.

Meanwhile, on May 1st, a joint US/ARVN force invaded the small triangle of Cambodian territory, known as the Fish Hook (a VC sanctuary a few miles north of the Parrot's Beak) which was believed to contain the COSVN and at least two VC divisions. The advances were preceded by concentration bombing by B-52s and an artillery barrage. The main object was to destroy or capture the COSVN, but again the VC avoided contact, and it was not until the 3rd, that US troops met their first resistance, being fired upon from the town of Memot. This town was occupied the next day and large quantities of weapons were discovered there. The next VC resistance was on the 5th, at the small town of Snoul, which was taken after an air bombardment. On the 7th, the US forces occupied a huge encampment area, known as the 'City', some seven miles south of Snoul, which contained 300 bunkers, 500 camouflaged huts and miles of tunnels, while the arms haul included one

* It was admitted by the US Defence Department in July 1973, that during the 14 months preceeding May 1970, some 3,630 B-52 bombing strikes had been secretly made over Cambodia.

million rounds of ammunition, 1,000 small arms, 120 machine-guns and over 40,000 lbs of explosive. Later (on the 11th) it was denied in Saigon that this had been the site of the COSVN, but this was not convincing.

On May 4th yet another joint US/ARVN force, of about 6,000 men, launched an airborne offensive in the Se Sam Valley of Ratamakiri province in north-east Cambodia, some 50 miles west of Pleiku. Along this valley Route 19 continued to the Mekong Valley and it was from this area that the VC had made incursions into SVN the previous year. On May 6th, US and ARVN troops opened up three other offensives into Cambodia. One, entering Prey Veng province, just to the north of the Parrot's Beak, was supported by a flotilla of river boats moving along the Kham Spean River; another entered Cambodia about ten miles to the north of the SVN town of Loc Ninh, and the third, an airborne one, crossed the frontier about 20 miles north of the SVN town of Phuoc Binh.

On May 3rd, a VC regiment had captured the town of Neak Long, commanding the ferry over the Mekong River on Route 1. Units of Khmer Kroms, serving with the US Special Forces, together with arms and ammunition for the Government troops, had been flown there on the 1st, but had failed to hold it. On the 8th, a flotilla of 90 US and SVN gunboats sailed up the Mekong to try and recapture Neak Long, but the US ships turned back on reaching the 21 mile inland limit set in Cambodia by President Nixon. The ARVN element continued, and on the 10th using armour and helicopter-gunships, re-took Neak Long, meeting little resistance. That day another 2,500 US troops joined those operating in the Fish Hook area.

On the 13th, 3,000 US troops were withdrawn from the Parrot's Beak and the Se Sam Valley, but on the 14th the ARVN launched yet another thrust into Cambodia, in the Ratamakiri province, some 15 miles south of the Se Sam Valley. On the 15th ARVN troops, advancing from Svay Rieng linked up with those holding Neak Long, and the next day, finding several arms caches, troops were withdrawn from the Se Sam Valley. On the 20th, the ARVN launched yet another operation into Cambodia, in the province of Mondolkiri. Generally, the VC withdrew before all the Allied advances into Cambodia.

On June 3rd, President Nixon stated in a broadcast that the US intervention into Cambodia had been "the most successful operation in this long and difficult war", adding that 43,000 ARVN and 31,000 US troops had taken part. He had already announced, on May 12th, that all US troops would be clear of Cambodia by June 30th. This occurred, the last group leaving on the 29th, but the following day, about 300 US military advisers returned to their SVN units in Cambodia. The invaders had left behind them damaged bridges, torn up roads and stocks of CS gas, which in favourable weather conditions should have remained effective for six months.

The original ARVN operation into the Parrot's Beak which had commenced on April 29th, ended on July 22nd. In this operation it was claimed that over 3,000 VC were killed for the loss of 313 ARVN dead and 1,460 wounded. Another similar ARVN operation was launched the same day, with the aim of clearing Route 1, to be succeeded by yet another on July 26th, which claimed to have killed 168 VC and captured 54 by the time it terminated on August 3rd. By the end of July, there still remained up to 10,000 ARVN troops operating in Cambodia. As other thrusts were withdrawn, B-52s bombed the 'sanctuary areas', to which the VC were reported to have returned. President Nixon pledged he would not again send US troops into Cambodia.

Elsewhere in Cambodia, the Communists had been all too successful, having flooded most of the country. Only the main towns were holding out and the Government controlled only the narrow region of the Mekong Valley, from Neak Long up to the Ton Le Sap Lake, the VC being within a few miles of Phnom Penh. In July the VC relaxed pressure on the capital, but remained active around Kompong Thom and Kompong Cham in the north-east (still held by Government forces) and in the south-western provinces. On August 9th, there was fighting only two miles from Phnom Penh, against small groups of VC trying to infiltrate.

The US and ARVN incursions into Cambodia had upset and retarded the VC programme of preparation, but that was all; due to their efficient intelligence network, they had at least a week's warning of the various offensives, and for example, the senior personnel at the COSVN were able to motor-cycle away almost leisurely to another sanctuary deeper in Cambodia. VC formations that were forced to withdraw temporarily, returned quickly to their former positions as soon as the invaders had gone, but they also began to establish new 'sanctuary areas' in the four Cambodian north-east provinces and on the Bolovens Plateau to the south. There was no doubt that huge quantities of arms and equipment had been captured, most estimates varying between 30 per cent and 50 per cent of all that possessed by the VC in Cambodia. Figures released on May 25th, claimed the Allies had taken 10,898 AK-47 rifles and sub-machine-guns, 1,269 mortars, 184 vehicles, including six armoured half-tracks, 1,505 tons of ammunition, and nearly 3,000 tons of rice. Some VC had been killed for the loss of 140 US and 472 ARVN dead. The US/ARVN intervention had the converse result to the one expected, for as the VC spread over parts of Cambodia, they established new sanctuaries that could only be rooted out by massive force, which General Lon Nol did not possess, and the USA had debarred itself from providing.

The question of invitation or permission for US troops to enter Cambodia arose, when on May 1st, General Lon Nol said he had not been consulted. However, on the 11th, President Thieu claimed he had been given permission, and added that his soldiers had been operating inside Cambodia since March 20th, two days before Sihanouk had been deposed. In any case there was good liaison between the US/ARVN forces and the Cambodian army, which within a month had suddenly swelled in size to about 100,000 men. Lon Nol, who formed a Government on July 2nd, with himself as Premier and Defence Minister, was clearly relieved that this course had been taken, and would perhaps have liked it to continue until all the VC were driven from his country. On October 9th, 1970, Cambodia was proclaimed a republic, and so the 1,168 year old Khmer monarchy was brought to an end.

Disappointed at US limitations, Lon Nol turned to SVN and resumed diplomatic relations with that country, which had been broken off in 1963, so there may be much in what President Thieu said. Diplomatic relations, having been broken off in 1965, were resumed between the USA and Cambodia.

The other traditional enemy of Cambodia – Thailand – also drew closer in the face of the Communist threat, and diplomatic relations were resumed between those two countries on May 13th. On the 22nd, the Thailand Government stated it would supply US military equipment, but not arms, to the Cambodians. Later, on the 27th, the Thailand Government was asked to send 10,000 troops to help defend Phnom Penh, but it refused, saying instead it would send more military equipment, to include reconnaissance aircraft and 20 gunboats to patrol the Mekong River. There had been frequent reports that Thailand troops had actually been in Cambodia fighting the VC in the western provinces for many months, but this was denied by the Thailand Government, which speculated there might be some Thailand irregular volunteers there.

Invasion of Laos–1971   12

"The longer the fight, the more mature our forces, and the weaker the enemy forces"   Vo Nguyen Giap *Big Victory, Great Task.*

The most notable event of the war in 1971, was the brief, unsuccessful invasion of Laos (the supply route and sanctuary of the VC) by ARVN troops. As the American Administration had decided in December 1969 not to send combat formations into either Laos or Thailand, American troops did not cross the border, but US air support was given.

Fighting in Laos between the Pathet Lao and the Government of Prince Souvanna Phouma had been renewed since January 1969, but it was largely a stalemate, until in May and June of that year the Pathet Lao overran the Plain of Jars, the main area in dispute. They remained there until, in turn, they were expelled by Government troops in August and September. Both sides received foreign support, the Pathet Lao being helped by the NVN, and the Laotian Government by the Americans, while for a long period US aircraft had been bombing Pathet Lao-held territory.

The Pathet Lao army, between 25,000 and 30,000 strong, was supported by a force of about 3,000, composed of left-wing neutralists and militia. The opposing Government army numbered about 60,000 men, all of whom were to the west of the 1962 Cease-Fire Line, backed by a force of about 8,000 right-wing neutralists, mainly at Muong Soui, Van Vieng and Souvannakhili. However, the brunt of the fighting was borne by a guerrilla force of Meo tribesmen, about 12,000 strong, of whom about 1,500 were full-time regulars. There was also another tribal guerrilla force of Kha tribesmen, operating on the Bolovens Plateau in the south, on the Government side. In addition to aerial support, a number of US Advisers were also helping the Royal Laotian forces* and the two CIA-run airlines (ostensibly civilian air charter companies) ferried in supplies and helped the small air force. US assistance to Laos was co-ordinated by the Combined Operations Centre at Vientiane. There were also about 5,000 Thailand troops in Laos, which fact was confirmed on March 20th, 1970, by the Americans, but formally denied (on the 22nd) by the Thailand Government, who admitted Thailand military personnel might be in Laos in a private capacity. The Pathet Lao alleged that Thailand troops had been in Laos since 1967, and that in March 1968 some had been killed when the Communists captured the town of Pha Thi.

About 6,000 VPA troops had remained behind in Laos in 1962, and the number had steadily risen to 55,000 by mid-March 1968, but only a small proportion were helping the Pathet Lao, the majority being employed guarding the Ho Chi Minh Trail, or administering it. The importance of the Trail was increased when the Cambodian port of Sihanoukville (Kompong Som) was closed to VC traffic in 1969, and in the spring of that year the number of VPA troops in Laos was increased to about 67,000.† In February 1970, the Pathet Lao carried out another offensive in the area of the Plain of Jars.

An Allied decision was taken to use ARVN troops to block the Ho Chi Minh Trail and in consequence the only major operations carried out by US and ARVN troops in January 1971, were the establishment of fire bases near the DMZ and at points near the Laotian frontier. During this month the VC made a number of harassing and sabotage raids on US posts. As a prelude, a force of about 9,000 US and 20,000 ARVN troops moved towards Laos from the base at Dong Ha, to clear Route 9, which runs just south of the DMZ. On January 30th, 1971, three battalions air-landed at the abandoned base of Khe Sanh, where the airstrip was made usable again, and elements pushed on to establish a fire base at Lang Vei; others established fire bases overlooking the A Shau Valley. There was little initial VC resistance to these moves.

On February 8th, the majority of the ARVN forces crossed the border into Laos with the intention of cutting the Ho Chi Minh Trail and occupying the town of Tchepone, an important VC junction.‡ The ARVN units met little resistance in Laos at first, but despite this,

* On March 6th, 1970, President Nixon stated that there were 1,040 US military personnel in Laos; but other sources variously estimated the number to be between 2,000 and 4,000.

† A Laotian Government statement indicated that over 100 NVN prisoners had been taken between 1964–1970, and indeed a few had been publicly exhibited in Vientiane.

‡ At a Press Conference on February 17th, 1971, President Nixon revealed that the possibility of blocking the Ho Chi Minh Trail had been under consideration since 1965.

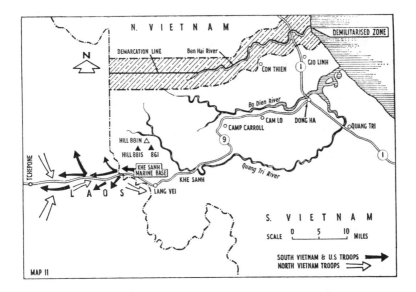

MAP 11

progress was slow, mainly due to bad weather, rain, mud and fog, which caused supporting aircraft and helicopters to be grounded. Once the weather cleared, VC resistance stiffened and the ARVN communications were harassed; 20 trucks were destroyed in ambush on the 12th, while back in SVN on the same day, Dong Ha was bombarded. On the 15th, the ARVN operational command HQ, established at Khe Sanh, claimed that the Ho Chi Minh Trail had been blocked and VC supplies stopped, but this was not so, and throughout this operation, VC traffic continued along roads and tracks slightly farther to the west. It was later estimated that the vehicular traffic actually increased from about 1,000 trucks daily moving along the Trail to about 2,000 daily during this period.

On the 19th, it was admitted that the ARVN advance had bogged down about 15 miles inside Laos due to bad weather, that the Ho Chi Minh Trail was not completely cut and that the VC were using trails farther to the west.

The ARVN had managed to establish a number of positions mainly to the north of Route 9 inside Laos, and were attempting to take up more when on February 17th, the VC began their counter-attack, commencing with an assault on a paratroop company which had just landed about five miles inside the border. The VC moved their troops into commanding positions and on the 23rd the ARVN HQ stated it had no intention of moving any further into Laos, admitting that for the previous 12 days VC units had cut Route 9 behind the forward troops. The forward commander was reported to have said that if his advance was still held up, his units would have to try and escape by jungle paths back to SVN before they were all blocked. On the 22nd, President Thieu claimed the operation to have been a success because it frustrated the NVN plan to occupy the central provinces of SVN in order to improve their bargaining position at the Paris Peace Talks. However, this rather cut across Thieu's earlier statement that the object of the incursion was to block the Ho Chi Minh Trail.

On February 25th, a VPA regiment, supported by 20 Soviet PT-76 tanks, attacked an ARVN position, held by a battalion, based on three adjoining hills, about six miles inside Laos and about six miles north of Route 9. After six hours fighting, they overran one hill (Hill 31) but fighting for the other two continued for three days, until they were evacuated by the ARVN defenders. Except for the capture of Lang Vei in 1968, this was the first use by the VPA of tanks in battle. On March 4th, President Nixon claimed at a Press Conference, that the operation had been a success, saying that 200,000 rounds of ammunition, and 2,000 guns had been taken, 67 tanks destroyed or captured, and that truck traffic along the Trail had decreased by 55 per cent. But the fighting was not yet over.

After these ARVN setbacks, commencing on March 1st, strong reinforcements were sent to Khe Sanh. The second phase of the operation was launched on the 4th, when troops were landed by helicopter about four miles from Tchepone, which was about 25 miles from the border, and the town itself – a deserted ruin – was occupied by them on the 6th. This brought the number of ARVN soldiers in Laos to about 24,500. At a Press Conference at Khe Sanh on the 8th, it was claimed the two main aims of the operation – to disrupt the VC network and restrict infiltration – had been achieved and that 6,000 VC had been killed in the fighting. These brave words were hardly justified, as Tchepone was evacuated on the 8th and 9th, although the information was not released until the 11th.

The VPA launched its counter-offensive on March 12th, against the many positions occupied by ARVN troops in Laos, and under powerful pressure, one by one they were abandoned, often in panic, being hastily lifted off by helicopter, the last troops leaving Laos on March 25th. The previous day, the Pathet Lao had claimed a great victory over the invaders. On the 26th, Lang Vei was evacuated; ARVN troops were withdrawn from Khe Sanh on April 6th, and President Thieu on the 9th, declared that the operation was officially at an end. In this incursion into Laos, the ARVN lost 1,445 killed, suffered 4,016 wounded, and 204 missing, while the Americans stated that 105 helicopters had been lost. To say the Laos incursion was unsuccessful was an understatement. Advancing without anti-tank weapons, the ARVN had suddenly found itself tangled up with about 150 VPA tanks, mostly PT-76s, but also a few T-34s, T-54s and T-55s; this could be marked down to faulty intelligence.

Following the retreat from Laos, the VC took the offensive in SVN again commencing on March 28th, when a number of bombardments and attacks were carried out, and this pattern continued with intensity for several days in the northern provinces. There was also fighting in the Central Highlands, especially around Fire Base Six, which was just six miles from the border junctions of SVN, Laos and Cambodia. A VPA regiment attacked the Fire Base at dawn, and after some fighting the ARVN garrison blew up its guns and withdrew. B-52 bombers were brought into action, but the VC remained in possession until the following day when they were driven out again. The Fire Base came under daily attacks from the surrounding VC until April 14th, when a force of about 6,000 was lifted in by helicopter; after a few days the VC faded away, the siege being declared to be at an end on the 20th. The SVN claimed that 3,454 VPA soldiers had been killed during the siege and the subsequent operations in the area, for the loss of 210 SVN killed and 589 wounded. The VC launched another wave of minor attacks on April 24th.

On April 14th, the ARVN opened an offensive in the A Shau Valley, where generally the VC avoided contact, but fighting developed on May 12th, terminating in a six hour battle on the 19th. On the 21st, the ARVN claimed to have killed 571 VC. In May, the VPA took the offensive just below the DMZ, and in the months of May and June, it was estimated that at least 6,000 infiltrated southwards through the DMZ. On June 2nd, ARVN troops began a Search and Destroy operation near the abandoned base of Khe Sanh, which ended on the 10th, when it was claimed that 225 VC had been killed for the loss of only 17 soldiers. On the 24th the VPA stormed Camp Fuller, the westernmost camp of a line of positions just south of the DMZ. It was considered to be a serious loss, but after aerial bombardment the VC evacuated it again.

By July 1st, the last US combat troops began to withdraw from the area of the DMZ, and after a period of six weeks of relative calm, the VC renewed the offensive in the north, to which the US replied by using their B-52s. The fighting declined in the latter part of August, and all but ceased during September, the NVN calling off the offensive as it had to withdraw at least three VPA regiments for relief work in the heavily flooded Red River Delta.

In the south, there was fighting in the U Minh Forest, where the resident VPA regiment was joined by another. On the 14th, the VC attacked several ARVN positions, routed an ARVN battalion and inflicted heavy casualties in actions that continued for eight days. Small attacks, bombardments and sabotage by the VC continued for the remainder of the year, pressure being applied in the Saigon area, especially on the occasions of the Presidential election and investiture.

Throughout 1971 US and ARVN aircraft gave close support to the ground troops, and the B-52s were frequently in action over NLA-held areas in SVN and over the Ho Chi Minh Trail. It had been admitted on December 2nd, 1970, that US aircraft had been flying over Laos, and had been authorised to attack the NVN-manned SAMs on the Ho Chi Minh Trail if they felt themselves to be threatened, while American pilots frequently bombed the anti-aircraft defences near the Laos border when they found their aircraft being tracked by radar. During November and December, NVN MiGs frequently harassed US aircraft bombing the Trail. On December 18th, three US Phantoms were lost while covering retreating Laotian troops during a Pathet Lao offensive. US aircraft also carried out 'protective reaction' air raids over NVN on 108 occasions in 1971, as against 21 the previous year.

The heaviest US air raids on NVN occurred during the period December 16th–30th, when over 200 aircraft, from bases in SVN and Thailand and from US aircraft carriers, made over 1,000 strikes. They met increased anti-aircraft activity and harassment by MiGs; three US planes were lost. It was stated by the US Military Command in Saigon on December 17th, 1971, that 8,051 US aircraft had been lost since the war began, and of these 4,454 were as the result of accidents and 'non-hostile' causes.

The main events on the political scene in 1971 were the Presidential election on October 3rd and the investiture on the 31st. President Thieu was re-elected without opposition with a huge majority, after his two opponents, Vice President Nguyen Cao Ky and General Duong Van Minh had withdrawn. During the voting there was rioting all day in Danang, Hue and a few other places, and several explosions in Saigon. Thieu granted an amnesty to 2,938 prisoners, of whom 618 were released immediately, most being either sick or disabled. The remainder were given 'returnee' status, which meant that after 60 days 'political training' they would be allowed to return home for six months before being liable for military service.

During 1971, there was a sharp reduction of US personnel (from January 1st, 1971 to February 1st, 1972) from 337,900 to 139,000, during which period the Australian and New Zealand contingents were being withdrawn, as well as 10,000 South Koreans.

US Disengagement 13

"The truth is that the American expeditionary troops are being defeated in the people's war of the Vietnamese"   Vo Nguyen Giap *Big Victory, Great Task.*

The year of 1972 was marked by the VC offensives in April and May (which had many successes), renewed US bombing of NVN, and the SVN counter-offensives which also had some success. In the first quarter of the year, apart from the (by now) customary run of scattered incidents, big and small bombardments, raids and sabotage, there was little heavy fighting, except in the Hue area. But it was the relative calm before the storm, as a VC offensive was expected. The NVN policy was again to use big formation attacks,* and the time was considered to be right because of the withdrawals of the US combat troops from vital areas, the weakness of the ARVN and because it was thought the three-man cells in the towns had done their preparatory work properly and the people generally were ready to rise in revolution in support of the VC. There was a build up of US air power to counter this anticipated offensive, while US 'protective reaction' raids over NVN increased, there being some 90 on SAM and anti-aircraft sites in the first 12 weeks of the year. On the 19th a MiG-21 was shot down, the first since March 1970, and on March 8th, yet another was brought down in an air battle. During February, the US aircraft carrier *Constellation* joined the *Coral Sea* and the *Hancock* in the Gulf of Tongking, and it was reported that reinforcements of B-52s were sent to Guam. Bombing raids by US and SVN aircraft continued to be carried out over the northern provinces of SVN and the Central Highlands, and on the 16th there was a 100-aircraft raid over NVN.

The long expected VC offensive which developed on four separate

* The decision to resort to large-formation warfare was made at a Lao Dong Party meeting in December 1970.

fronts began in the early hours of March 30th, after a heavy bombardment of the ARVN positions just south of the DMZ, in which it was estimated that over 5,000 shells, bombs and rockets rained down on the defenders. Much unexpectedly new Soviet equipment was revealed, the VC using 122 mm rockets, 130 mm field guns, and also firing 152 mm howitzers from the Khe Sanh plateau. The VPA infantry, about 15,000 strong, supported by about 100 Soviet tanks, advanced and by April 2nd all the ARVN positions in the northern part of Quang Tri province had fallen; only the towns of Dong Ha and Quang Tri, and the narrow coastal strip remained in Government hands. The VPA advance was helped by rain and low cloud which prevented effective US air intervention. On the 3rd the naval base at the mouth of the Cua Viet River was taken and the next day VPA amphibious tanks crossed the river at two points, despite a saturation bombing strike.

The ARVN managed to establish a defensive line on the south side of the Cua Viet River, which it held for about three weeks, repulsing on April 9th a major attack on Dong Ha, 12 miles south of the DMZ, and another on Fire Base Pedro, about 10 miles south-west of Dong Ha. In both battles the VPA used tanks, including T-54s, but handled them badly, at least 40 being knocked out, many by the US M-72 anti-tank missile; also about 1,000 VC were killed. On the 18th and 19th further VPA attacks west of Quang Tri were beaten back with the aid of B-52s. On the night of the 22nd, VPA infantry and tanks, under cover of a heavy artillery barrage, crossed the Cua Viet River at another point, and a battle raged the following day.

To the south, on April 4th, Fire Base Anne, 18 miles west of Hue, and Fire Base Bastogne, 12 miles south west of Hue, came under attack, and eventually after 25 days siege, the latter Fire Base was evacuated on the 29th. To the west, other VPA units were advancing down the A Shau Valley to move into the offensive just to the west of Hue.

Meanwhile on April 27th, the VPA renewed pressure when at dawn its infantry and tanks made a three-pronged thrust towards Quang Tri town. The next day, Dong Ha on the Cua Viet River was overrun. The area around it northwards to the DMZ was declared to be a Free Fire Zone, so that US ships could shell VC moving through it, and aircraft could bomb them; but bad weather restricted aerial activity. The population of Quang Tri, almost en bloc, fled southwards along the roads and were deliberately shelled by VC guns, and enormous casualties were inflicted on civilians. On May 1st, VPA tanks broke through the defences on the northern side of Quang Tri, when ARVN Commander,*

---

* On October 2nd, 1973, Brigadier-General Vu Giai was sentenced by Court Martial to five years hard labour with loss of rank and decorations, being charged with disobeying an order and abandoning a position in the face of the enemy. This was the first time the GRVN had tried and sentenced a general for a defeat.

staff officers and US Advisers were flown out by helicopter – a bad psychological move. During the night, after some resistance, the defending ARVN division broke and evacuated in panic, vehicles being commandeered at pistol-point. By the 3rd, undisciplined soldiers reached Hue, causing chaos on the streets and general apprehension, and the following day when he visited Hue, President Thieu ordered strong measures to be taken to restore order. Thieu later said, on the 9th, that in this disastrous three-day rout, the VC had inflicted about 25,000 casualties on the SVN. This ARVN defeat was put down partly to disagreement between senior officers, and partly to the blind reliance placed by the soldiers on the 'air kill' concept, which had given them over-confidence.

Farther south, on April 5th, the VPA had opened a 'second front' offensive, in the Binh Long province, next to the Cambodian border. On the 7th it occupied the town of Loc Ninh and laid siege to An Loc, the provincial capital. The VPA had chosen Binh Long as it had been an established VC stronghold, with many sympathisers amongst the population, and the withdrawal of US and ARVN troops from Cambodia left that part of the SVN frontier open. Also, three regiments of the SVN Rangers had been withdrawn suddenly to take part in the defence of Quang Tri in the north. Route 13 from Saigon (68 miles away) to An Loc came under VC pressure, and repeated attempts to re-open this route and push reinforcements through were unsuccessful. Soon An Loc was completely besieged, and Route 13 blocked firmly at Chon Thanh, 37 miles from Saigon.

On the 8th, an ARVN force of about 15,000 men with armoured vehicles was mustered to re-open the route, and by the 11th had suc-ceded in relieving Chon Thanh. But its further advance was slowed down by repeated ambushes and rocket attacks. On the 13th, VPA infantry and tanks broke through the outer defences of An Loc and managed to occupy part of the town. There had been a confused un-comprehending advance of the VPA tanks, unco-ordinated and without infantry support,* some 37 being destroyed by M-72 anti-tank missiles, B-52 bombers or guns firing at point blank range. The next day, ARVN paratroops were landed to reinforce the garrison, which was ordered by President Thieu to "fight to the last man", and the VC were ejected, only to force their way back into the defences on the 15th, after which a stalemate set in. The VPA maintained a heavy, continuous bombardment on An Loc, but in turn suffered considerably from the B-52 saturation bombing. On May 3rd, a relief force that had been

* Prisoner interrogation established that at least 3,000 NVN tank crewmen in these several offensives had only four to five months earlier graduated from the Russian armoured school at Odessa.

flown in, pushed the VPA units back about four miles, while the same day a road convoy reached An Loc, the first for 22 days, bringing in supplies and munitions. The 500 ARVN wounded were then able to be taken back by road, but still Route 13 was not properly open.

The 'third front' of the VC offensive took place in the Central Highlands in the first part of April, when VPA troops, amounting to two divisions and five independent infantry and artillery regiments, began to advance with the objective of cutting the two strategic roads in the area, Route 19 and Route 14. By the 7th, Route 14 from Pleiku through Kontum to Danang, was severed in several places, and by the 11th, Route 19 from Pleiku to Qui Nhon was blocked at the An Khe Pass. Next, the VPA attacked a series of five fire bases on a line of hills, known as Rocket Ridge, which guarded the approaches of Kontum from Laos and Cambodia, one base being overrun on the 15th, and another on the 22nd. On the 25th, Tan Canh, 25 miles north-east of Kontum was overrun by VPA infantry and tanks: the previous day Dak To, with the only airfield in the northern part of Kontum province had been captured by the VC.

The retreating ARVN then tried to establish a defensive line about eleven miles north of Kontum, but it was outflanked and was abandoned therefore on April 26th, the same day on which the last remaining positions on Rocket Ridge were evacuated. The only outlying base still held by the ARVN was at Ben Het, which was soon encircled. By the 28th the town of Kontum was being surrounded and VPA tanks were reported to be within six miles in the north and five miles in the south. On the 29th, the last outlying defensive position on the north side was abandoned, and the defenders withdrew to other positions about two miles from the town which, crowded with refugees, was shelled on the 30th.

Just previously, the VC block on Route 19 at the An Khe Pass had been broken by South Korean troops on the 26th, after a 16 day struggle. A military road convoy reached Pleiku, the first since April 9th, but the GRVN admitted that the road could not be regarded as permanently open. On May 4th, ARVN paratroops were dropped between Pleiku and Kontum, and were able to prise open Route 14 long enough for one road convoy to reach Kontum; but the VC snapped it shut again on the 6th.

The VC began the 'fourth front' offensive on April 14th, in Binh Dinh and Quang Ngai provinces. When, on the 19th, they advanced on the town of Hoai An, about 45 miles north of Qui Nhon, ARVN regular troops and Popular Force personnel abandoned their weapons, took off their uniforms and fled, allowing the VC to walk in unopposed. On the 26th, a Fire Base on Route 1 was taken by the VPA, when the 300 defending Regional Force members simply changed sides. On the 29th, the town of Bong Son fell as did that of Tam Quan on May 1st; in both instances no defence was put up by the Regional Force garrisons. On the 2nd, the last ARVN-held base, Landing Zone English, in the north, was evacuated by sea. By the 3rd, the VC controlled the whole of the northern part of Binh Dinh province, while in the southern part there was fighting near the Phu Cat airbase, ten miles north of Qui Nhon. On the 17th, for the first time VPA tanks were on Route 1, about 60 miles south of Danang.

Farther south, in the Saigon area, during April, the VC intensified their activities, trying to block roads into the capital, while in the Delta, they sought to re-establish control over areas regarded as 'pacified' since the ARVN–US incursion into Cambodia in 1970.

By April 1972, over 25 ships of the US 7th Fleet were concentrated in the Gulf of Tongking area. They fired at shore targets and were themselves attacked occasionally, one MiG-21 being brought down by ships' anti-aircraft fire on the 19th. The four aircraft-carriers in the Fleet brought the number of available US fighter-bombers up to about 600, in addition to about 100 B-52s. On two days, April 3rd and 4th, US aircraft had carried out nine 'protective reaction' raids, but on the 6th, this pretence was abandoned and mass air raids began on NVN, aiming first of all at SAM sites within the DMZ, and then ranging farther northwards. On the 10th, the B-52s joined in raiding NVN, to bomb the area of Vinh, about 145 miles north of the DMZ. Although they had taken part in the bombing of NVN in 1966–7, they had never penetrated so far north, and since 1967 had been used solely on targets inside SVN or along the Ho Chi Minh Trail, as their comparatively slow speed made them vulnerable to SAMs. On April 16th, Hanoi and Haiphong were hit.

During May and June, heavy bombing of NVN continued, hitting communications and strategic targets, including the oil pipeline running through the DMZ, set up by the VC, which was able to pump about 1,300 metric tons of fuel daily for VPA vehicles operating in SVN. On May 10th, both Hanoi and Haiphong were again bombed, but the heaviest US air strike of the war occurred on June 19th, when over 300 sorties were made over the NVN anti-aircraft defences. On this occasion it was claimed that 76 SAM launchers were destroyed, while another 46 were destroyed on the 21st. The pace of the bombing caused a NVN fire-power shortage, and the number of SAMs fired against Allied aircraft was daily reduced.* As the NVN were short of SAMs, of which by early July it was estimated that over 1,600 had been fired (since early

* On June 8th, 1972, the Defence Department stated that the number of shells fired at the besieged An Loc had been reduced from about 8,000 daily in April, down to less than 300.

April), the MiG-21s were pushed into action, and by the end of July about 40 of some 200 possessed by NVN, had been brought down.

Bombing by US and SVN aircraft continued during the year, reaching peak intensity on August 15th–17th, when over 1,000 sorties were flown in the three days, while on the 17th, there were over 270 raids on NVN.

The effectiveness of the American bombing was largely put down to the new Smart or Laser bomb, which enabled a system of precision bombing to be developed. A specially equipped fighter-bomber laid down a Laser beam on to the target below, and then the following strike-aircraft released the Smart bombs containing guidance systems which 'homed' on to the Laser beam, giving pin-point accuracy. If the Laser beam was laid accurately on to the target, the Smart bomb could not miss, but it was not so effective against moving targets. Whereas formerly in visual bombing, large numbers of aircraft were employed against single targets, often repeatedly hitting them without causing lasting damage, with the Smart bombing method, only five or six aircraft were required. On June 8th, for example, the US claimed to have destroyed 15 key bridges and to have put over 3,000 trucks out of action, which in turn caused a shortage of fresh food in Hanoi.

A controversy arose over whether the US aircraft were bombing the dikes in the Red River Delta. Annually during the monsoon season and immediately afterwards large quantities of silt were brought down by the river and deposited in the Delta, where the waters slowed down, so much in fact that the river bed became far higher than the surrounding countryside, so that dikes had to be built to contain the waterways. Photographic evidence showed that NVN anti-aircraft guns were mounted on the high dikes in many places, but on June 29th, President Nixon declared that orders had been given not to bomb the dikes, and that no dikes had ever been bombed. But on July 6th, Defence Secretary Melvin Laird admitted that on occasions dikes and dams might have been hit by accident. Had the dikes been seriously bombed up to one million people might have lost their lives in the resultant flooding and the economy of the country brought to a halt.

On April 26th, President Nixon had said that the US troop withdrawals would continue, but that air and naval attacks on NVN would carry on as long as the NVN offensive lasted, adding that the only limitations would be that no US combat troops would be sent back into action and that nuclear weapons would not be used. He said the Paris Peace Talks, suspended on March 23rd, would be resumed. Nixon spoke well of the performance of the ARVN, saying that 'Vietnamisation' had proved itself sufficiently and the programme of the withdrawal of US troops could therefore continue; that all VC attacks had been resisted on the ground by SVN troops, aided by the South Koreans, and that no US ground forces were involved. He said that preparatory to the VC offensive, three NVN divisions had entered SVN through the DMZ and another three farther south, indicating that there were about 120,000 regular VPA troops in SVN. This meant that 12 regular divisions had left NVN. General Abrams insisted that with US air and sea support, the ARVN could hold out against the VC.

On May 8th, President Nixon said that all NVN ports would be mined and the bombing of NVN intensified until all US prisoners were released and there was a cease-fire. The following day, in the morning, US naval aircraft commenced dropping mines outside Haiphong, two ports to the north of it (Hon Gai and Cam Pha) and four to the south of it (Than Hoa, Vinh, Quang Khe and Dong Hoi). During the mining of Haiphong port, two Soviet ships were machine-gunned and four Soviet sailors wounded. On the 10th, it was stated that when the mines were laid there were 36 ships in Haiphong harbour, including 16 Soviet and five Chinese; others had slipped away the previous night. This action was condemned by the Soviet Union and China, while US Press comment was that the mining of NVN ports had been under consideration since 1964. While this mining undoubtedly hindered NVN, it did not completely blockade the country, as the bulk of munitions and supplies came by rail overland across China. Smaller ships were used that were able to offload at smaller, unmined quays and jetties along the coast, or on sandy stretches of beach, while some goods were transhipped at sea into barges at night. This blockade did not stop flow of fuel oil to the VPA, as an oil pipeline from the Chinese border to Hanoi and Haiphong had been completed by July 1972, and a second one by the end of September, the latter being a 'double pipeline', which in fact meant there were three pipelines pumping oil through into NVN.

After their misfortunes in the VC spring offensive, the ARVN with US air support launched a summer counter-offensive, which achieved a number of successes. In the north, after the fall of Quang Tri (on May 1st), the ARVN had established a defence line along the My Chanh River, about 12 miles south of the town and 20 miles north of Hue, and was able to beat off a heavy VC attack on the 21st, after the VPA had forced a crossing over the river at several points. On the 25th, using tanks, the VPA managed to get behind the ARVN defence line, when the situation momentarily stabilised, although ARVN Marines made a number of raids on VC positions in Quang Tri province. On May 10th, President Thieu had declared martial law in SVN, and he was empowered to legislate by decree on matters of defence, national security and economy.

The ARVN opened its offensive to regain Quang Tri on June 28th, using some 20,000 troops, supported by probably the largest concentration of fire-power employed so far in the war, which included shelling from 17 US cruisers and destroyers, and bombing by B-52s. Four separate groups advanced on Quang Tri town, one from the south-west, another landed on the coast and advanced from the south-east, while two others were landed by helicopter to advance from the east and north-east. The VC put up strong resistance, and it was not until July 11th, that the ARVN troops reached the outskirts to become involved immediately in house-to-house fighting.

Parts of the town fell to the attackers, and on the 25th, ARVN soldiers penetrated the Citadel, a fortress-like construction, but were driven out again two days later. An artillery duel had developed, and for the first time the VPA brought their 152 mm howitzers, which had a range of about ten miles, into action. On August 3rd another assault was mounted to drive the VC from the town, but it was not successful, and certain ARVN formations had to be replaced, before another could be made. On the 23rd, ARVN Marines entered the Citadel, but were driven out again. On September 11th, fierce fighting began which terminated on the 15th, when the whole of the town of Quang Tri was once again in ARVN hands, with the exception of the Citadel, where about 600 VPA troops held out for several days longer. When President Thieu visited Quang Tri on the 20th, to declare that the territory between Quang Tri and the DMZ was to be a Free Fire Zone, he was not able to enter the Citadel.

There was also fighting around the Hue area as the ARVN troops pressed their offensives, and on July 26th, Fire Base Bastogne once again changed hands, this time being taken by the VC, but it was recaptured by the ARVN on August 2nd. However, the worst ARVN defeat was yet to come, when early in August, the VPA division that had been in the Que Son Valley, just south of Danang, since March moved over to the offensive, and on the 19th, captured Que Son town and Camp Ross, two miles from the town. It was reported that the ARVN regiment fled in panic, leaving about 40 guns behind on the field, and much other equipment. The fall of Que Son opened the way to Danang itself, which was now periodically shelled. An ARVN counter-offensive was mounted in which the Rangers played a prominent part, entering the outskirts of Que Son town on the 25th. By September 1st, the whole town was again in ARVN hands, and Camp Ross was re-taken on the 8th. In this instance the ARVN had responded quickly to avenge a defeat.

Farther south the three towns in Binh Dinh province, which had fallen to the VC, were re-captured in July; that of Bong Son on the 21st, Tam Quan on the 23rd, and Hoai An on the 28th. About 8,000 ARVN troops had launched this successful offensive from Phumy on the coast, commencing on the 20th. A new threat appeared against the Pleiku area by VPA troops entering SVN from Cambodia towards the end of August. On September 4th the VC were repulsed with heavy loss when they attacked an ARVN Ranger camp at Bau Can, but on the 8th, it was admitted by the GRVN that nine such frontier camps had been abandoned. In Quang Ngai province, another ARVN offensive began on September 16th, to clear part of Route 1, and after three days fighting the town of Dak To was taken, but the offensive failed to recapture the town of Mo Duc. The momentum of this offensive died down by the 21st.

In the Saigon sector, where the VC concentrated upon cutting road communications, an ARVN mobile force of about 8,000 men (three infantry, an armoured and a Ranger regiment), was formed to patrol the territory up to a radius of about 40 miles from the capital, a task which, until July, had been carried out by US forces.

Two other creditable battles fought by the ARVN were that of Kontum and the relief of An Loc. On the night of May 25th, the VPA managed to penetrate the Kontum defences on the north-west side, and the following night VC infantry and armour broke into the town from the south. At one stage the ground fire was so intense that helicopters could not land, and ammunition and supplies had to be dropped on to the garrison. On the 28th, by which time the VPA held about a quarter of the town, waves of B-52s pounded the attackers. After street fighting on the 29th, the VC began to withdraw, and by June 6th, the last had been expelled by the ARVN.

After a heavy bombardment early on May 11th, the VPA, with tanks, attacked An Loc, and the next day compressed the defenders into a small space. Meanwhile, the ARVN division trying to open Route 13 was making slow progress, the main body, based at Chon Thanh 19 miles south of An Loc, had taken nearly five weeks to clear five miles of roadway, and a paratroop brigade that had been landed only five miles from An Loc, was also bogged down. On the 14th, another ARVN division was called in, but on the 20th, VPA formations, with tanks, moved against it and were advancing along this Route, attacking from both flanks, forcing it back and blocking the route behind it.

On June 7th, advanced units of the original ARVN division at last reached An Loc, and helicopters evacuated the wounded. By the 12th, all the VC, except for a small pocket in the north-west corner of the defences, were ejected and the 12,000 refugees, who had been living underground since the siege began, were evacuated. The bombardment by the VC continued for another month, and Route 13 remained dangerous, there being frequent skirmishes along it. On September 1st, for example, in an ambush only 40 miles from Saigon, 73 ARVN soldiers were killed, and another 100 wounded. All ARVN positions along Route 13 between Chon Thanh and An Loc were evacuated by the end of August.

For the remainder of the year, VC pressure remained intense in places, especially around Danang, Pleiku, Saigon and in the Delta, without the overall situation changing drastically, although the VC filtered back into areas from which they had been ejected, or from where ARVN posts and troops were withdrawn.

On January 2nd, 1972, President Nixon had said that if all US prisoners were released he would withdraw all US troops from SVN by November 1972, an offer that was ignored by the GDRV. Despite this rebuff, however, the programme of US disengagement and withdrawal continued. On June 28th, the President of the USA said that another 10,000 US troops would be brought home from SVN during the following two months, to reduce the total remaining to 39,000 by September 1st, and that the US force level should be down to 27,000 by December 1st. He added that new US conscripts would not now be sent to SVN unless they volunteered to serve there. On June 28th, General Frederick Weyand was appointed Commander of US Forces in SVN, in place of General Abrams, who was appointed Army Chief of Staff, and his task was to speed the US policy of disengagement. The last US ground combat unit, an infantry battalion, guarding the Danang base, stood down on August 11th, leaving the ARVN completely responsible for all ground operations.

The 'third Nation' forces were also disengaging rapidly, and on March 1st, the last Australian and New Zealand combat troops left SVN; about 150 personnel remained behind (in Laos and Cambodia as well as SVN) as military advisers, instructors and engineers, but it was firmly stated that they would not take part in any fighting. On September 7th, the South Korean Foreign Minister announced that the remaining 37,000 South Korean troops would be withdrawn between December 1972 and June 1973. Previously, on July 8th, 1971, the Thailand Government had stated that about 600 of its 1,200 troops in SVN would be repatriated by the end of that month, and the remainder in early 1972, only a token contingent of 100 remaining.

In adjacent Cambodia, Premier Lon Nol had assumed increased powers; on March 10th, 1972 he dissolved the Constituent Assembly, and on the 13th he took the title of President and openly ruled by decree. Commencing in October 1971, his military forces suffered a series of setbacks at the hands of the VPA and the supporters of Prince Sihanouk. By May 1972 they had begun to extend their control in Cambodia, until by August it was estimated they controlled about 80 per cent of the country and half the population. In the east, they virtually

174

held the whole area between the SVN border and the Mekong River, in the south they overran much of the provinces of Kampot and Takeo, while in the north and west, Government forces only held isolated towns, and Phnom Penh itself was subject to periodic raids and bombardments, all roads into the capital being cut. The eastern and northern portions of Cambodia were now secure springboards for the VC to operate into SVN.

To the north of Cambodia, in adjacent Laos, the situation was equally favourable for the VC, where for some time there had been a continuing struggle between the Pathet Lao, supported by the VPA, and the Government troops, backed by US air power. Eventually, on October 17th, 1972, cease-fire negotiations began, but made little progress because the Laotian Government would not accept the Pathet Lao demand that any cease-fire must be accompanied by a political settlement. On December 12th, the Pathet Lao presented demands that included the establishment of a National Political Council and a coalition government, but on the 19th, the Government rejected them.*

Meanwhile fighting continued in Laos during 1972, as both sides sought to obtain more territory so as to be in a more advantageous position in the event of a cease-fire. For example, the Pathet Lao claimed to have won a major victory on the Plain of Jars on October 26th, killing and wounding over 1,200 Government troops, and reports indicated that the Communists were in control of most of the Plain. In southern Laos, Government troops launched two offensives, one of which was along Route 9, towards Muong Phalaine, captured by the Pathet Lao the previous year, which was taken on November 26th, but when the Laotian soldiers attempted to advance farther eastwards, they were driven back. The other offensive was on the Bolovens Plain, but it did not have much success. US aircraft continued to bomb Pathet Lao territory.

The Paris Peace Talks which had been broken off on May 4th, 1972, were resumed on July 13th, but little progress was made, mainly owing to the divergent views of the USA and President Thieu. They broke down again on December 18th, owing to renewed US bombing of Hanoi and Haiphong, but were resumed on January 8th, 1973. Signs of progress in the Talks caused President Nixon on January 15th, to order the bombing of NVN to stop, but on the 18th, the 174th session of the Peace Talks ended without a date being fixed for the next meeting. However, private meetings and contacts continued, and largely due to the efforts of Dr Henry Kissinger, President Nixon's Assistant for

* A Standstill Cease-Fire eventually came into effect on February 22nd, 1973, which left the Pathet Lao in possession of two-thirds of the country. US bombing of Pathet Lao territory continued until the cease-fire in Laos.

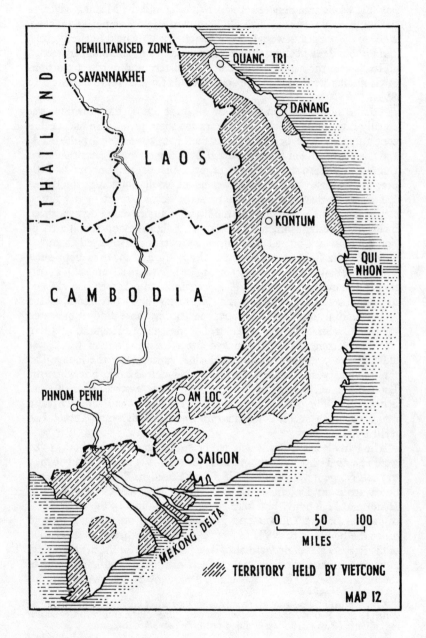

THAILAND

DEMILITARISED ZONE

○ SAVANNAKHET

QUANG TRI

L A O S

○ DANANG

○ KONTUM

C A M B O D I A

QUI
NHON

PHNOM PENH ○

○ AN LOC

○ SAIGON

MEKONG DELTA

0   50   100

MILES

TERRITORY HELD BY VIETCONG

MAP 12

176

National Security Affairs, they led to a peace agreement being initialled on the 23rd. On the 24th, President Thieu claimed the agreement represented a victory for SVN, and on the same day, Le Duc Tho, the NVN representative at the Talks, conversely claimed it was a victory for the NVN.

The agreement, signed on the 27th by the Foreign Ministers of the USA, GRVN, GDRV and the PRG, provided for a cease-fire the following day, the 28th, which came uneasily and warily into fleeting effect. It provided for the withdrawal of US forces, the release of US prisoners within 60 days, the formation of a Four Party Joint Military Mission, the establishment of an International Commission of Control and Supervision, the clearance of mines from NVN waters and for elections. So terminated the War in Vietnam, or the long phase in the fighting in Indo-China, that perhaps more properly could be regarded as the Second Vietnamese War, as in true Communist character and dedication, the VC disregarded the cease-fire and continued to surge forward wherever and whenever they could: within days the Third Vietnamese War was in full swing.

The Communist Guerrilla Way of War 14

"When the enemy retreats – we follow" Mao Tse-tung *The Golden Rules of Warfare*, 1928.

The war in Vietnam, the second Vietnamese War, lasted nearly 19 years, and was another example of Communist guerrilla power struggling to take over a country by force and to imprint its creed on the people, and additionally in this case, to cause a friendly power that had intervened, to disengage. For the Communists at the best it had been only a partial victory, although they made many gains: they had succeeded in forcing America to withdraw its combat element, but they had not toppled the GRVN, nor had they forced the USA to withdraw its support and other military assistance. But the VC had obtained a firm hold on perhaps 75 per cent of the countryside of SVN, while the initial tattered guerrilla body had developed into the 225,000-strong NLA, comparatively well armed, indoctrinated, disciplined and well-trained. Poised, the impatient NLA was only too anxious to plunge into the Third Vietnamese War, just as soon as US combat troops were withdrawn – the Communists in their revolutionary, single-minded political zeal, never lose sight of their ultimate aim, to impose their beliefs and domination upon the world; they pause when they have to, and give way when they must, but these tactics are customarily used in temporary unfavourable situations, to be corrected as soon as possible.

The strategy, tactics and conduct of this war were based on the Four Golden Rules, evolved by Mao Tse-tung in his refuge at Chin Kan Shan in 1928, and which have since become firm articles of faith for the guerrilla fighter of any persuasion. In Chinese they each consist of four written characters only, and their usual translation is

1. When the enemy advances – we retreat.
2. When the enemy halts – we harass.

3. When the enemy avoids battle – we attack.
4. When the enemy retreats – we follow.

To put these Rules successfully into practice certain conditions must be present, and these are basically space, population, external support and a secure supply line. The first condition, that of space, is essential to enable the guerillas to "retreat when the enemy advances", and with this must be coupled inaccessible terrain in which to hide, where Government troops cannot easily follow. This enables the guerrillas to observe the first principle of guerrilla warfare, "to preserve oneself". In SVN there were ample stretches of dense forest, swamp, mountains and poor road communications, and many areas where central government control had been absent for decades. In these areas the VC were able to observe another principle of guerrilla warfare, that of "expanding and developing a conventional force" ready to fight the last battle – the Dien Bien Phu to gain the ultimate victory by destroying the opposing forces on the field of battle.

Next, the population must be of sufficient size, and being mainly a country of villages, with a few towns and even fewer cities, SVN was eminently suitable for the guerrillas to gain a grip on the majority of the people, which they did in the first instance by terrorism. They also needed to turn the villagers into the 'sea' in which the 'fish', the guerrilla fighters, could safely swim. The VC had almost continuous success in the countryside, and almost consistent failure in the cities and towns.

Left alone without external support or sympathy, under pressure from strong Government forces, the VC would probably have eventually withered into insignificance, like some of the groups in Cambodia and Laos, such as the Khmer Serai or Kong Le's 'neutralists', but they had the full support of the Politburo of NVN, which instigated and directed the war in SVN. Also, the two Communist Super Powers were firmly in sympathy with the VC, and both supplied munitions of war. The other vital condition that enabled the VC to exist and fight, was a secure route for such munitions and supplies to reach the guerrillas. At first the DMZ was blocked, but soon the Ho Chi Minh Trail was discovered and developed through adjacent Laos, and then the Sihanouk Trail through Cambodia followed, the territory through which these two broad routes passed being grasped and firmly held by the Communists.

President Diem missed a good opportunity to deal with the VC who had been left behind in SVN in 1954. They were then at their perilous and uncertain 'survival stage' in their remote areas, but Diem consistently ignored the countryside and minimised the problem until it was too late. By 1960, Ho Chi Minh, his own domestic problems solved to a degree, realised that guerrilla force would have to be used to unite Vietnam under his leadership, so the direction of the war in the South was assumed by the Politburo of the GDRV. The VC in SVN were shaken up, re-organised and invigorated, and men and supplies moved slowly down the Trail. The Generals who in turn ruled SVN after Diem's assassination were no better at perceiving the ultimate danger of the growing VC monster, or of combating it, and for about three years, from 1962 until US combat troops intervened in SVN in 1965, the US Green Beret Advisers, with their sections of CIDGs, composed largely of hill tribesmen, stood practically alone against the waves of VC lapping at the frontiers of SVN. ARVN troops still mainly garrisoned the towns and were reluctant to get out into the jungle, forest and swamplands to fight the VC on his own ground. Slowly, but surely, villages were taken over by the VC and the ARVN was compressed into the population centres, as progressively the railways and the main routes were blocked.

The bogy of creeping Communism from the East frightened Western nations and appeared to be a very real threat in the 1950s and early 1960s, and so American aid was unstintingly given to SVN. The firm US belief was that just a little more military help would tilt the scales decisively against the VC – but it never did, and always more was required, and given in pursuit of this false hope. This optimistic belief remained especially among US military leaders, even after it was abandoned by McNamara in 1966, but by then the USA was deep in the morass, and in its struggle to disengage was sinking deeper. As each fresh escalation was made to try to over-awe the VC, by shows of strength, aerial activity or massive fire-power, it was nullified by guerrilla tactics and a further one had to be considered. US aircraft was brought into action under this theory, that just a little bombing of VC concentration areas would bring them to the point of surrender, but it did not, and so further escalations followed, until US planes were heavily bombing NVN. As had been shown in previous wars, there are distinct limits to the effectiveness of bombing enemy territory, and contrary to what had been expected by the US, it just made the NVN more determined to fight and win. This encouraged the Soviet Union to send 'defensive weapons', such as anti-aircraft guns and SAMs to NVN, which took a great toll of US aircraft, while the VC in SVN simply dug themselves underground and took to living and fighting in tunnels.

The Neutrality of Laos settled in 1962 had enabled the VC to further develop the Ho Chi Minh Trail and make it secure, and also to establish sanctuaries in both Laos and Cambodia, neither of these two states having sufficient armed force to remove them. The Trail was a vital factor to the VC and could it have been eliminated, VC strength and capacity would have rapidly waned, and indeed, would never have risen as quickly as it did. The US had considered blocking the Trail since 1966, but had not taken up the idea because it would use up so many men, and the rate US Servicemen were being absorbed into SVN for so little result, had begun to alarm the American Administration. The idea of 'defensive barriers' was briefly tried near the DMZ, but was found to be ineffective because they immediately became fixed defences at the mercy of prowling, mobile VC. In 1970, when US and ARVN troops were stung into invading Cambodia to attempt an elimination of the VC sanctuaries near the border, the VC formations and the mobile COSVN simply moved deeper into the country to avoid them, thus practising Mao Tse-tung's First Golden Rule – "When the enemy advances – we retreat". Similar tactics were used during the ill-fated ARVN invasion of 1971.

Throughout, the VC concentrated upon building up and training its full-time Main Force for the final conventional battles. The long dragging, protracted stage of guerrilla warfare was wearing the Allies down, but instead of continuing to outlast and outstay the Americans, after argument within the NVN Politburo, early in 1968, Giap launched the VC into the Tet Offensive, in which he planned to take most towns, including Saigon. The VC were not ready for such a test of strength and so the battle was lost, the VC having to revert to protracted warfare once more.

ARVN strategy seemed to be to sit on the population centres and hope the few Ranger units would 'pacify' the countryside, the main tactic being to take up a position, construct defences and then wait for the VC to attack, but under strong US urging, the ARVN took part in the elephantine sweeps through the countryside. After American ground involvement, the ARVN usually copied US tactics, especially in the use of helicopters. Whenever possible, the ARVN stayed in large formations, having been trained for conventional warfare.

US strategy was to base its military strength on coastal enclaves (there were exceptions) which could be supplied and evacuated by sea, so there would never be any danger of a Dien Bien Phu-type defeat. At first the US troops carried out Search and Hold operations of increasing size, but finding it unwise to try to hold on to any part of the countryside, they switched to Search and Destroy methods, and then tried a mixture of both. With their troops remaining in large formations, with massive air support, the American generals longed to bring the elusive VC to battle but seldom succeeded on their own terms.

The VC also varied their tactics, sometimes concentrating upon assaults using large formations, and on other occasions using smaller ones, as they practised Mao Tse-tung's dictum of "first take small cities, and then large ones", without a great deal of success. When they entered SVN, the VPA troops remained in their larger (usually divisional-sized) formations, and as a result suffered heavily from aerial bombing, as did the VC, especially from saturation raids by the B-52s. Briefly, the VC relied upon marching infantry and Mao Tse-tung's Golden Rules, while the road-bound US and ARVN troops relied upon aircraft and fire-power. In the latter stages the VPA used armour, but used it badly and without comprehension – they were far better at infantry battles, although the VC offensive from May to July 1972 failed, because the ARVN stood fast and allowed US air power to come into play.

When they landed in SVN in 1965, and in the years immediately following, the US troops created a good impression as an efficient combat force. They had stepped in at the right moment. Had they not appeared when they did, the GRVN would most probably have been toppled by the VC, who were almost ready to make their 'final offensive'; because of American ground intervention this had to be postponed until 1968. Highly trained and technical, US troops tended to place over-reliance on sophisticated weaponry and fire-power, and apart from the Green Berets, stuck as far as they could to the conventional warfare they knew. Gradually they felt the frustration of never being able to pin down the enemy in number to fight him, and the fact that all the people back home in America were not fully behind them tended to affect morale in the latter years.

The picture projected to the world of the ARVN as a second-rate army, unreliable, unfit to take its place alongside US Forces in the battle line, and looked down upon by the US top brass, is an unfair and also very untrue view. Throughout, ARVN soldiers had been in the thick of the fighting, and bore the brunt of it in the provincial capitals and the countryside, as witnessed by the very heavy casualties incurred. Its morale and leadership had varied, and it had a poor start in that being originally French-officered and French trained, it was tainted with defeat. But concurrent with increased US military aid it was re-organised and re-trained, and had so improved that during the Tet Offensive of 1968, when the VC deliberately hit at ARVN units thinking they were the weaker, not a single one broke and ran and most managed to drive off the enemy.

The ARVN had always been a poor relation, and was never as well equipped or armed as the US Force alongside which it was fighting, but when Vietnamisation became a reality and not just a promise, in the latter months of the war, weapons and equipment in quantity were sent to it. Its main handicap was that it was consigned to the role of pacification, which was regarded by the MACV as a secondary objective

In retrospect the main reasons why complete victory eluded the Allies were US (and ARVN) failure to appreciate guerrilla warfare and Mao Tse-tung's Four Golden Rules; failure to arm and train the ARVN adequately, self-imposed US restrictions, and lack of complete unity amongst Allied statesmen and military leaders. There were other contributory factors of course, such as the failure of the Strategic Hamlets Programme, a hostile American and World Press, and the general unpopularity of the war, especially in America.

The Golden Rules were formulated to defeat conventional armies, and provided conditions (such as there being ample space in which manoeuvre) allowed them to be adhered to, the conventional forces could not win – it was only a matter of time. The only way to counter guerrilla warfare, such as the VC were practising, was to operate anti-guerrilla tactics – to get in amongst them and beat them at their own game. For the Allies it should have been a war of small 'killer' units, thousands of them prowling the jungle like tigers in search of prey, all constantly on the move and seldom staying more than 24 hours in one location. With command of the air, plenty of helicopters and good field communications, this concept would have been possible and would have produced drastic results, as the VC must have safe areas, for training, administration and rest, and many supply routes, all of which are vulnerable. Imagine, for example, the chaos and apprehension, if the Ho Chi Minh Trail was kept constantly under surveillance and attacked by hundreds of small 'tiger' units, that leapt into the kill frequently. Vulnerable spots would have to be strongly guarded, and as in SVN, the VC would probably have had to use up to 75 per cent of its personnel on defensive tasks, while the other small proportion would have to be employed on hunting the 'tiger' units: few would be left to carry out the main Communist aim. This concept was unconventional, it was an untidy way of fighting a war, with little chance of glory for the senior commanders, and did not commend itself to MACV. On the whole the US Green Berets, with their CIDGs, and the SVN Rangers, did good work, but they were too few, too static and were stifled or ignored. Perhaps the only real criticism that could be levelled against them was that when they set up jungle camps, they stayed in them too long, causing them to be turned into defensive posts: they should have moved their camps far more frequently.

As has been mentioned, the ARVN was treated by MACV as a second-class army, and Vietnamisation was a joke for a long time, both of which were detrimental to a combined war effort, and played into the hands of the VC. This neglect also retarded the US disengagement programme.

The self-imposed US restrictions, often loudly announced to placate

184

with only second-rate prestige and priorities. Like the US Forces, the ARVN placed greater importance on conventional, rather than guerrilla, warfare (having only 20 Ranger battalions as opposed to over 150 infantry ones), and became affected by expressions like 'air-kill capacity', 'Free Fire Zones', 'reconnaissance by fire', 'preparatory bombing' and 'vertical envelopment'.

The jungles and swamps were the natural elements of the VC, while conventional forces were road-bound, which gave the advantage to the guerrillas, who could block roads and mount ambushes almost at will, as the French Expeditionary Force had discovered. This tended to cause Government forces to withdraw into defended localities and become immobile, and so the VC, who could walk anywhere, gained the freedom of the countryside. The US brought helicopters in number to SVN, and so to a degree regained mobility, being able to lift troops quickly to any vital spot: later their 'gun-ships' would fly low to attack the VC on the ground. Good VC camouflage, living in tunnels and mass firing of all weapons available at helicopters whenever they came near enough, tended to neutralise this advantage, but helicopters continued to be used extensively and many techniques were developed. Without US helicopters the VC would have had a far easier task, but there was an Allied tendency to place too much reliance on them.

Aircraft of the GDRV played only an insignificant part in the war, but as soon as the US and SVN began bombing NVN, a formidable anti-aircraft defence system was developed, which cost the Americans dearly in planes. When Soviet SAMs arrived in NVN an electronic struggle began as US Electronic Counter Measures, ECM, were introduced to enable pilots to have warning of approaching missiles – the SAM Song – a variation in the pitch of the sonic wave, in time for them to take evasive action. Improved Soviet electronic guidance systems nullified this warning, until in turn, the Americans produced ECM that could "jam and divert" missiles. It became a war of electroni[c] progressions, a "mad scientists" war. The main fact that emerged fro[m] this electronic struggle was that the SAMs were not as effective as t[he] Soviet Union had anticipated, or the USA feared, and only a sm[all] proportion of US aircraft were brought down by missiles.

What really did prove to be effective were the World War II-t[ype] anti-aircraft guns, which threw up a solid wall of fire, which was [hit] when attacking aircraft ran into it; these weapons accounted for [a] large majority of US and SVN aircraft losses over NVN. The mil[itary] prophets had been confounded as the old-fashioned anti-aircraft [gun] with its 'uncontrollable projectile', which was about to be phase[d out] in many national defence forces, proved more deadly than the s[ophis]ticated 'controllable' missile that was to replace it.

world opinion, were gifts to the Communists. Examples were that the dikes and certain places in NVN would not be bombed, that a 21 mile penetration limit in Cambodia was set, and that US combat troops would not again enter Cambodia, or go into Laos. In warfare the object is to keep the enemy guessing and to be unsure of what is going to happen next, not to tell what will not happen. However to put forward the American view, it should be realised that the Cold War was still in progress, and the USA had to be cautious as to how far it could really go, without provoking either the Soviet Union or China into action. Differences in view between personalities, such as Robert McNamara, Generals Harkins, Taylor and Westmoreland, and SVN statesmen and generals, and also between the US Army and the US Marine Corps, did not help to project a united and determined front against the VC.

On the Communist side, the NLF and the GDRV considered they had gained a great victory, though not the ultimate one, but they felt they had taken a gigantic step towards their ultimate aim of uniting Vietnam. Apart from their previously mentioned advantages, such as support from the Soviet Union and China, and the existence of the Ho Chi Minh Trail, the main reasons for their degree of success were united leadership, a clear objective, disregard for human life and adherence to Mao Tse-tung's Golden Rules.

Unlike scarcely veiled Allied disunity, the Politburo of NVN, despite internal differences at times, remained intact for nearly 20 years, and of the original eleven members appointed in 1945, nine were still serving in 1973; the other two (Ho Chi Minh and Nguyen Chi Thanh) having died in office, were not replaced. Once decisions were made, no matter what private views were held, all loyally worked to put them into effect, as for example, Giap; although he felt the VC were not ready for the Tet Offensive, he launched it nevertheless. This united leadership, solid and all-powerful, had a clear definition of their ultimate objective, which was for all Vietnam to be under Communist rule, and this was never lost sight of. This determination did not wax or wane with victories or defeat, nor did it deviate, but it remained constant. The Politburo was prepared to continue the struggle for 20 years or more, if necessary, and to out-wait the Americans, and its patience in this respect in direct contrast to the impatience of the US, which was hoping for a quick victory and then rapid disengagement.

Essential support for the villagers of SVN for the VC was gained by terrorism, the Communists having an absolute and complete disregard of the sanctity of human life. Their programme of callous elimination of Government officials (killing over 1,000 annually for the first ten years of the war), and their methods of rough justice, torture, and of dealing with defectors, spies, prisoners and others who offended, were deadly advantages. No Western country could even contemplate using such a means, let alone carry it through.

The VC never forgot the Four Golden Rules, and although at times they stayed in divisional-sized formations, notably the VPA, these formations were marching infantry, that could move through jungle and swamp, and were not tied to roads. This mobility enabled them to practise the Rules, which they invariably did, and on the few occasions they did not, they suffered heavy casualties and setbacks. The NLA, and the VPA, were built upon a mobile guerrilla basis, which they used as a spring board to launch conventional operations as and when opportunity presented itself, while the Allied Forces were built on a conventional basis, to fight a conventional war, and only reluctantly and with poor grace, did they stoop occasionally to dabble rather ineffectually in guerrilla warfare concepts. Unlike the Allies, the VC placed no restraints on themselves, but on the contrary they pursued the war relentlessly by every means in their power: they had no intention of fighting 'half-a-war' as the Allies were doing.

Terrorism was an accepted weapon of war to the VC, who used it profusely, carrying out untold assassinations and atrocities. Examples are the mass graves unearthed at Hue after the Tet Offensive, with victims tied together, many having been tortured and their bodies mutilated before being killed; the victims included women and children and many were buried alive: the killing and burning to death of 114 Montagnards in their village of Dak Son in 1967; and the tying together and shooting of 18 people, including three girls, in the village of Suoi Chan in the same year, to deter the villagers from voting in the local elections. Terrorism became commonplace and part of the accepted way of life for the VC, a point that was frequently overlooked, or glossed over, by their supporters and sympathisers the world over.

American and ARVN prisoners were tortured and killed, and in the face of such extreme barbarism the restraint shown by the Allied soldiers, who stuck to the accepted rules of warfare and the Geneva Conventions, was extremely commendable. This conduct was highlighted by a few exceptions that proved this general rule, notably the My Lai Incident, to which great publicity was given, not only by the World Press, but by the American Press as well. It was alleged in November 1969, that US troops had killed a number of civilians on March 16th, 1968 at My Lai, which was a village about six miles north of the town of Quang Ngai, right in the heart of VC country, which had been designated as a Free Fire Zone. On March 29th, 1971, Lieutenant Calley was convicted by Court Martial. Other alleged incidents by US and ARVN troops came to light, but they simply emphasised the self-control exercised by the Allies in this one-sided war. In all wars the cost in human suffering is great, and this was no exception. Casualty figures are contradictory, and some have been amended several times, so no one can be sure of the truth. According to US sources, between January 1st, 1961 and January 28th, 1973, they lost 45,941 killed in action, 300,635 wounded, 1,811 missing, captured or interned, while another 10,298 died from other causes in SVN. In 12 years of war the price of intervention and partial success had been high in human terms for the Americans. The US Defence Department stated that 31,463 SVN civilians had been killed, and 49,000 abducted by the NLF between 1966 and 1972, while a US Senate Sub-Committee on Refugees estimated that 415,000 SVN civilians had been killed and 935,000 wounded between January 1965 and October 1972. The ARVN said it had lost 183,528 killed and 499,026 wounded during the war, but claimed the NLA and the VPA had lost 924,048 killed. The Third Nation forces, that is Australia, New Zealand, South Korea and Thailand, lost 5,225 killed.

On the other side claims were more inflated, and accordingly more suspect, and for example, between March and October 1972 alone, the NLF said the ARVN had lost 80,000 killed and 240,000 wounded, while the Agency for International Development stated that between January 1968 and May 1971, as the result of action by the GRVN against suspected NLF sympathisers, that 20,587 SVN civilians had been killed and 28,978 imprisoned. Figures are still incomplete and confusing.

When considering how this war will reflect in history, perhaps it can be said that it was one of a series fought with dubious success by Western nations in Asia as part of the general Crusade of the 1950s and 1960s against the forces of Communism. The prospect must be the dark one of continuous Communist pressure on small South-East Asian states.

The Third Vietnam War: 1973–1975 15

"We have not asked President Thieu. . . ."   Henry Kissinger: Press
Conference, 24th January 1973

President Nguyen Van Thieu, of South Vietnam, was a reluctant
signatory to the Paris Agreement of the 23rd January 1973, and to
the subsequent Cease-Fire of the 28th of that month, and there is
little doubt that pressure was applied to make him accept it. In
particular, he objected to countenancing the presence in SVN, after the Cease-Fire, of some "300,000" Communist troops – at that
time the officially accepted figure – of North Vietnam and the
Provisional Revolutionary Government of SVN. He wanted them
to be quickly phased out, but the Communists would not agree,
and so to conclude the Paris Agreement, the United States forced
this condition on the SVN President. On the 24th January, Henry
Kissinger said at a press conference, the day after the agreement
was signed, "We have not asked President Thieu, nor has he accepted the presence of South Vietnamese troops in South Vietnam". The Cease-Fire came into effect at 0800-hours on the 28th
January 1973, the troops remaining in position where they were.
    NVN and PRG troops were in actual possession of the wide
western strip of territory, stretching the whole length of SVN, adjacent to Laos and Cambodia – the expanded Ho Chi Minh Trail
in fact – together with parts of the Central Highlands and the Mekong Delta, and including a few enclaves on the coast and in remote areas. The ARVN held the major eastern half of the country,
and most of the Central Highlands, based on the main north-south
coastal road, Route 1; in its possession were all the ports and coastal
towns, as well as all cities and inland provincial capitals, with
strings of defensive posts thinly covering vulnerable approaches.
Allied contingents, including the 37,000 South Koreans, and lesser

numbers of Thais, Filippinos, Chinese Nationalists, Australians and New Zealanders, had already gone or were in the process of departing, and all were to leave within weeks of the Cease-Fire.

Fighting between the ARVN and Communist troops had continued with ferocity right up until the last minutes, and in many sectors beyond the deadline, as NVN and PRG soldiers sought to gain as much territory as possible before the Cease-Fire brought hostilities to a halt. US B-52 aircraft had been brought into action again over parts of SVN occupied by groups of Communist forces. Later, a SVN spokesman stated that in the 24-hour period previous to the Cease-Fire, "378 engagements had taken place – the largest number recorded in a single day in the war so far". The withdrawal of US combat forces left the ARVN to fight it out alone on the ground. At the time of the Cease-Fire, about 23,000 American servicemen were in SVN, but over half of them were quickly repatriated. Later, a NVN spokesman alleged that 10,000 US combat troops remained behind "in disguise", but the US authorities maintained that only 8,500 US servicemen stayed in SVN, of whom 5,000 were on contract to maintain ARVN equipment and communications.

On the 25th January, the governments of Canada, Hungary, Indonesia and Poland agreed to supply contingents for the International Commission of Control and Supervision, the ICCS, and for the Joint Military Commissions, to supervise the Cease-Fire, and other provisions of the Paris Agreement. Arrangements began for the exchange of prisoners-of-war. The US stated that ownership of all American bases and all military equipment in SVN passed to the SVN Government. In France, talks were to continue to find a political solution for SVN, which meant looking for a way to involve the PRG in the democratic processes of the country. On the 13th February, President Thieu formed a "Popular Front" coalition as a broad organisation to "fight for peace and the right of self-determination," and to contest the promised forthcoming free elections against the Communist National Liberation Front of SVN.

The Communists had no intention of honoring the Paris Agreement, and they blatantly and cynically used it to handicap the ARVN, and to enable them to continue the fight with advantage against the Thieu Government. Just before the Cease-Fire came into effect, NVN and PRG troops had been steadily closing in around Saigon, and had indeed blocked off most of the routes into that city. They continued this pressure after the 28th. The ARVN rallied, counter-attacked, and by the 3rd February had succeeded in re-opening them again, after which fighting generally seemed to quiet down in SVN.

The Communist forces in SVN now concentrated upon building up their strength for planned battles ahead, and brought in more arms, supplies and reinforcements from NVN. They began to convert the jungle paths of the Ho Chi Minh Trail into all-weather motor roads. US aerial reconnaissance had ceased, as had SVN air activity, so the Communist troops were able to use this route by day as well as by night. Before the Cease-Fire it had taken Communist troops and equipment four months, travelling only by night because of US and SVN air interdiction along the Ho Chi Minh Trail through Laos and Cambodia, from NVN to the Delta area. Soon they were able to make the same journey in daylight, by shorter routes, often part way in trucks, although mainly still on foot, in less than three weeks. On the 21st March, a SVN spokesman alleged that "More than 50,000 North Vietnamese troops, 300 tanks, and hundreds of extra guns" had been moved into SVN since the Cease-Fire. The following month, on the 17th, a US spokesman alleged that since the 28th January, over 27,000 tons of military supplies had moved through the Demilitarised Zone, the DMZ, in the north of the country, into SVN, and that over 30,000 North Vietnamese troops had also moved into SVN through Laos and Cambodia, a number that included completely new formations, some of them anti-aircraft ones.

On the 19th April, the US announced that its mine-clearing operations, part of the Paris Agreement, were suspended because of Communist breaches of the Cease-Fire conditions, and that aerial reconnaissance flights by pilotless aircraft over NVN had been resumed. By this time SVN aircraft had again become active over the country, but they tended to keep their distance from enemy ground forces, owing to the lethality of the one-man operated Soviet SAM-7's. There was still no sign of any NVN air force activity over SVN, and the SVN air force accordingly had the skies to itself.

Meanwhile, talks between the SVN Government and the PRG, which had begun on the 19th March, at La Calle-Saint-Cloud, near Paris, to try to find a political solution between the two sides, continued fitfully with intervals of suspension on one pretext or another. President Thieu was struggling hard to exclude the PRG from any future involvement in SVN, and eventually, on the 29th December 1973, he stated that the general election would not take place, and that neither would he agree to any politically negotiated solutions that embraced the PRG, as he declared the Communists could not be trusted to act in a democratic manner. This was a great disappointment to the American Administration, which wanted this political problem solved quickly so it could extricate itself from the Vietnam morass, in which it had been so deeply, and disastrously, involved since 1965. President Thieu had become the US stumbling-block.

During 1973, the Communist armies concentrated upon stockpiling arms, ammunition and supplies inside SVN, and deploying their divisions, but at the same time they eased themselves forward whenever possible. In particular, they pressed against the small defended posts, usually manned by SVN Rangers, often isolated in hostile territory, designed to protect vulnerable areas. After outbreaks of fighting, another cease-fire was declared on the 15th June, but it was hardly effective, as it only lasted as long as was convenient to the Communists.

From September 1973 onwards, the tempo of the fighting steadily increased, although there were no large scale engagements, NVN pressure being directed against the Central Highlands area from Laos, and towards the Mekong Delta area from Cambodia. Additionally, pressure against the ARVN positions shielding Saigon was intensified. In that month, NVN troops used tanks in action in the Central Highlands for the first time since the January Cease-Fire. Apart from assaults on ARVN and Ranger positions, the fighting consisted mainly of the usual Viet Cong jungle tactics of harassing fire and ambushes, the bombardment of towns, base camps and storage centers with mortar and rocket fire, and the occasional attempt at sweeping through villages in order to overrun the local Self-Defence units, and so bring the villagers under their control.

Although there had been no spectacular battles or sieges during 1973, on the 27th January 1974, a SVN spokesman stated that "In this 'First Year of Peace' 57,835 soldiers have died in combat in South Vietnam", and claimed that three-quarters of them had been Communist troops. He also said that in the same period, from the January Cease-Fire to the end of the year, that 59,009 SVN troops had been wounded "in Cease-Fire violations", that another 4,000 were "missing," and that about 2,000 civilians had been killed and about 6,000 wounded. This indicated the continuing volume of low-level guerrilla activities of the Communist armies. One reason for the seeming restraint on the part of the Communist armies in SVN, in just keeping up steady military pressure, was the hope of the Hanoi Government that the Paris talks would produce a favourable political settlement, when the NVN and the PRG troops would not have to fight at all, but would be able to obtain their aims at the negotiating table.

An estimate of comparative military strengths, made in November 1973, indicated that SVN had about 1.5 million men under arms, of whom about 500,000 were in the ARVN, while the opposing Communist numbers in SVN were about 180,000 NVN regulars and about 60,000 Viet Cong fighters under the PRG command. This leaves a discrepency of over half a million in President Thieu's calculation at the time of the Paris Agreement, which could be partly explained by his having exaggerated and partly because some of them may have been somewhere along the Ho Chi Minh Trail, technically outside the boundaries of SVN. Certainly, the ARVN outnumbered Communist troops; but it was at a disadvantage because it had a defensive task, and the Communist forces had an aggressive one, which allowed them to concentrate superior forces at weak vulnerable points, while their defence was simply to withdraw into the jungle.

By this time President Thieu had become more reluctant than ever before to respond to US persuasion to be moderate and accommodating to the PRG, because of continuing Communist breaching of the Paris Agreement and their ignoring the Cease-Fire within SVN. President Thieu had had enough, and on the 4th January 1974, in an aggressive speech, he stated, "As far as the armed forces are concerned the war has begun again". President Thieu called upon his commanders to seek out the enemy in their base areas. Until this moment, Thieu, ostensibly at least, had adopted a defensive posture in the field, but now he openly ordered the ARVN to attack the Communist armies in his country. Thieu still quoted "300,000" as the figure for NVN personnel in SVN. The SVN air force, which had been frequently in action in 1973, now began to make bombing raids on territory controlled by the PRG, and on the 9th January 1974, it stated that it was regularly attacking "Communist build-ups".

The exchange of prisoners had been subjected to many petty delays, hesitations, and suspensions, but eventually, by the 8th March 1974, they were essentially completed, but deep US concern remained on account of a number of "untraceable missing", as the NVN authorities were extremely unhelpful. It was suspected that a few American, and other, prisoners of war were being deliberately retained for political, or blackmail, reasons. The atmosphere of the discussions on the POW issue was one of distrust on the non-Communist side. Also, an obligation taken on by the US under the Paris Agreement was mine-clearing in certain areas.

On the 18th July 1973, the Defense Department announced it had completed its task of clearing mines from NVN waters. In 1972, about 8,000 US mines had been dropped in NVN coastal waters, and another 3,000 in inland waterways.

In June 1974, President Thieu withdrew his delegation from the negotiation talks in Paris with the PRG. In turn, the PRG withdrew its representatives from the Joint Military Missions of the ICCS, and in consequence the ICCS had to suspend its activities. Within the ICCS there had been differences between national contingents, and for example, the Canadians had disagreed with the Poles, and had withdrawn: their places were taken by the Iranians.

Now openly alarmed by Thieu's stubborn attitude towards the PRG, and his refusal to come to any agreement with it, the US Administration, in the hope that if financial pressure was applied, Thieu might come to heel, proposed to the US Congress that the $11.4 Billion allocated to SVN, might be reduced to $7 million. Also, President Thieu was strongly advised by the US to come to some political arrangement with the PRG by the end of August: but Thieu still refused.

As hope of a negotiated political settlement waned during 1974, the Hanoi Government ordered the resumption of full-scale operations in SVN, and from May onwards, NVN and PRG troops concentrated on seizing and occupying key territory, and depriving the Saigon Government of control of its inhabitants. Owing to lack of government control, especially at night, and incomplete Communist control, a degree of anarchy reigned in many areas. Practically the whole of the Central Highlands was by this time in a state of seething unrest because of rebellion on the part of the Montagnards, who, never good friends with any central government, considered that they had been badly treated – used and then abandoned by the Saigon Government.

Throughout 1974, Communist troops exerted pressure in many regions, and flurries of small and not so small engagements flared up continually. Brief mention can be made of a six-week battle that began on the 17th May, around Ben Cat, only 24 miles from Saigon, in which the ARVN suffered heavy casualties. In July and August, Communist troops carried out major offensives to the southwest of Danang, in an effort to cut that city off from the south. August was a bad month, when about 600 of the approximately 3,000 defended posts in the north, and containing the Ho Chi Minh Trail, were either overrun or abandoned, partly because of desertions, and partly, according to the Saigon Government, because of cuts in US military aid. On the 16th May, NVN troops had captured a district capital in Kontum province (they had only taken one district capital the prevous year, and then had held it but for a few days). In August, district capitals fell to the NVN troops in the northern provinces of Quang Nam, Quang Ngai and Kontum; and yet another in Kontum in October. In all, in the northern sector of SVN, in the area of the DMZ and the northern part of the Ho Chi Minh Trail, about 150 SVN outposts fell in the last three months of 1974.

The open resumption of the war by the Hanoi-led Communist troops brought unpopularity to President Thieu. One of the first manifestations of the change occurred on the 8th September 1974, when Father Tran Huu Thanh, a right-wing Catholic priest, issued his "Public Indictment No 1", accusing Thieu of personal corruption. Father Thanh, who had attracted a following, led the "People's Anti-Corruption Movement". Other political factions and organisations in Saigon, including the Buddhists, also began to mutter discontentedly against Thieu.

Events in South Vietnam affected next-door Laos, where on the 22nd February 1973, a "Standstill Cease-Fire" agreement was signed, which called for the formation of a Provisional Government and a National Political Consultative Council, that would contain both right-wing and neutralist elements, and an equal number of Pathet Lao members. The agreement provided for the removal of foreign armed forces from Laos, which meant non-Communist ones, as mention of the NVN contingent was deliberately omitted.

Negotiations for this agreement had hung fire, mainly because the Pathet Lao, combined with the NVN forces, physically occupied two-thirds of the country, and insisted that a cease-fire be linked to a political settlement. The Pathet Lao had no part in the "Royal Government," at Vientaine, headed by Prince Souvanna Phouma, which was composed of both right-wing and neutralist elements. The "neutralists" broadly wanted Laos to be completely neutral, and rid of all foreign armed force, including NVN ones. The Royal Government's writ only ran in the region of Vientaine and in parts of southern Laos. There was also a virtually independent neutralist army, based on the town of Vang Vieng. Prince Souvanna, the Prime Minister, was a neutralist.

In collaboration with the Vientaine Government, US aircraft had been bombing Pathet Lao concentrations inside Laos for some time, as well as, of course, NVN troops in that part of the Ho Chi Minh Trail that lay in Laos. The US CIA had been largely responsible for paying the Vientaine troops, the neutralist ones, and the mercenaries. The Pathet Lao headquarters was at Sam Neua.

On the 3rd February 1973, a Pathet Lao representative, the Secretary General of the Meo Lao Hakset (the political wing), arrived in Vientaine with full powers to negotiate an agreement. The Prime Minister, Prince Souvanna, wanted the prevailing "tripartite" system to continue, in which he expected the Pathet Lao to be content with a one-third representation in government. The US Administration had wanted a quick political settlement in Laos, to be concluded before the Conference on Vietnam was due to begin in Paris on the 26th February. When the Pathet Lao representative hesitated, and put forward other demands, US bombing of Pathet Lao areas was increased. A US spokesman said on the 15th February, that the bombing of Laos had "increased from 280 bombing raids a day in the previous week, to 380 raids a day". It must have considerably concentrated the minds of the Pathet Lao, and an agreement was reached which came into effect on the 22nd February.

When this Standstill Cease-Fire agreement came into effect, US bombing raids immediately ceased, but ground fighting, which had been in spasmodic progress for some considerable time between Government forces, neutralist ones, the mercenaries and the Pathet Lao, continued. The Pathet Lao was accused of seizing the town of Paksong before the cease-fire deadline. The Vientaine Government requested US bombing sorties, and with them the town was retaken two days later. The US had warned the Vientaine Government against attempting a right-wing coup, supported by army officers, which was thought very probable, as many considered that too many concessions were being given to the Pathet Lao. Later, in April, when the Plain of Jars was overrun by NVN troops, the Vientaine Government again requested US bombing support. After that fighting seemed to gradually die down to a wary, hostile stalemate.

On the 20th August 1973, there was an attempted right-wing military coup in Vientaine, led by officers in exile, who had crossed the Mekong River from Thailand; the coup was crushed within a few hours. The Vientaine Government owed its survival to the support of senior army officers who objected to proposed concessions to the Pathet Lao, which further delayed negotiations.

Talks between the Pathet Lao and the Vientaine Government on implementing the agreement dragged on for months thereafter. One of the sticking points was that the Pathet Lao wanted to station units of its troops in both Vientaine and Luang Prabang to protect its own ministers and representatives, a proposal that both the right-wing and neutralist elements objected to. It was not until April 1974 that a Provisional Government of National Union, with Prince Souvanna Phouma as the Prime Minister, was established in Vientaine, which contained members of the Pathet Lao and of right-wing and neutralist factions. The Defense Minister was a Pathet Lao man, and in June, he stated that there were between 26,000 and 29,000 NVN troops in Laos: he was in a position to know. It was also estimated that there were about 14,500 NVN troops with the Pathet Lao army. The leader of the Communist Pathet Lao was Prince Souphanou Vong, half-brother to the neutralist Prime Minister, Prince Souvanna Phouma, although it is doubtful whether he ever held very much real power. Their father was King Savang Vatthan, the shadowy Head of State. In 1963, the Vientaine Government had split into the present two factions, referred to as "right-wing" and "neutralist," but generally they worked well together.

The government and Pathet Lao retained their separate armies, each suspicious and hostile towards the other, each continuing to independently hold its ground, as did the much smaller "neutralist" one. Also in the country were several thousand Special Forces, or Rangers, of Meo, Lao and Thai tribesmen, recruited, trained, led, and paid for by the US CIA. Other groups of mercenaries, over 17,000 in all, paid for by the same source, include, for example, 9,000 Thais, who should in theory have been merged into the Vientaine army but had been reluctant to do so. Supported by air from Thailand by the CIA, which considered them to be the only reliable bulwark against Communist armies in Laos, they retained a precarious independence.

The National Political Consultative Council, of Pathet Lao and other factions, which had been formed in Vientaine, produced and adopted in May 1974, an "18-Point Programme." This document, couched in high moral terms, pontificated on freedom, rights and democracy, and aimed "to unite the people of all nationalities, tribes, religions and classes ... to struggle for the full implementation of an independent neutral Laos". "Neutralism" came to mean the removal of all foreign troops from Laos, especially those from North Vietnam. The US Military Mission, of about 180 personnel, had all left by the 1st June, and that month about 7,000 Thai mercenaries were flown back to Thailand. The Lao National Assembly was later (13th April 1975) dissolved.

There was a mutiny on the 24th December 1974, in Houei Sai, near the Thai border, by a small group of Meo Special Forces, in territory dominated by the Pathet Lao, who were still resisting integration into the Vientaine army, and who demanded implementation of the neutralisation of Laos. They were calmed down, and the government made some trifling concessions. In January, 1975, demonstrations were made in the southern town of Thakhet by civilian organisations, who demanded, amongst other things, the implementation of the 18-Point Programme. Laos had huge economic and other problems; for example, it was estimated that about one-quarter of the population of just over six million people, were "displaced" because of the continuing war and the recent US bombing. These groups, which included students, trade unions and political organisations, became known as the "21 Mass Organisations", and also began to demonstrate in Vientaine, the capital.

By mid-April 1975, the Pathet Lao were ready, and moved in to attack the groups of Special Forces and such other mercenaries as remained in Laos. The Meos had always fought on the side of the Vientaine Government against Communist forces. The fighting continued until the 6th May, ending in the complete defeat and mass evacuation of the Meo, with their families, westwards across the Mekong River. This mass grouping of Meo, and other Laotian, exiles in adjacent Thailand caused alarm in Laos, in case they combined with the right-wing exiled elements, to launch either a military invasion against the Pathet Lao forces, or guerrilla operations from the sanctuary of Thai soil. However, on the 21st May, the Thai Government stated that it would not permit the Laotian exiles to establish a government-in-exile on its territory. Nevertheless, relations between Laos and Thailand continued to be poor.

The defeat of the Meo and other tribesmen, indigenous to Laos, broke the political and military stalemate in Laos which had been in being since before 1973. On the 9th May 1975, several right-wing ministers resigned, and with others, fled to Thailand. In southern Laos, in a series of mutinies, Government army units rejected their right-wing and neutralist officers, and during the latter part of May, and the beginning of June, Pathet Lao officers moved in, and by invitation, took command of these formations, which now openly threw in their lot with the Pathet Lao. In short, the Communist Pathet Lao swept into power quietly and firmly, with hardly any bloodshed. Several thousands of Vietnamese and Chinese, living and working in Laos as traders and small businessmen, and members of traditional ruling and landed families, hastily left the country.

At last a Communist government was in control of Laos, which co-operated fully with the NVN forces in the country, and listened to advice from the Hanoi Government. At the beginning of March

1975, there had been about 26,000 NVN troops in Laos, but by the end of May, they had been reduced to less than 12,000: the Pathet Lao no longer had to rely upon them for their survival. On the 12th May, the US Government informed the Laos Government that the Agency for International Development Programme would cease; and the last remaining US AID personnel left Laos on the 25th June.

Under Pathet Lao urging, on the 6th June, senior officers of the Vientaine army adopted a resolution that Pathet Lao officers take over senior military posts; that the Pathet Lao army, of about 14,000 well-trained and well-armed soldiers, be integrated into the government army; that the former Vientaine army be reduced from about 50,000 men down to about 30,000; that the soldiers take part in productive labour; and that all Special Forces, Rangers, and mercenary units be disbanded.

Cambodia was also influenced by events in South Vietnam and Laos. Following his overthrow by General Lon Nol in 1970, Prince Norodom Sihanouk, the former Head of State of Cambodia, made an alliance with the Khmer Rouge Communist guerrilla fighters, who then numbered about 3,000. Sihanouk's "Royalist" supporters were about of equal number. Although in exile he resided in Peking, he kept his "government" in being, receiving encouragement and support from both the NVN and Chinese governments. Some ministers were with him in Peking, and others remained in Cambodia in the countryside. During the period 1970 to 1972, NVN regular forces in Cambodia did most of the fighting against Lon Nol's government troops. As the Khmer Rouge increased in strength, the NVN troops were gradually withdrawn, but by the beginning of 1973, about 7,000 of them still remained as advisers and training staff. The Khmer Rouge had set up its own High Command in the Cambodian countryside, with Khieu Samphan as the Commander-in-Chief, and Son Sann as Chief of Staff. Although this coaliton went under the name of "Royalist Forces", because of Prince Sihanouk's nominal leadership, its solid main core was Communist, being the Khmer Rouge. The other small groups involved were of the same political persuasion, and included the Communist Party of Cambodia. Eventually, this coalition came to be called the National United Front of Cambodia.

On the 29th January 1973, Lon Nol ordered his army to cease fighting, and on the 30th, Prince Sihanouk stated that his "Royal Government of National Unity" was also prepared to suspend military operations and negotiate, if the Lon Nol Government would sever itself from all US support. Thus condition was rejected, and on the 2nd February, the National Unity forces resumed offensive operations, which they continued until July. The US air force, at Lon Nol's request carried out bombing missions over Cambodia.

The National Unity forces claimed to have about 100,000 men under arms, equipped with both Chinese and Soviet weapons, which had been channelled through Hanoi along the Ho Chi Minh Trail, and also a few US ones that had either been secretly purchased or obtained in battle. In Ferbruary 1973, the NVN contingent in Cambodia was increased to about 10,000 combat and 13,000 support troops. Opposing them, the Lon Nol Government forces, which had numbered about 300,000 in 1972, had sunk to less than 180,000, and conscription was introduced in March.

By the end of March the National Unity forces had cut all roads leading into the Cambodian capital, Phnom Penh, and the army of Lon Nol's regime was only able to hold them back because it had intensive US bombing support, which had re-commenced on the 8th March. US bombing in Indo-China had become a particularly unpopular and sensitive subject to Americans at home, and on the 31st May, the Senate voted to cut off all funds allocated for bombing in Cambodia. Just previously, on the 8th, for the first time, Lon Nol, who had reformed his government on a broader base, offered to negotiate with Prince Sihanouk. But Sihanouk refused: his forces were doing well in the field, despite American aerial bombing.

Despite adverse American public opinion, US bombing continued in Cambodia, and concern arose in America over alleged bombing errors which had cost civilian lives. For example, it was alleged that on the 6th August 1973, a US B-52 bomber aircraft had dropped its bomb-load on the small town of Nek Luong, killing 56 Lon Nol Government soldiers and 81 civilians, wounding 268 soldiers and civilians, and destroying half the town.* Eventually, US bombing of Cambodia was terminated on the 15th August 1973. It was stated by a US spokesman that in this period, from the 8th March to the 15th August, the US Air Force had dropped over 240,000 tons of bombs on Cambodia, which he said was 50% more than the weight of all conventional explosives dropped on Japan in World War II.

It was widely expected that Phnom Penh would fall to the Communist National Unity forces after US support-bombing ceased, but that did not happen. Instead, they pulled back from the outskirts of the Capital, and the fighting in that sector died down. On the

* This was the worst incident of its kind reported since 1967, when US aircraft bombed the South Vietnamese village of Lang Vei by mistake, killing 83 villagers and wounding 176.

31st August, Prince Sihanouk, still in Peking, stated that the Hanoi Government was resuming military aid to his army in Cambodia, but there is some doubt whether this did actually happen. Next, a section of the National Unity army moved off to launch an attack on the port of Kompon Son (formerly Sihanoukville), which was repulsed after some heavy fighting. Sihanouk blamed this defeat on a shortage of ammunition, and accused both the Hanoi and Peking Governments of not supplying sufficient military aid to his forces in Cambodia, and of prevaricating in this respect because they were interested in bettering their relations with the United States.

On the 9th November 1973, the National Unity Government announced that its Ministries would be transferred from Peking to Cambodia, and others formed in the "liberated areas"; and that Ministers working outside the country would be dismissed. Prince Sihanouk remained in Peking, and although still the nominal Head of the Royal Government of National Unity, the real power had passed to the leader in the field, the Khmer Rouge man, Khieu Samphan.

From November 1973, National Unity forces maintained a stranglehold on Phnom Penh, again isolating the Capital, and blocking off all approach roads. From mid-February 1974, as fresh supplies of weapons and ammunition reached them, they were able to continually bombard the outskirts with mortar and rocket fire. However, by the end of February, the Lon Nol defenders rallied and made a successful counter-attack which pushed the besiegers back a considerable distance.

After this setback Khieu Samphan tried a different strategy, one aimed at further dispersing the Lon Nol republican forces. Lon Nol probably had an army of about 200,000 men by this time, of which the best four divisions, about 50,000 soldiers, were defending Phnom Penh, while the remainder were dispersed to provincial capitals, which had to be held for national prestige reasons. On the 18th March 1974, the National Unity forces captured the small provincial capital of Oudong, about 24 miles north of Phnom Penh, which was the first such town they had seized since 1970. This was a great psychological victory, as Oudong was both a religious centre and an ancient Royal Capital. However, Oudong was recovered by Lon Nol's troops on the 9th July. Then in April, Khieu Sampham turned, and put renewed pressure on Phnom Penh.

After the termination of US Air Force bombing of Cambodia, at Lon Nol's request the American CIA organised a civilian air service, known as "Bird Air Company", to fly in supplies, make reconnaissance flights to obtain information for the Cambodian Air

Force bombing raids, and check results. This airline used former US Air Force aircraft, with the old markings painted out, and the pilots were ex-US servicemen. Especially were these "civilian" aircraft used to drop supplies by parachute to besieged towns and garrisons. On the 5th June, James Schlesinger, US Defense Secretary, stated that this airline was "carrying out 690 missions a month in Cambodia".

Throughout 1974, the National Unity forces concentrated mainly upon keeping a stranglehold on Phnom Penh, although other far-ranging operations were also carried out. The National Unity Government controlled, or influenced, most of the countryside, while the Lon Nol Republican troops held all the towns, and were able to continue to hold them because they had superior arms and equipment, good aerial transport facilities, and a small but efficient Cambodian air force.

On the other side, the National Unity army was neither large enough nor strong enough to achieve its objectives, and was not as well armed as its enemy. Only comparatively small amounts of weapons and ammunition trickled through from China, North Korea and North Vietnam, and none at all from the Soviet Union. Such as arrived had to be paid for in cash; in the summer of 1974, the National Unity Government sold about 50,000 tons of rice to the PRG in SVN, to pay for weaponry. Both field and anti-aircraft guns had been captured, as had ammunition for them, which had to be carefully husbanded. On the 26th August, National Unity soldiers captured some villages near the famous Angkor Wat ruins, near Siem Reap, in the western part of the country, which they wanted to make into a base, but they were expelled on the 4th October. Khieu Samphan's army did not seem capable of holding on to any objectives it captured.

Beginning in January 1975, the National Unity forces, with some help from NVN troops, launched a major offensive against Lon Nol's army, and soon gained control of the southern Mekong sector, to the east of the river. By the end of the month, Phnom Penh was completely blockaded by land and water, and normal supplies ceased to reach the capital, which became entirely dependent upon supply by air. Two more "civilian" airline companies quickly came into being, similar to the Bird Air Company, and for the same general purpose. As the National Unity troops closed in towards the city, the delivery of airborne supplies became more precarious.

On the 15th January 1975, a reshuffled National Unity Government was announced, with Penn Nouth, a long-time friend of Prince Sihanouk, as Prime Minister. Aged 69, Penn Nouth was very much a figurehead, so the real power continued to rest with

Khieu Samphan, as Deputy Prime Minister and Defence Minister. On the 28th March, the Soviet Government sent a note to Prince Sihanouk, still in Peking, and still the official Cambodian Head of State, recognising this Penn Nouth Government. This was a surprising change of Soviet policy, as the Soviets had previously recognised Lon Nol's Government as the legal one of the country, but they had never formally broken off diplomatic relations with Prince Sihanouk.

In February, a National Unity Congress was held in the "liberated area" of Cambodia, which approved the Five Principles of Peaceful Coexistence (of 1954), and called on all Cambodians to join it. The Congress made a list of "Seven Traitors", who were Lon Nol and his immediate colleagues, but offered an amnesty to all others who surrendered to them. The US Administration was desperately anxious to persuade both sides to enter into political negotiations, but the National Unity Government was both elusive and evasive.

On the 28th January 1975, President Ford had, in a special message to Congress, asked for extra military aid to help the Lon Nol regime in Cambodia withstand pressure from the Communist National Unity army. Henry Kissinger, US Secretary of State, in particular, was loath to accept a Cambodian Government, negotiated on a local political basis, that contained declared and dedicated Communists, such as the Khmer Rouge, because he felt they would certainly be puppets of the Hanoi Government. On the 3rd February, the National Unity Government alleged that Lon Nol's Cambodian air force, in its bombing raids near the Mekong River, was using the US "Cluster Bomb", the CBU-55, which on explosion instantly consumed all the oxygen within a radius of a hundred feet or so, thus destroying human and animal life. This was the first instance of Cluster Bombs being used in the Southeast Asian theater.

From mid-January 1975, Chinese rockets in the hands of National Unity troops, began to fall on Pochentong airport, outside Phnom Penh, and the outskirts of the city. The Capital was now under severe siege, being blocked off by both land and water routes. Previously, about 80% of the provisions had been brought in by river. The usual population of Phnom Penh, about 600,000 people, was increased by floods of refugees to over two million. Hunger began to be the problem, and civilian deaths from starvation increased daily. At the end of February, the hired aircraft of all three civilian airlines was harnessed to fly in rice for the people to eat, and ammunition for the defenders.

In Phnom Penh, President Lon Nol was facing opposition and

meeting criticism of his handling of the war against the National Unity army. On the 7th March, a majority in the Cambodian Assembly called on him to resign, which he did on the 11th, leaving the country on the 1st April. On the 17th March, the US State Department announced that the US Defense Department, in an audit of the military aid programme, had discovered that through an accounting error, Cambodia had been "over-charged" some $21.5 million. Previously, it had been stated that all US money allocated for Cambodian military aid had been expended. Had this announcement come earlier, it might have given Lon Nol a belated boost that might have helped him, but by this time it was far too late to be effective. And massive saturation bombing of jungle areas, which had been constantly asked for, was not the correct counter to guerrilla armies and guerrilla tactics.

In Phnom Penh the end was near, and after the last US Embassy personnel had left the city on the 12th April, airborne provisions ceased to arrive in the Capital. On the 14th, in Peking, Prince Sihanouk, intimated he would like to retire from public life. Resistance quickly crumbled, and on the 17th, National Unity soldiers, meeting hardly any opposition, walked in and took over the city. Cambodia had effectively fallen under the Communist control of Khieu Sampham and his National Unity Government. Only two of the Seven Traitors remained in the Capital, one of whom took refuge in the French Embassy.

The Communist National Unity victory was due to superior tactics, while the Lon Nol Republic defeats were due to a combination of shortage of manpower, low morale, and widespread corruption. Certainly, they were not due to lack of weapons and ammunition. In theory the Republican Government had over 200,000 men under arms, but only about 80,000 of them remained as combat troops, as there had been a considerable desertion problem throughout the war, and especially in the closing months of the Lon Nol regime. Over half this number of soldiers available were tied down in isolated garrisons, and there was no battle reserve available to counter-attack at the vital moment. On the other hand, the Communist National Unity army had about the same number of combat troops, over 70,000, but having no positions or towns to defend, and freedom of movement in the countryside, they could all be concentrated to strike at key points when required, and to put pressure on the noose slowly tightening around Phnom Penh.

Meanwhile, Communist forces in South Vietnam had made ready for the offensive against the SVN Government, led by President Thieu. At the beginning of 1975, the ARVN consisted of about

465,000 regulars, who were basically formed into eleven infantry and one airborne division, two independent infantry regiments, eighteen units of armour and another three motorised ones. In addition there were 43 units of Rangers in the Special Forces, composed mainly of Montagnards, and a marine division. Also, there were about two million men in the para-military forces scattered across the country, of which 1.4-million were in the armed village Self-Defence units. But these were "paper figures", and the true number of effectives was far less, although how much less is a matter of speculation and guesswork. For example, during the first quarter of the year, the desertion rate from the regular element exceeded an admitted 24,000 a month. The SVN air force had about 60,000 men, and some 500 US aircraft.

ARVN weaknesses lay not in lack of weaponry and equipment, as it had plenty of the best Americans could supply, but in poor morale and poor discipline, due to the uncertain political situation, despair that the war could ever be won, and corruption that permeated all military levels. On the 30th January, the SVN Government dissolved the "General Civil Guard" group, the Buddhist Hoa Hao sect militia, which it accused of harboring deserters, and helping people to avoid conscription. This group had been responsible for village defence in areas in the Delta. It was ordered to hand in its arms, but many members resisted and had to be forcibly disarmed: many were detained. Gaps were left in the nationwide Self-Defence network by this disbandment for unreliability.

On the Communist side estimates, even official ones, are still contradictory, but in January 1975, there were probably at least 160,000 regular NVN troops inside SVN, and about 120,000 "support" troops, largely controlling and operating the Ho Chi Minh Trail, making a probable total of almost 300,000. Their strength lay in their inculcated sense of mission and purpose, their military aggressiveness and discipline; although out-numbered and out-gunned, they continued to take offensive action continually even though generally they suffered twice as many battle casualties as their SVN counterparts. Regular NVN formations were now equipped with the one-man portable SAM-7, able to bring down aircraft flying below about 8,000 feet, and in the four-day period commencing on the 22nd January, the SVN air force lost five fighter-bombers in the Mekong area to these missiles. The Hanoi Government still did not commit any of its aircraft into battle over SVN.

The strength of the PRG troops, the Viet Cong, seemed to remain fairly constant at about the 60,000 mark, adequately armed by NVN standards, but there seemed to be a distinct lack of encouragement for this number to be expanded. It seemed the Hanoi Government did not want a large PRG army that might begin to flex its muscles and develop independent thoughts. NVN troops dominated the situation in SVN, and for many months the PRG troops had been playing secondary roles.

A Communist offensive began on the 6th December 1974, in the Mekong Delta, and continued to the end of January 1975. On the 6th January, NVN troops won an important battle for the provincial town of Phuoc Binh, which had a mainly Montagnard population. The town was at an important "turning off" point of the Ho Chi Minh Trail, and had been reinforced in December by SVN formations. A SVN division had been badly ambushed; SVN aircraft had caused casualties among their own forces; and many of the garrison deserted in battle. The Battle of Phuoc Binh marked a turning point of the war: it was the first provincial capital the NVN army had captured for some three years. (NVN troops had taken Quang Tri in 1972, but had only held it for about four months). On the 13th January, NVN tanks had been brought into action in the Kien Tung province, this being their first appearance in this sector. Also, in January, NVN troops overran the province of Phuoc Long, adjacent to Cambodia, another important "turning off" point on the Ho Chi Minh Trail.

Although NVN pressure was maintained on SVN forces in most places, February was a comparatively quiet month, in which Communist troops carried out some considerable redeployment. It should be remembered that this was necessarily a slow process, as whole divisions still marched on foot by night, carrying all their equipment with them, since they were subjected to SVN air strikes and exposed to reconnaissance in daylight.

American public opinion was running strongly against continued involvement in the war in Vietnam, and when on the 28th January 1975, President Ford asked Congress for additional sums of money to help save SVN from defeat (and also Cambodia), he came up against strong new opposition instead of only reluctance, and eventually in March, moves were made in Washington to halt all military aid to SVN. On the military side, the rules were bent by the US to help the ARVN. On the 12th January, a US spokesman admitted that American military aircraft were regularly carrying out reconnaissance flights from bases in Thailand, over North Vietnam and Cambodia, contrary to the Paris Agreement, which forbade the "introduction of foreign military personnel, including technical military personnel". In view of the volume of reinforcements, weaponry and ammunition pouring into SVN from NVN, these puny measures were thought by many to be more than justified. On the 7th February, a US spokesman confirmed that US Air Force technicians were in SVN, helping to distribute aircraft spares.

In Saigon, opposition to President Thieu mounted, and on the 13th January, Father Tran Huu Thanh, leader of the now flourishing People's Anti-Corruption Movement, published another accusation, alleging that Mme. Thieu, wife of the President, had received $7 million from the US Government at the end of 1972 to persuade the President to sign the Paris Agreement, which was so detrimental to him. Father Thanh followed this up on the 1st February, with another indictment, accusing the President of accepting the presence of "300,000 North Vietnamese troops" inside SVN, in exchange for US support for his continued political survival. Father Thanh made other accusations, including the general one that President Thieu and his officials were corrupt, and that because of this territory had been lost in battle to the Communists.

The Hanoi Government launched a general offensive in March, which began in the Central Highlands on the 10th, when with the assistance of the Montagnards, who by this time were almost in a state of rebellion against the Saigon Government, the veteran NVN 316 Division took the town of Ban Me Thuot. The SVN garrison had been depleted on the 5th March, when a SVN division had been sent from Ban Me Thuot to reinforce Pleiku.

On the 14th March, President Thieu flew to Cam Ranh town, and on assessing the situation, ordered what was virtually the total military evacuation of the Central Highlands, telling his commanders to abandon all sectors the ARVN could not supply by road or sea. The next day he ordered the evacuation of the garrisons of Kontum and Pleiku, mainly held by Rangers. A NVN division had made a feint attack on Pleiku on the 4th March. About 100,000 civilians were forced to accompany this military withdrawl, and a 50-mile long convoy moved out down Route No. 7 towards the coast. It was a sad story of chaos and panic, and of officers abandoning their units, and leaving the soldiers and irregulars without fuel, food or instructions. The last vehicles of this tragic refugee evacuation, since known as "The Convoy of Tears", reached the coastal town of Tuy Hoa on the 28th. On the 19th, Thieu had ordered the complete evacuation of the northern province of Quang Tri, from which, two days previously, he had withdrawn the SVN airborne division for the defence of Saigon.

On the 24th March, the towns of Quang Ngai and Tam Ky, both on the coast some miles south of Danang, fell without a fight, there being a panic exodus of the garrisons and sections of the population. Danang was now cut off from Saigon by road. On the 26th March, Hue, just to the north of Danang, also fell to the Communist invaders without a fight, there again being a rout with fleeing soldiery and refugees intermingled, hastily falling back on Danang, whose normal population of about 500,000 was suddenly doubled. On the day Hue was abandoned, the 26th, President Thieu announced that a new defence line was to be based on Danang, and demanded that his ARVN defend it to the death. Danang was now an isolated garrison that backed on to the sea, and Communist forces marched to surround it from the land side. On the 29th, Danang fell with hardly a fight. Over 100,000 regular SVN troops were taken prisoner; the general in command fled by sea; hordes of undisciplined soldiers, deserters and refugees mobbed evacuation ships and aircraft in their efforts to escape from the Communist victors.

By the end of March NVN forces, which three weeks previously had held only one province (out of 44), now held at least thirteen, and controlled the main coastal road as far south as the outskirts of Qui Nhon. The result of President Thieu's panic decision of large-scale evacuation was that the Communist forces now held all the vital northern provinces and the northern part of the Central Highlands. Their battle casualties had been slight. ARVN forces were now in an acute state of disarray and demoralisation, and their huge desertion problem increased. At least four SVN divisions and over a dozen Ranger units had ceased to exist. The maximum effective SVN numbers of combat soldiers could not be more than 160,000, and for the first time in the war, the NVN armies, which by this time must have exceeded "300,000" men, as more reserve formations had filtered into SVN during March, outnumbered those of the South Vietnamese.

On the 25th March, President Thieu formed a War Cabinet, which lowered the age of conscription, but otherwise seemed indecisive and helpless in the demoralised atmosphere. Demands that Thieu resign increased, some voiced in the National Assembly, while Father Thanh suggested that Thieu should hand over to a "collective coalition". Marshal Nugyen Cay Ky, who had taken no part in politics since resigning from the Vice Presidency in 1971, came to the fore again, and on the 27th March, demanded the formation of a "Government of National Salvation". Ky obviously saw himself as its Prime Minister, and perhaps visualised himself saving his country from Communism, and much as a Churchill at Dunkirk. However he obtained little support, and although he urged everyone to stand and fight to the death, hastily left Saigon in the final evacuation. On the 31st March, another figure from the past reappeared, Tich Tri Quang, the Buddhist leader, who in 1963 had led demonstrations that had brought about the downfall of President Ngo Dinh Diem, but had been politically inactive since. He also loudly demanded the removal of President Thieu.

As Communist troops flooded into the evacuated areas as fast as they could march on foot, the expected blood-bath did not occur. In fact, a semblance of law and order was quickly and firmly clamped on these occupied regions. On the 1st April, the PRG published a "Ten-Point" statement, outlining the need to quickly restore order, to get the people back to work, and to establish a Socialist order in SVN. However, it was the Hanoi Government that called the tune, and Hanoi troops who provided the efficient military administrations set up to control the newly occupied provinces and towns. No reliable evidence has yet been produced of any major atrocities committed by the Communist forces in this phase, and there were comparatively few executions. The people were "vetted" and new identity cards were issued to them. Where possible they were sent back to their villages to work on the land to prevent mass starvation, while others were put to work repairing roads, bridges and irrigation systems, clearing war debris, and restoring communications.

The Roman Catholic clergy co-operated with the new NVN administrations, and urged their flocks not to flee south, as had happened in 1954, but to stay where they were. In the Central Highlands, the Unified Front for the Struggle of the Oppressed Races, FULRO, the Montagnard organisation, openly collaborated with the NVN administrators, but the Buddhists remained wary. Neutral observers later commented upon how quickly order was restored under NVN supervision; for example, on the 24th April, Danang was re-opened under a Communist military administration, as its normal life resumed.

On the 1st April, the coastal town of Qui Nhon, now in the front line against NVN troops advancing from the north, fell without a fight, as did Nha Trang the same day. The following day, Tuy Hoa, in between those two towns, was hastily evacuated. Elsewhere, the previous month, on the 18th, the town of An Loc, on the route north from Siagon, had been captured, and on the 28th Bao Loc also fell. On the 2nd April, Dalat surrendered, as did the two coastal towns of Phan Rang and Phan Thiet. The main Saigon defence now rested on Xuan Loc, on the main coastal road, less than 40 miles from the Capital.

Meanwhile, in Saigon pressure continued to be put on President

208

Thieu to resign, but he still refused, and when news of the loss of coastal towns reached him, he merely reshuffled his Cabinet. On the 8th April, a South Vietnamese pilot, in a SVN aircraft, made a lone bombing raid on the Presidential Palace, but Thieu was unhurt. This act appeared to be an isolated one, unconnected with any political motive. The previous day, Nguyen Huu Tho, Chairman of the South Vietnamese National Liberation Front, stated that the US must agree to completely terminate all military involvement in SVN of any sort, and added that he was prepared to talk to any government that was alternative to that of Thieu. On the 18th, when formations of marching NVN soldiers were steadily deploying towards the Capital, Thieu refused yet another request to resign. On the 20th, the US Ambassador to SVN, Graham Martin, asked for an urgent interview with President Thieu, at which he handed him an ultimatum received from the PRG delegation in Paris. It said that if Thieu did not resign, an all-out Communist military offensive would be launched against Saigon.

The following day, the 21st, Xuan Loc, the main SVN bastion defending the Capital on Route No. 1, fell to the Communists. In this battle, despite the demoralisation and hopelessness of the military and political situation, the SVN troops fought well, but they were unlucky; for example, one division ran into an ambush. It was later confirmed by both the US and SVN military authorities, that Cluster Bombs, the CBU-55's, had been used in what proved to be the final major battle of the war.

The day Xuan Loc fell, the 21st, President Thieu at last resigned, making a televised recriminatory farewell speech in the National Assembly, in which he largely blamed the US for his misfortunes. He alleged that the US Administration had gone back on a secret commitment made to him by President Nixon, according to which the United States would "react violently and immediately" to any NVN offensive. Thieu also blamed Kissinger for forcing him to allow the "300,000" NVN troops to remain in SVN under the Paris Agreement. He said he had wanted a gradual reduction in their strength until they disappeared. He also alleged that President Nixon had put pressure upon him to sign the Paris Agreement, and he blamed the Americans for standing passively by while the NVN forces in SVN were built up "to 570,000 men". A major, long-time difference between President Thieu and Kissinger, was that Kissinger was of the opinion that there should only be three states in Indo-China – Vietnam, Laos and Cambodia, while Thieu insisted there should be four, meaning that Vietnam was two nations.

Thieu's place was taken by the Vice President, Tran Van Huong, who temporarily became acting President: Thieu left SVN on the 26th. On the 28th, Huong handed over the office of President to General Duong Van Minh – Big Minh – who was persuaded to step forward into the political arena again at this last hour. He called for an immediate cease-fire, and the opening of peace negotiations, but the PRG, in whose name the Hanoi Government was fighting this war, refused.

Despite Thieu's resignation speech on the 21st – or perhaps because Thieu had remained briefly in Saigon for a few days after it, and it was not believed – after a four-day pause, the NVN offensive against Saigon again moved forward, pressure being exerted on all sides to slowly compress the cordon. One incident of interest occurred on the 28th April, when three American A-37 fighter-bombers bombed the Tan Son Nhut airport near Saigon, which at first was thought to be part of an attempted coup by Marshal Ky. It turned out to be the first-ever operation by the newly formed PRG air force, using captured US aircraft, which destroyed about a dozen US helicopters on the ground.

During the first quarter of 1975, there had been a steady evacuation of American citizens, but about 7,500 still remained at the end of March. On the 16th April, President Ford ordered all "unneeded" Americans to leave SVN. The same day the PRG announced that the evacuation of Americans would be no obstacle. More to the point was the large number, at least 50,000 or more, South Vietnamese who had collaborated with the Americans over the years, and who were classified as "high risk", as it was anticipated that dire Communist retribution would fall on them if they were caught. During April, many of them quietly began to leave the country, or were officially evacuated by US aircraft. Alarmed at the large numbers of both military and civilian personnel leaving, the SVN Government, on the 27th, refused to grant any more exit permits, which caused alarm and some panic. The 28th was the day of mass evacuation of SVN top brass and officials, and also of many National Assembly members.

Early on the 29th, while coming in to pick up more "high risk" SVN personnel from the Tan Son Nhut airport, two American C-130 transport aircraft were unable to land because massed crowds were waiting on the runways hoping to be evacuated. This was the last attempt at evacuation by American transport aircraft. Helicopters now had to be relied upon, to land on the flat tops of buildings in order to pick up Americans and "high risk" South Vietnamese. Later, on the 29th, a huge operation was launched, involving 81 helicopters, with a force of 1,000 US Marines to protect them, control the evacuees, and prevent the machines being mobbed in panic, while US fighter aircraft gave protective cover. In a period of about four hours, 395 Americans and 4,475 South Vietnamese were evacuated by this method to US naval craft lying a couple of miles offshore.

There were wild, final scenes at the US Embassy in Saigon, as people fought to get on to the helicopters, of which only two at a time could land on its flat roof. It took some sixteen hours to lift off 978 Americans and 1,120 South Vietnamese. US Marines at times had to use tear-gas to keep the mob back. This helicopter "lifting off" operation at the US Embassy terminated about 0800 hours on the 30th, after which the angry mob broke into the building and looted it. The last American servicemen to be killed in this Third Vietnam War, were two US Marines, whose helicopter crashed into the sea. Many refugees fled by other means, particularly along the coast in small craft to be picked up by cruising US and allied warships. It was later stated that the US Navy picked up over 32,000 refugees in this way.

Left alone in Saigon in a hopeless situation, Big Minh ordered the SVN forces to cease all resistance, and about noon, on the 30th April 1975, NVN troops walked unopposed into the Capital. The Third Vietnam War was over. The Communists had won it, as they had won the previous two. Some spasmodic resistance continued in a few sectors of the Mekong Delta and in the Central Highlands for a few weeks, although much of the latter might be regarded as plain banditry.

The undoubted military master-mind behind the Communist victory was General Nguyen Vo Giap, the NVN Defense Minister and Deputy Premier. Giap had expected to have to fight on for another year, anticipating not being able to defeat the SVN Government until some time in 1976. The panic moves by President Thieu in ordering mass evacuations of the northern provinces and the Central Highlands, were an unexpected gift to Giap, as they caused the ARVN to crumble prematurely. Thieu had practically opened the road to Saigon to Giap.

On its surrender on the 30th April 1975, Saigon was taken over by a PRG Military Management Committee, which eventually, on the 21st January 1976, handed over to a People's Revolutionary Committee. There was no blood-bath, although a great many people were detained, and order was soon restored. The Roman Catholic church co-operated with the new Communist regime, but the Buddhists still remained aloof and suspicious. Most SVN officers, and some soldiers, were sent to "re-education camps", but the majority were released after a few days when they had agreed to become part of the new Communist society. The SVN soldiers underwent short indoctrination courses, and together with refugees, once they had been "vetted" and new identity cards were issued to them, were sent back to their villages to work on the land. Senior officers, officials, and others suspected of "war crimes", remained in detention; many were later put on trial, a few of whom were executed. A Five Year Plan for economic recovery was hastily put together.

During the summer of 1975, the Military Management Committee imposed Communist control on the people, especially in Saigon and other cities and towns, by organising "solidarity cells", consisting basically of ten neighbouring households. Each head of a household was responsible for all members in it, and had to account for their whereabouts and actions at all times to the "cell leader", who was part of the Communist organisation. Although thousands of people were rounded up and sent back to their villages to work on the land, thousands more seemed to remain in Saigon, where a huge unemployment problem and a crime wave developed. At one stage there were some three million unemployed, but this was solved by putting them all to reconstruction or productive work. The crime wave was more difficult to cope with. Special courts were set up to deal with offenders, who included drug pedlars, prostitutes, gangsters, protection-racket organisers, thugs, and petty thieves. Most were sent for "re-education" and put to productive work, but a few criminals were publicly executed as a deterrent.

Elections were held in both South Vietnam and North Vietnam on the 25th April 1976, as a prelude towards re-unification, for a combined National Assembly, which met for the first time in Hanoi on the 24th June. On the 2nd July NVN and SVN were formally declared to be one country, to be known as the Socialist Republic of Vietnam. The capital was to be Hanoi, and Saigon had already been renamed Ho Chi Minh City. A Government was formed under Prime Minister Pham Van Dong, containing representatives from both the north and the south, with northerners in the majority. On the 2nd September, Prime Minister Pham Van Dong offered to normalise relations with the US, his object being to qualify for US financial and economic aid, but President Ford refused. The issue of "unaccounted-for" American prisoners was still a sore one in America.

The China-Vietnam War: 1979   16

"Vietnam must be punished severely, and China is considering taking appropriate counter-action." Teng Hsiao-ping, Chinese Vice Premier, and Chief of Staff of the People's Liberation Army: 7th February 1979

The fall of South Vietnam and the reunification of Vietnam effectively removed the last traces of American influence in Indo-China, where Communist regimes were in power in Vietnam, Laos and Cambodia. In Hanoi, Le Duan, First Secretary of the Vietnamese Workers' Party (soon to become the Vietnam Communist Party), expressed gratitude to both the USSR and China for the assistance they had given during the last thirty years of war. The Hanoi Government had been extremely careful to walk the tightrope of neutrality over the ever-widening Sino-Soviet rift that was first exposed to the world in 1960. Both these powers began to show great interest in the Indo-China region.

The Soviet Union in particular stepped in to assist Vietnamese economic recovery, and indeed the Soviets had been the major supplier of munitions during the wars in Vietnam. Technical help was certainly needed at this time, since large areas of arable land had been laid waste by US defoliants, and it was estimated that about 150,000 tons of bombs (out of the some fifteen million tons dropped on Vietnam) had failed to explode. Soviet economic aid, expertise and money flowed into Vietnam: The US Congress had repudiated President Nixon's promised post-war aid to "South Vietnam", saying that it was no longer binding, as the Hanoi Government had so obviously breached the Paris Agreement.

On the 13th December 1976, the first through train from Ho Chi Minh City arrived in Hanoi, a distance of over 1,000 miles. The reconstruction of this battered railway line had been carried out by military labour, and Soviet engineers and materials. Regular train service between these two major cities began on the 15th January 1977. Roads and bridges were also repaired as quickly as possible. A Five Year Plan for the whole of reunified Vietnam had begun in 1976, but was retarded by a prolonged drought and short rainy season in 1977.

On the 30th September 1976, the US used its veto in the United Nations to block Vietnam's application for membership, but Vietnam was finally admitted on the 20th September 1977. In September 1976, reunified Vietnam had been accepted as the successor to South Vietnam and granted membership in the World Bank. It was not until the 23rd March 1977, that President Carter decided the US should resume discussions with the Vietnamese Government, and these began on the 3rd May.

In Laos the revolution which had begun in May 1975, was completed by the end of the year, leaving the Pathet Lao solidly in power. The Pathet Lao set up "People's Revolutionary Administrations" in Vientaine, other cities and towns, and "revolutionary committees" in the villages. This process of stamping Communist control on the whole of the population was completed by August 1975. In September, the joint Pathet Lao-Vientaine government army detachments in Vientaine and Luang Prabang, were replaced by newly formed "worker's militia" units. On the 7th October, the last members of the French Military Mission left Laos.

During 1975, relations between Laos and Thailand became worse owing mainly to the large number of Laotian refugees who had fled westwards across the Mekong River. One set of UN figures showed them to number 54,821 by the end of the year. On the 17th November, after a clash between the frontier forces of both sides, the Laos Government closed its frontiers to Thailand, which caused internal hardship, as large quantities of food, and other essentials such as fuel oils, came from that country by river transport. On the 19th, the Hanoi Government announced its support for Laos in its dispute with Thailand, and sent in food convoys to Laos by road, and also flew in certain provisions by aircraft. The USSR, now deeply involved with Vietnam, in order to back that country, mounted a daily airlift of essential supplies from Hanoi to Vientaine, beginning on the 22nd December. The International Commission of Control Supervision, the ICCS, set up under the Geneva Conference decision of 1962, which had never worked well, and lately had been plagued by differences among its national representatives, was terminated in December 1975.

On the 1st December 1975, a Congress was convened by the

Lao People's Front (Neo Lao Haksat), more commonly referred to as the Pathet Lao, which formally accepted the resignation of the Provisonal Government of National Union, headed by Prince Souvanna, and proclaimed Laos to be a People's Democratic Republic, with Prince Souphanou Vong, Chairman of the Pathet Lao, as President. The shadowy King Savang Vatthana abdicated. A People's Supreme Council was formed to be the highest executive authority, and it approved the formation of a government headed by Kaysone Phomvihan, General Secretary of the Communist People's Revolutionary Party.

The Communist regime which had established itself so firmly in power in Laos in 1975, had to face some serious problems in the following two years or so. The economic blockade from Thailand, started by the Laotians, had proved to be double-edged, and coupled with a poor harvest in 1976, and a drought in 1977, resulted in such chronic economic distress that the Government had to ask for international aid. The other problem was that of the dissident Meo tribesmen, and their resistance to being communised and brought under the thumb of the central government; they were provoked into insurrection in the spring of 1977. A major military punitive campaign was launched against them in November and December, which caused several thousands of the Meo to flee across the River Mekong to take refuge in Thailand. Vietnamese military help had been given to subdue the Meo rebels, and five divisions of Vietnamese soldiers, about 50,000 men, remained in Laos. On the 18th July 1977, the Laos Government signed a treaty of Friendship and Co-operation with Vietnam.

When the Khmer Rouge took over Cambodia on the 17th April 1975, much of the country was devastated by the ravages of war, so the whole population was mobilised to reconstruct the economy. The entire population of Phnom Penh, and other towns, was evacuated into the countryside, and put to work on the land, and to repair bridges, roads and railways during the last few months of the year. Money was withdrawn from circulation, and replaced by ration tickets, which had to be earned by productive labour. In this period of mass migration from the towns, thousands died of starvation and medical neglect, while thousands of others escaped into Thailand, or fled to the border regions near Vietnam. Practically the whole of the ethnic Vietnamese community, estimated to be about 600,000, fled the country, due to fear of Khmer Rouge hostility and possible recriminations. When the Khmer Rouge party split in 1973, the Vietnamese element, the Khmer Vietminh, had been completely eliminated, and traces of this antipathy remained.

215

Few foreigners were allowed to visit Cambodia, so little reliable news of what was really happening was available to the outer world.

On the 5th January 1976 a new Communist Constitution was promulgated, which changed the name of Cambodia to Kampuchea. On the 2nd April, Prince Norodom Sihanouk, who had paid a brief visit to his own country from the 9th to the 28th September 1975 before returning to Peking, resigned as Head of State; on the 11th, Khieu Samphan, the Khmer Rouge leader, became President of Kampuchea; and a Cabinet headed by Pol Pot, another prominent Khmer Rouge leader, was formed. A statement made in Phnom Penh, on the 31st March 1976, alleged that about 800,000 people had been killed during the war, and about 200,000 wounded: the population of Kampuchea was then claimed to be about 7.7 million. This was regarded as gross exaggeration, and it was suspected these figures had been quoted to shift any blame there might be for the regime's own atrocities.

There had long been differences and disputes over the precise Kampuchea-Vietnam common border, which had been demarcated in colonial days by the French, and frontier clashes in 1975 and 1976, between the troops of the Khmer Rouge and Hanoi Governments developed into more serious fighting during 1977. By this time both the USSR and China were struggling for influence in Indo-China. From September onwards this fighting intensified, and the Hanoi Goverment claimed that at least four Kampuchean divisions had invaded its Tay Ninh province, while the Phnom Penh Government made similar counter claims. On the 31st December 1977 Kampuchea broke off diplomatic relations with Vietnam, and a Hanoi offer to negotiate was rejected.

Apart from traditional and deep-rooted ethnic rivalries in the Indo-China region, and the confused border issues, there were other reasons for the quarrel that was developing between these two Communist regimes. They were becoming puppets of the USSR and China respectively, and their forces proxy ones. The Khmer Rouge Government, led by Pol Pot, alleged that the Vietnam Government was trying to force Kampuchea into an "Indo-China Federation," which it would dominate. Each accused the other of harbouring its dissidents amongst the mass of refugees who had fled to the other's territory. A propaganda and an economic war developed.

Another point of dispute was that the Kampuchean Government claimed the former province of Cochin China, now incorporated into Vietnam, because of its large indigenous Khmer population, and the sovereignty of the small islands in the Gulf of Thailand.

The latter issue might have been influenced by hints of oil potential under the seabed. In 1960, the Saigon Government had laid claim to seven of these islands, including the largest, Phu Quoc, on which were now posted Vietnamese troops. During 1977, border fighting escalated in the jungle provinces lying between the Mekong River and the coast, which began to spread northwards along the common frontier areas. On the 12th April 1978, Pol Pot confirmed Kampuchean claims to Cochin China and the offshore islands, and accused the Hanoi Government of collaborating with the American CIA against it. From that month onwards, Vietnamese propaganda broadcasts urged the Kampuchean army to overthrow its government, and on the 24th June, alleged there had been an unsuccessful coup in Phnom Penh, which had been preceded by earlier ones.

The eastern part of Kampuchea had been used by the North Vietnamese as the southern part of its Ho Chi Minh Trail, and they had gained the collaboration of certain sections of the population. As opponents of the Pol Pot regime fled to these remote border areas, the Hanoi Government organised many of them into anti-Khmer Rouge forces, which fighting on the Vietnamese side regularly clashed with Kampuchean regular army formations. Much of this fighting centered around the Parrot's Beak area, and a fairly significant Khmer resistance movement developed during 1978. In June of that year, the UN High Commissioner for Refugees stated that 331,000 Kampuchean refugees had entered Vietnam, of whom at least 150,000 urgently needed help, and that another 75,000 had been driven into Vietnam from their homes by the fighting.

From June 1978 onwards, the Vietnamese air force came into action against Kampuchea government forces in the border regions, and commencing in August, Chinese-trained Kampuchean pilots began flying captured US aircraft against Vietnamese units on the ground. Several proposals by the Hanoi Government to negotiate were rejected by Pol Pot.

Little hard news came out of Kampuchea, but many alarming rumours that could not be verified, did. The Hanoi Government constantly alleged that the Pol Pot regime was annihilating the Kampuchean nation, and on the 8th October 1978, Radio Hanoi stated that over two million Kampucheans had been massacred. This was thought to be an exaggeration, but the figure of half-a-million was then regarded as being more credible. Refugees and survivors brought tales of executions and mass killings, but no independent verification was available, and also many reports were contradictory.

A concensus of rumour was that when the Khmer Rouge took over the country in 1975 there had been a series of mass executions, which appeared to diminish, but not cease, during 1976. Another outburst of government massacres occurred after the discovery of an alleged plot against the Pol Pot Government in April 1977, and a third wave of massacres began in September of that year after another attempted coup, which continued on into, and throughout, 1978. From July 1978 onwards a purge of the Kampuchean Communist Party, and presumably also the Khmer Rouge administration, had begun. Several military mutinies had occurred, which had been suppressed by mass killings. Throughout 1978, Pol Pot faced other crises, that included alternate floods and drought, which caused an acute food shortage. Kampuchea, which could produce two rice crops a year, and was regarded as the rice bowl of Southeast Asia, was reduced to starvation.

As relations between Vietnam and Kampuchea deteriorated towards the end of 1978, the Communist governments of the world began to divide in their support for one or the other. By this time Vietnam was well on the way to becoming a Soviet satellite country, having become dependent upon Soviet aid, and so was openly backed by the Moscow Government and by most of the Warsaw Pact countries. Other Communist governments, such as those of Cuba, Mongolia, Angola, and Mozambique also supported Vietnam. China, although pretending to be neutral, was backing Kampuchea, and giving some military assistance, as was North Korea. Laos tried to remain neutral but was unable to do so, being so much under Vietnamese influence; in fact the only real Communist neutrals were Yugoslavia and Rumania.

On the 3rd December 1978, representatives of several factions hostile to the Pol Pot regime, under Vietnamese auspices, met together somewhere in the "liberated areas" in the Parrot's Beak region, and formed the "Cambodian National United Front for National Salvation," usually shortened to the "Kampuchean United Front." A Central Committee was formed, and Heng Samrin, a Khmer Rouge defector, was made its Chairman, and the Kampuchean resistance army, which had increased in strength to about 20,000 men, was placed under his command.

Vietnamese regular forces launched a major offensive on the 25th December 1978, on a wide front into Kampuchea, and slowly converged on Phnom Penh. A Soviet-Vietnam Friendship and Cooperation Treaty had been signed on the 3rd November, under which Soviet support had been promised to back up this operation. The initial thrust into Kampuchea was made by twelve regular

Vietnamese infantry divisions, over 120,000 men, and within days this number was increased to about 200,000, who were supported by Heng Samrin's Kampuchean resistance army.

Pol Pot's armed forces consisted mainly of about 60,000 Khmer Rouge troops, formed into four small divisions and three independent regiments of infantry, equipped with a mixture of Soviet, Chinese and American weapons. On the 1st December, the Kampuchean Government had received six MiG-19 aircraft from China, to add to its dozen or so American ones. The main invasion force closed in on Phnom Penh, while other divisions branched off to seize Kompong Cham and Kompon Thom in the hinterland, and Kampot and Kompon Son to the southwest.

Faced by this overwhelming enemy strength, the Khmer Rouge army did not stand and fight, but abandoned the towns and withdrew into the countryside to carry out guerrilla warfare against the invaders. On the 7th, Heng Samrin, his small army, and Vietnamese troops, literally walked unopposed into Phnom Penh, and by the end of the month all provincial towns were in Vietnamese hands. On the 8th January 1979, a People's Revolutionary Council, with Heng Samrin as President, assumed power in Kampuchea, maintaining it only with Vietnamese military support. This new government was immediately recognised by the USSR, Vietnam, Laos and other Communist States, but not by China. On the 14th January, the Soviet Union used its veto in the UN against a Security Council Resolution demanding that foreign troops be withdrawn from Kampuchea. The Chinese Government was very angry at the Vietnamese invasion as it considered that Kampuchea was in its own sphere of influence, and on the 7th February, Teng Hsiao-ping, the Chinese Vice Premier and Chief of Staff of the People's Liberation Army, said "Vietnam must be punished severely, and China is considering taking appropriate counter-action." Prince Sihanouk was brought out of retirement in Peking, and sent to New York to try to retain the Kampuchea UN seat for the Heng Samrin Government, and not let it be used by the deposed Pol Pot administration.

On the 18th February, a Peace and Friendship Treaty with the Hanoi Government was signed by President Heng Samrin; on the 22nd March, he signed a Co-operation and Economic Agreement with Laos; and on the 30th March, some Laotian military units moved into part of Kampuchea to relieve Vietnamese ones. A Vietnamese occupation force of about fourteen divisions settled on the country. Pol Pot, with his Khmer Rouge army, now down to about 25,000 men, had moved out into the countryside to organise guerrilla warfare, concentrating in the northeast area near the Thailand border. Military supplies were sent from China, and as China did not have a common frontier with Kampuchea, these were channelled secretly through Thailand.

During 1979 and 1980 the situation in Kampuchea was that the Capital and all provincial towns were held by Heng Samrin's Vietnamese troops, while the Khmer Rouge army, which soon expanded to about 45,000, largely had the freedom of the countryside. Several of the refugee camps adjacent to the Thailand border, which received international aid, became virtually Khmer Rouge "No-Go Areas" to Kampuchean officials. This Vietnamese conquest of Kampuchea caused some alarm in Indonesia, Malaysia, the Philippines, Singapore and Thailand, most of which were comparatively defenceless.

A People's Revolutionary Council spokesman said that when Phnom Penh was entered only about one hundred people remained in the city, and that buildings and houses were deserted and empty; hospitals, schools and factories had been vandalised; and Western goods and appliances such as radios, typewriters, telephones, cars and electrical gadgets had been systematically destroyed as the people were forced back into a primitive existence. The country was without medical or educational facilities. In the four years of the Pol Pot Khmer Rouge regime a large section of the population had been annihilated, which mainly included the professional, administrative and educated classes, merchants and traders, and others with any skills at all. Especially had the Buddhists suffered, and their Pagodas been damaged or destroyed. In February, the first mass graves were discovered. International press representatives were invited to Kampuchea, and the world at large saw on their television screens and in their newspapers ghastly scenes of emaciated children, opened mass graves and heaps of skulls and human bones. Perhaps over two million people were killed in this four-year period in Kampuchea. No one really knows yet – perhaps the figure should be higher. It was certainly a holocaust of Hitlerian proportions. This holocaust left Kampuchea without any economic or administrative capability, so Vietnamese had to be employed to start the life of the country again, which further consolidated the Hanoi Government hold over it.

Meanwhile, hostility between Vietnam and China had risen to a peak. Relations had been deteriorating since April 1975, when the Hanoi Government had occupied the Paracel and Spratly Islands in the South China Sea, claimed by China. Another cause of dispute was the territorial waters in the Gulf of Tongking, demarcated by the French, the Chinese claiming jurisdiction over two-thirds of the Gulf and complaining that the boundary line was far too close to Hainan Island, part of China. The underlying reason in both these issues was the suspected oil potential under the seabed.

The more immediate cause of the quarrel was the disputed 50-mile frontier between the two countries, which had been demarcated in colonial days by the French, although only a very few square miles of territory were actually in dispute. Frontier incidents began in 1974, and increased in number annually, until, as alleged by the Vietnamese, there were 2,175 of them in 1978; the Chinese made similar allegations. Negotiations between Vietnam and China over the frontier dispute had commenced in October 1977, but were broken off in the summer of 1978.

Another huge tragedy was occurring in Southeast Asia, which came to be known as that of the "Boat People". Vietnam had about 1.5 million, or more, inhabitants of Chinese descent, the "Hoa", whose families had been there for generations, of whom about 1.2 million lived in what had been South Vietnam, the largest concentration being in Cholon, the Chinese section of Saigon, or Ho Chi Minh City as it had become. The large majority of the Hoa retained Chinese nationality, and refused to become Vietnamese citizens. From 1975 until March 1978, when private trading was abolished, private traders, most of whom were Hoa, had been allowed by the Communists to continue to operate in Vietnam, for the simple reason that they were essential to the economy. Once state-owned shops appeared, private traders were no longer necessary, and were ordered to register for productive work. This would have meant the dispersal of the Hoa on to the land, so many crossed the border into China. In the spring and summer of 1979, about 250,000 Hoa fled from Vietnam by other means, many trying to escape by sea to Hong Kong or other Southeast Asian countries.

This massive exodus was promoted by "agents", who incited the Hoa to flee from Vietnam, telling them that war with China was inevitable, when they would be treated by the Hanoi Government as enemies, traitors or spies. Not enough information has yet been forthcoming about these "agents", who they were, and what their precise motives were. One theory was that they were a group of Chinese criminals, who stimulated mass fear amongst the Hoa, to extort gold, money and property from them, in return for providing an escape by sea. Another theory was that these "agents" were working with, or for, the Hanoi Government, which wanted to expel its "capitalist-natured" Hoa ethnic minority, as it would not fit comfortably into the Communist pattern; but this was denied by the Vietnamese Government.

There had been a steady stream of "boat people" from Vietnam since 1975, but the volume had increased so much by the latter part of 1978 and during 1979 that it became an international problem because of the number of penniless Hoa refugees. This problem reached crisis proportions in May and June 1979, when over 50,000 "boat people" arrived unwanted in Southeast Asian countries and Hong Kong, many in small, unseaworthy craft, packed like sardines in tins. Many such craft sank at sea without trace, and in other cases refugees were plucked from sinking boats by passing ships.

On the 15th June, Malaysia, which already had some 76,000 Hoa in refugee camps, said it would take no more. However, other countries for humanitarian reasons were persuaded to accept numbers of Hoa; these offers amounted to taking 260,000 "boat people" in all. Protests were made to the Vietnamese Government by several nations, and in July 1979 the Hanoi Government undertook to make efforts to prevent further "illegal" departures of its Chinese population, after which the flow of "boat people" slackened off, but still continued at a trickle. The Chinese Government accused Vietnam of deliberately ejecting them, which was another major cause of friction between them.

At dawn on the 17th February 1979, a large Chinese military force invaded Vietnam, and the short Sino-Vietnamese War began. A vast country with a population officially quoted as being 970 million, China's military statistics were equally staggering, since that country had a regular army, the People's Liberation Army of over 3.6 million, an armed militia of well over seven million, and millions more men and women in other types of militia service. The PLA was a huge shambling army, basically an infantry one, equipped mainly with out-of-date infantry weapons, short of motor transport, and bereft of any quantity of modern sophisticated weaponry. The PLA had gone into massive infantry action during the Korean War of 1950, but apart from a brief 33-day invasion of India in 1962, had seen no active service since. Its senior commanders were extremely old by Western standards.

Since the Vietnamese invasion of Kampuchea, as indicated by Vice Premier Teng Hsiao-ping's threat to punish Vietnam, the PLA had been preparing for this punitive operation. Over eighteen divisions, of which three were artillery ones, about 180,000 men in all, were slowly assembled near the Vietnam border. The plan was that eight such divisions would form the initial attacking waves, the others having a follow-up or reserve role. Additionally, more Chinese divisions were being moved up in support, which brought the numbers available for this operation to over 600,000. It was basically an infantry force marching on foot. The commander of the Chinese invasion force was General Hsu Shih-yu, aged 73 years, and his Chief of Staff for the operation was General Chang Ting-fa, aged 70, who was also the Commander of the Chinese Air Force. On the 9th February, Chinese troops began to move to their forming-up areas. The plan was to enter Tongking, the northern part of Vietnam, by the six main entry routes, and then to converge towards Hanoi, the Capital, situated in the Red River basin.

The Vietnamese regular armed forces amounted to about 615,000 men, comparatively well equipped, well disciplined and battle experienced, the ground element being basically formed into 25 divisions of infantry. Additionally, there were independent regiments with specialist roles. Six of the infantry divisions were stationed in Laos and fourteen in Kampuchea, with four of the best protecting Hanoi. The border with China was defended by a 70,000-strong Border Security Force, equipped with field guns, mortars and infantry weapons, and this was supplemented by the armed militia of the area, which was specially mobilised, and amounted to about 50,000 men. The frontier mountain passes, and the roads to them from the actual frontier, were strongly defended by fortified, bunker-like positions, protected by minefields, barbed wire and booby traps, all heavily covered by artillery and mortar fire.

The Chinese made about 43 simultaneous attacks along the frontier, but most were feints, the main strength being concentrated upon the six routes into Tongking. From west to east, these were: towards Lai Chau, on the Black River; towards Lao Cai, on the Red River; towards Ha Giang; towards Cao Bang; through the Friendship Pass towards Dong Dang and Lang Son; and along the coastal route towards Mon Kai. Preceded by heavy artillery and mortar barrages, Chinese troops pushed forward on these main invasion axes, each division moving independently with instructions to quickly force the well-defended jungle-clad frontier passes at all costs. Units within the divisions acted on the "granular" principle, fighting their way individually forward as best they could, and disregarding what was happening on their flanks.

It was a scene of mass infantry attacks reminiscent of Korean War days. It took the leading Chinese divisions at least two days to force their way through these mountain passes, against intense opposition from the Vietnamese soldiers and militiamen, who knew every inch of the ground, and were well prepared for such tactics. Dong Dang fell on the 17th, and Lao Cai on the 19th, both being railhead towns. Then, although the average depth of Chinese penetration into Vietnam was little more than five miles, the Chinese invasion force halted for several days, to wait for more ammunition, supplies and reinforcements. Soon there were about 200,000 Chinese soldiers on Vietnamese territory.

Cao Bang and Ha Giang fell on the 22nd, by which time all the frontier passes were held by the Chinese, who resumed their advance on the 23rd. On that day the Vietnamese defenders made two small counter-attacks into Chinese territory: one in the north near Lao Cai, and the other on the coastal route, both having very limited success. The Chinese had deliberately paused, hoping to scare General Giap, still the Defense Minister (although otherwise slightly down-graded in the Hanoi hierarchy) into deploying and dispersing some of his divisions from around Hanoi, and also to withdraw some of the Vietnamese divisions from Kampuchea and Laos to take the pressure from the Pol Pot Khmer Rouge guerrillas. The Chinese could envelop single divisions by sheer numbers. Giap kept his head and his nerve, and did not initially commit any of his regular divisions. He wanted to see where the main thrust was going to develop first. He was content for the moment to let the Border Security Force and the militia take the brunt of the fighting.

As the frontier towns began to fall one by one, Giap had to move, and he rushed one division from the Hanoi area, the 308th of Dien Bien Phu fame, to join in the battle for the town of Lang Son, where the toughest fighting was developing. Chinese infantry had entered part of Lang Son on the evening of the 2nd March, but the Vietnamese division did not reach that town until the 3rd, too late to prevent this happening. About the same time Giap moved another regular division from the area of Danang, forward to support the battle in progress around Mon Kai on the coastal road. One other division only was withdrawn from Kampuchea, but did not arrive in Tongking until the Chinese had left.

By the 1st March, it seemed as though the fighting on all six fronts had bogged down in stalemate only about, on average, twenty miles from the frontier, and an impasse continued for about a week. Suddenly, on the 5th March, the Chinese announced they were withdrawing, having attained the goals set them by the Peking Government. They said their main objective had been to capture

Lang Son, which they had achieved. The Chinese troops began to withdraw at once, and the Vietnamese defenders simply watched them go. During the withdrawal, Chinese forces carried out scorched earth tactics, taking with them everything of value that was movable, and destroying what was not. By the 15th March, all Chinese troops were clear of Vietnamese territory.

This 18-day war had been a hard fought one, and although the claims of both sides were suspect, it is thought that the total casualties of both were about 45,000. Later, in batches, 238 Chinese prisoners were exchanged for 1,636 Vietnamese ones. The Chinese had badly under-estimated the capability of the Vietnamese frontier troops; they had used "human wave" tactics; they lacked adequate field communications, having still to rely upon the bugle and whistle to control formations in the attack; their weaponry was inferior to that of the Vietnamese; and they mistakenly thought that the people in the frontier regions would rise up against the Communist Hanoi Government, and fight with them against it. Other Chinese drawbacks became evident, such as insufficient motor transportation. The outstanding leader in this war was again General Giap, who refused to be panicked into prematurely deploying his regular divisions, and it was not until the 5th March, that he ordered general mobilisation. Had the Chinese continued their advance in mass down the valleys towards Hanoi, he would have had to quickly withdraw formations from Kampuchea.

The remarkable feature about this war was that although both sides had air forces, there was no aerial activity at all. The Chinese had concentrated about 1,000 aircraft in southern China (its air force had about 4,700 combat aircraft) to support this campaign, but did not use any of them over Vietnam. The assumed reasons are lack of ground control facilities, suspected unairworthiness of aircraft, and lack of combat capability generally. Why the Vietnamese did not use their aircraft (they had about 485 combat planes), even for reconnaissance purposes, remains a mystery so far.

On the 22nd February, the Soviet Union mounted an airlift to Vietnam to deliver urgent supplies. There were about 3,000 Soviet advisers and technicians with the Vietnamese armed forces, a number that doubled during the following twelve months. A Soviet naval task force of about twelve ships was already in Vietnamese waters when this war began, and early in March it was joined by the *Admiral Senyavin*, flagship of the Soviet Pacific Fleet, but otherwise no major movement of ground or air forces in Siberia was detected by US Intelligence, nor were any other significant naval moves made. In May 1979, the first Soviet submarine entered Cam Ranh Bay, where the USSR had been granted naval facilities by the Hanoi Government.

From March 1979 through to the end of 1980, the tense, suspicious status quo in Indo-China has smouldered on, with the two giant powers, the USSR and China, intriguing in the background for "hegemony" in the region, each striving to extend its influence at the expense of the other. Vietnam is now firmly in the Soviet camp, and thousands of Soviet and East European advisers are busily turning the country into an armed camp, ready for the next conflict. About 200,000 Vietnamese troops remain in Kampuchea, not so much as a garrison to protect the Heng Samrin regime against the Khmer Rouge army of Pol Pot, but rather as a potential springboard for incursions into Thailand. The much scorned Domino Theory, that if one Southeast Asian state falls to Communism, it will lean on, and knock over, the next one to it, is once again a real talking point. Thailand may well be the next domino to fall.

In Laos over 50,000 Vietnamese troops remain as a warning to right-wing and neutralist elements inside the country, and the exiled dissidents on the other side of the Mekong River. Reinforced, these Vietnamese divisions could be another threat to Thailand, but perhaps what is more likely is that the Pathet Lao army will be encouraged to raid into its territory to try to destroy camps in which Laotian dissidents are plotting and planning. It may seem that the Hanoi Government has put all its military eggs into one main basket, Kampuchea, and would have little reserve in hand should the Chinese again decide "to teach it a lesson." General Giap would not be so foolish. Practically the whole of the able-bodied manpower of Vietnam, and much of the woman power, is being conscripted into a huge milita, which is being armed and trained for guerrilla defence.

However, it is doubtful whether China, not yet as expert in subversive and proxy war as the Soviet Union, would allow the Thailand domino to fall unaided. The Khmer Rouge army, in the countryside of Kampuchea, has already been increased to over 50,000 guerrilla fighters, and for months Chinese weapons, ammunition and supplies have been trickling in to them through the adjacent jungle areas of Thailand. The year of 1981 can be predicted as being one of a proxy struggle in Kampuchea between regular Vietnamese divisions and the Khmer Rouge guerrillas: a reversal of military roles for the Hanoi Government. The huge expanses of jungle in Kampuchea, merging as they do with the border jungle areas of Thailand, are a suitable cockpit in which to carry on this struggle, which may be a lengthy one. China may seek to enlist other Kampuchean factions, such as Heng Samrin defectors, to fight against the Phnom Penh Government, while Heng Samrin may seek to enlist Khmer Rouge defectors (there are already reports of large sums of money being expended for this purpose) and other anti-Pol Pot groups, such as the right-wing Khmer Serei (Free Khmers). Defection and counter-defection have become almost a way of life in Kampuchea during the past decade. It is equally certain that if Vietnamese divisions were withdrawn from Kampuchea, there would be little to stop Pol Pot from sweeping back to power in Phnom Penh.

The spectre of famine has disappeared in Kampuchea, and the sight of horribly emaciated children is no longer to be seen, while Phnom Penh is once again a bustling city of some 500,000 people. The last day of 1980 saw the end of the combined relief programme mounted by UNICEF and the IRC, with the help of some 27 voluntary relief agencies, a programme that in fifteen months had distributed over 250,000 tons of food to refugee camps in the Kampuchea-Thailand border area. It had been alleged that much of the food had been diverted to feed the Khmer Rouge army, often by means of intimidation.

The danger to Thailand from Soviet proxy attacks by the Vietnamese must be seen in the larger context of the Association of Southeast Asian Nations, ASEAN, of which Thailand is one, which as a group is as yet comparatively toothless. Perhaps the two latter Vietnamese wars may sound warning notes of the militant advance of Communism, and stimulate some form of regional defence pact against Communism, whether of the Moscow or Peking variety. In January, the Hanoi Government again reiterated its total opposition to the suggested Western solution for an international conference to be held on the future of Kampuchea. Attitudes are hardening.

Abbreviations

Unfortunately several sets of initials are necessary to abbreviate the often-used and sometimes lengthy, titles of organisations. The main ones are:

ARVN Army of the Republic of Vietnam (used at times to include all the South Vietnamese Forces of all types, including the Air Force and the Navy).

CIA Central Intelligence Agency (American).

CIDG Civilian Irregular Defence Groups (Trained by the US Special Forces, and mostly composted of Montagnards, or hill tribesmen).

COSVN Central Office for South Vietnam (The Communist combined political and military HQ for directing the war in South Vietnam).

CRA Central Research Agency (A NLF organisation for collecting intelligence).

DMZ De-Militarised Zone.

DRV Democratic Republic of Vietnam (North Vietnam).

GDRV Government of the Democratic Republic of Vietnam.

GRVN Government of the Republic of Vietnam (South Vietnam).

ICC International Control Commission.

MAAG Military Assistance and Advisory Group (The American military organisation in SVN).

MACV Military Advisory Command, Vietnam (The American Command HQ in SVN).

NLA National Liberation Army (of the NLF).

NLF National Liberation Front (The Communist Political 'front' in whose name the war in SVN was being fought).

NVN North Vietnam(ese).

PRG	Provisional Revolutionary Government (of SVN – Communist).
PRP	People's Revolutionary Party of SVN (Communist).
RDT	Revolutionary Development Teams (SVN).
RVN	Republic of Vietnam (South Vietnam).
SVN	South Vietnam(ese).
VC	Viet Cong (Vietnamese Communists – used at times to include all Communists of all types in SVN, including the VPA).
VPA	Vietnamese People's Army (The armed forces of NVN – used to include all types of NVN formations).

Appendix I

A Chronological Sequence of the Main Events

1945

September 2nd — Ho Chi Minh entered Hanoi and established the GDRV.

1954

May 8th — End of Battle of Dien Bien Phu.

June 16th — Ngo Dinh Diem became Premier of SVN.

July 21st — Geneva Agreements came into effect.

October 5th — Last French troops evacuated Hanoi.

October 23rd — President Eisenhower decides to send Premier Diem direct aid.

1955

May 10th — The USA formally asked to train the armed forces of SVN.

October 23rd — Referendum held in SVN – Diem becomes President and declares a Republic, the RVN.

1956

July 16th — President Diem cancels the re-unification elections.

November — Ho Chi Minh takes over as Secretary-General of the Lao Dong Party.

1957

May 5th–19th — President Diem visits President Eisenhower.

September — General election in SVN won by President Diem.

Throughout 1957 — Ho Chi Minh engaged in re-organising the Lao Dong Party.

1959

April	A SVN branch of the Lao Dong Party formed.
July	A small VPA force invades Laos.

1960

April 30th	Personalities arrested for asking President Diem to liberate his regime.
May 5th	MAAG increased from 327 to 685 members.
August 9th	Captain Kong Le seizes control of Vientiane, Laos.
November 11th	Attempted military coup against President Diem.
December 20th	NVN assumes responsibility for the direction of the war in SVN.
December	The NLF established as a coalition front.
December	Le Duan appointed Secretary-General of the Lao Dong Party.

1961

May 11th–13th	Vice President Johnson visits SVN.
April 9th	President Diem re-elected for a further five-year term.
October 19th	General Maxwell Taylor, Special Military Adviser to President Kennedy, arrives in Saigon.
October 26th	President Kennedy renews pledge of aid to SVN.
October	Flood disaster in Mekong Delta.

1962

January 19th	US State Department confirms that chemical compounds are being used in SVN.
February 3rd	Strategic Hamlet programme launched.
February 8th	MACV formed under General Harkins.
February 27th	Two SVN aircraft attacked the Presidential Palace in Saigon.
April	Operation Sunrise to publicise the Strategic Hamlet scheme.
August	First Australian military personnel arrive in SVN.

1963

January 2nd	ARVN defeat at Battle of Ap Bac.
April	The Chieu Hoi (Open Arms) Amnesty scheme begun.
June 3rd	Buddhist disturbances in Hue.

June 11th	Buddhist monk immolates himself in Saigon.
August 22nd	Special Force police raid pagoda and arrest monks.
October 2nd	Defence Secretary McNamara declares the US military task would be completed by 1965.
October 31st	General Harkins says that 1,000 US troops are to be withdrawn by December 31st.
November 1st–2nd	President Diem killed.
November 6th	Revolutionary Military Committee formed, with General Duong Van Minh as Chairman.

1964

January 1st–8th	Second Congress of the NLF.
January 30th	General Minh ousted from power: General Nguyen Khanh takes over as Premier.
March 16th	Cambodian village of Chantes bombed by SVN planes.
March 29th	US admits supplying napalm to SVN.
June 20th	General Westmoreland appointed to succeed General Harkins in command of MACV.
July 2nd	General Maxwell Taylor appointed US Ambassador to SVN.
August 2nd	US destroyer attacked in Gulf of Tongking by NVN ships (another similar attack on the 4th).
August 5th	US aircraft strike NVN naval bases.
August 11th	The Tongking Resolution became law.
November	A small SVN military psychological warfare branch formed.

1965

February 1st–6th	The Tet Truce.
February 7th	VC raid on Pleiku.
February 7th	US and SVN aircraft strike at targets in NVN.
February 24th	US admit for the first time that American pilots are flying on operational missions against the VC.
March 8th	First US combat troops land in SVN.
March 29th	Soviet Union complains that China is delaying material destined for NVN.
April	Psychological Warfare branch began dropping leaflets over VC territory.
April 13th	The GDRV announced a Four Point Programme.

May 13th	The commencement of a five-day bombing 'pause' by the US and SVN.
June 15th	US combat troops take part in their first ground operation against the VC.
July 12th	A Moscow communiqué announced defence aid was to be given to NVN.
July 24th	The first US plane brought down by a SAM over NVN.
November 14th	The VPA in action for the first time against US troops at Ia Drang.

1966

January 24th	It was confirmed that SVN aircraft were regularly bombing the Ho Chi Minh Trail.
January 31st	Bombing of NVN resumed after a 37-day 'pause'.
February 27th	Political Action Teams formed in SVN.
March 10th	Premier Ky relieves commander of 1st Corps, and sets off Buddhist demonstrations.
April 21st	Soviet Union again complains the Chinese were delaying aid to SVN.
April 23rd	The first major air battle over NVN.
May 3rd	Chinese deny they were delaying aid to NVN.
May 31st	Big US and SVN raid on Yen Bay munitions complex.
July 27th	Premier Ky urges invasion of NVN.
August 21st	President Johnson says he has informed the GDRV that if it stopped sending men southwards into SVN, he would stop bombing NVN.
August 28th	The Soviet Union admitted it was training NVN pilots.
October 2nd	Soviet Union training NVN SAM crews.
October 3rd	Soviet Union announced new economic and military aid agreement with NVN.
October 24th–25th	The Manila Conference.
October 26th	President Johnson visits Cam Ranh Bay.
December 23rd	US aircraft ordered not to bomb within ten miles of Hanoi.
December 24th–26th	Christmas Truce.

1967

February 8th–12th	Tet Truce.
September 3rd	Elections in SVN.

| October 31st | President Thieu takes office. |

1968

January 21st	Siege of Khe Sanh begins (to last 77 days).
January 15th	Bombing of Haiphong area suspended by US.
January 18th	Bombing of Hanoi area suspended by US.
January 31st–	Period of the VC Tet Offensive.
February 26th	
February 6th	Fall of Lang Vei.
February 10th	US aircraft resumes bombing of Haiphong area.
March 19th	Operations begin in the A Shau Valley (lasting until May 17th).
March 31st	President Johnson orders cessation of bombing NVN, except near the DMZ.
March	General Westmoreland succeeded by General Abrams as Commander MACV.
April 1st	Clark Clifford succeeds Robert McNamara as US Defence Secretary.
April 3rd	GDRV accepts President Johnson's offer to negotiate.
April 7th	Khe Sanh relieved.
May 13th	Peace Talks begin in Paris.
July 5th	Khe Sanh abandoned.
July 18th–20th	Honolulu Meeting of President Johnson and President Thieu.
October 31st	President Johnson orders bombing of NVN to cease.

1969

January 25th	Paris Peace Talks opened formally.
March 16th	Alleged massacre at My Lai by US troops.
June 10th	Formation of the Provisional Revolutionary Government of SVN.
July 25th	The Nixon Doctrine enunciated.
September 3rd	Death of Ho Chi Minh.
November 15th.	Moratorium against the war in Vietnam in USA.

1970

March 13th	Prince Sihanouk, of Cambodia, visits Moscow.
March 18th	Prince Sihanouk deposed.
April 29th	ARVN invasion of Cambodia.
May 1st	US troops enter Cambodia.

June 24th	US Senate repeals the Gulf of Tongking Resolution.
June 29th	Last US troops leave Cambodia.
October 9th	Cambodia declared a Republic.
November 21st	US commando raid on Son Tay POW Camp, in NVN.

1971

February 8th– March 25th	ARVN invasion of Laos.
October 3rd	Presidential election in SVN.
October 31st	Thieu installed as President of SVN.

1972

March 23rd	Paris Peace Talks resumed.
March 30th	VC offensive begins in SVN on four Fronts.
April 5th	Siege of An Loc began (relieved on June 12th).
April 6th	US and SVN bombing of NVN resumed.
April 28th	Dong Ha overrun by the VC.
May 1st	Quang Tri fell to VC.
May 4th	Paris Peace Talks broken off (resumed again on July 13th).
May 9th	NVN ports mined by US aircraft.
May 10th	Martial Law declared in SVN.
June 28th	General Weyand relieves General Abrams as Commander US Forces in SVN.
September 15th	Quang Tri retaken by the ARVN.
December 18th	Paris Peace Talks suspended.

1973

January 8th	Paris Peace Talks resumed.
January 15th	President Nixon ordered bombing of NVN to cease.
January 23rd	A Peace Agreement initialled.
January 27th	The Peace Agreement signed.
January 28th	Cease-Fire came into effect.
February 13th	President Thieu forms Popular Front coalition to contest elections with National Liberation Front.
July 18th	U.S. Defense Department announces completion of mine-sweeping in North Vietnamese waters.
August 15th	U.S. bombing of Cambodia ended.

1974

March 8th   Exchange of POW's essentially completed.

1975

March 14th   President Thieu orders military evacuation of Central Highlands

March 29th   Danang falls to North Vietnamese troops.

April 17th   National Unity troops seize Cambodian capital.

April 21st   North Vietnamese capture Xuan Loc. President Thieu resigns.

April 30th   North Vietnamese occupy Saigon unopposed.

May 6th   Defeated Meo Tribesmen flee from Laos to Thailand.

1976

April 25th   Elections for National Assembly held in North and South Vietnam.

June 24th   National Assembly meets in Hanoi.

July 2nd   North and South Vietnam declared a single country, The Socialist Republic of Vietnam.

1977

January 15th   Regular train service inaugurated between Hanoi and Ho Chi Minh City (Saigon) on reconstructed railway.

September 20th   Socialist Republic of Vietnam admitted to the UN.

December 31st   Kampuchea (Cambodia) breaks off diplomatic relations with Vietnam.

1978

April 12th   Prime Minister Pol Pot reaffirms Kampuchean claims to Cochin China.

December 3rd   Factions hostile to Pol Pot proclaim Kampuchean United Front.

December 25th   Vietnamese begin a general offensive converging on Phnom Penh.

1979

January 7th	Heng Samrin takes Phnom Penh unopposed.
January 8th	Heng Samrin, as President of People's Revolutionary Council, assumes power in Kampuchea.
February 17th	Chinese invade Vietnam.
February 22nd	The Soviet Union mounts airlift of supplies to Vietnam.
March 5th	Chinese announce their withdrawal.

Appendix II

The Political Testament of Ho Chi Minh dated May 10th 1969.

Tu-Fu, the well known poet of the Tang epoch, wrote, "In all times, few are those who reach the age of 70". This year with my 79 years, I count those "few" people still. My mind is lucid, though my health has somewhat weakened in comparison with previous years . . . But who can forecast for how long I can continue to serve the revolution, the fatherland, and the people? That is the reason why I leave these few lines in anticipation of the day when I go and join venerable Karl Marx, Lenin, and other revolutionary elders . . .

First I will speak about the party. Thanks to its close unity and total dedication to the working class, the people, and the fatherland, our party had been able, since its founding, to unite, organise, and lead our people in an ardent struggle and conduct them from victory to victory.

Unity is an extremely precious tradition of our party and people. All comrades, from the central committee down to the cell, must preserve union and unity of mind in the party as the apple of their eyes. Within the party, to achieve broad democracy and to practise self-criticism and criticism regularly and seriously is the best way to consolidate and develop union and unity of mind in the party. Genuine affection should prevail among all comrades.

Each party member, each cadre, must be deeply imbued with revolutionary morality and show industry, thrift, integrity, uprightness, total dedication to the public cause, exemplary selflessness. Our party should preserve its entire parity. It should remain worthy of its role as the leader and a very loyal servant of the people . . . Training and educating the revolutionary generation to come is a highly important and necessary task.

Our labouring people, both in the plains and in the mountains areas, have for ages suffered hardships, feudal and colonial oppression and exploitation. Furthermore, they have experienced many years of war. Yet our people have shown great heroism, great courage, and ardent enthusiasm, and are very hard working. They have always followed the

238

party since it came into being, and have always been loyal to it. The party must work out a good plan for economic and cultural development with a view to ceaselessly raising the living standard of the people.

The resistance war against US aggression may drag out. Our compatriots may have to undergo new sacrifices in terms of property and human lives. In any case, we must resolve to fight against the US aggressors until total victory. Our rivers, our mountains, our men will always remain. The Yanks defeated, we will build our country ten times more beautiful.

No matter what difficulties and hardships may lie ahead, our people are sure to win total victory. The US imperialists will have to pull out. Our fatherland will be re-unified. Our compatriots in the North and in the South will be re-united and under the same roof.

Our country will have the signal honour of being a small nation which, through a heroic struggle, has defeated two big imperialisms – the French and the American – and made a worthy contribution to the national liberation movement.

About the world Communist movement: Having dedicated my whole life to the cause of the revolution, the more proud I am to see the growth of the international Communist and workers' movement, the more deeply I am grieved at the dissensions that are dividing the fraternal parties [a reference to the Sino-Soviet ideological quarrel].

I wish our party to do its best to contribute effectively to the restoration of unity among the fraternal parties on the basis of Marxism-Leninism and proletarian internationalism, in a way consonant to the requirements of heart and reason. I am sure that the fraternal parties and countries will unite again.

About personal matters: All my life I have whole-heartedly and with all my forces served the fatherland, the revolution, and the people. Now if I should depart from this world, there is nothing that I am sorry to have done. I regret only not to be able to serve longer any more. After my passing away, great funerals should be avoided in order not to waste the time and money of the people.

Finally, to the whole people, the whole party, the whole army, to my nephews and nieces, youths and children, I leave behind my boundless affection. I also convey my fraternal greetings to the comrades, friends, youth and children of the world.

My ultimate wish is that our whole party and people, closely united in the struggle, should build a peaceful, unified, independent, democratic, and prosperous Vietnam and make a worthy contribution to the world revolution.

Acknowledgements to Keesing's Contemporary Archives.

Index

The following words or abbreviations are not included in this Index as they appear on a majority of pages:
America(n)(s); ARVN; DRV; GDRV; GRVN; NLA; NLF; NVN; SVN; US(A); VC; VPA

244

Air Forces and Aircraft

Artillery and Small Arms

Missiles and Bombs

Armoured Vehicles

Naval

Ships